LIVE AND WORK IN DUBAI

Visit our How To website at **www.howto.co.uk**

At **www.howto.co.uk** you can engage in conversation with some of our authors – all of whom have 'been there and done that' in their specialist fields. You can get access to special offers and additional content but, most importantly, you will be able to engage with, and become a part of, a wide and growing community of people just like yourself.

At **www.howto.co.uk** you'll be able to talk to, and share tips with, people who have similar interests and are facing similar challenges in their lives. People who, just like you, have the desire to change their lives for the better – be it through moving to a new country, starting a new business, growing their own vegetables, or writing a novel.

At **www.howto.co.uk** you'll find the support and encouragement you need to help make your aspirations a reality.

You can go direct to **www.live-and-work-in-dubai.co.uk** which is part of the main How To site.

How To Books strives to present authentic, inspiring, practical information in their books. Now, when you buy a title from **How To Books**, you get even more than words on a page.

LIVE AND WORK IN DUBAI

MEERA ASHISH

howtobooks

Acknowledgements

Firstly, a big thank you to those who have helped put this book together – Celene Tud, Rholan Veslino and Raps Middle East, Miruna Toma and Kensington Dubai, Rebecca Ghalayini, Ahuti and Siya Chug ... and, of course, Ashish! A special thanks to Aysha Butti Al Muhairi, for helping me out and introducing me to so many interesting people; to Moza Al Youha and the Department of Tourism and Commerce Marketing (www.dubaitourism.ae) for their assistance and for all the pictures; to Marcel van Mourik (www.simplyweb.nl), Nikhilesh Kumar Singh (www.nikhileshsingh.com) and artist Nivedita Saha, who also provided some fantastic pictures. Without the continued support of Nikki Read at How To Books, this book would not have been possible.

How To Books Ltd
Spring Hill House, Spring Hill Road
Begbroke, Oxford OX5 1RX, United Kingdom
Tel: 01865 375794 Fax: 01865 379162
info@howtobooks.co.uk
www.howtobooks.co.uk

British Library Cataloguing in Publication Data
A catalogue record for this book is available from the British Library.

First published 2010

ISBN: 978 1 84528 353 7

Cover design by Baseline Arts Ltd, Oxford
Typeset by *specialist* publishing services ltd, Montgomery
Produced for How To Books by Deer Park Productions, Tavistock

Photos: see acknowledgements above, except for p30 © dblight/iStock 2009; p42 © Paul Cowan/ iStock 2006; p46 © Gordon Dixon/iStock 2007; p50 © Alexander Hafemann/iStock 2007; p74, © Kohlerphoto/iStock 2007; p118, © Kirby Hamilton/iStock 2009
Printed and bound in Great Britain by Cromwell Press Group, Trowbridge

Contents

Preface

There is something exhilarating about travel, about discovering, unravelling and exploring. It's not just the famous sites in a city, not just the night life or simply having good food, but an amalgamation of all these things and more. A city's heart lies in her people, in her culture, in her history and it is this, ultimately, that defines her.

However, the city also has an identity of its own, as unique as each of us yet more obscure, and this character of a breathing city can only be understood when you quietly peek out late at night, walk across its empty bridges and on the silent streets, or tread on pavements and grass very early in the morning when the sun has just risen, when the birds are waking ...

These extremities of time are when only the city is present – no people, no busy-ness, no confusion. And when all the heaving and quiet, cheerful and livid streets of a city come together, that's when you can really begin to understand the different attributes of the character of the city which has lived through centuries of people and eras of change.

And so, when I travel, I try to understand a city without a plan. From the modernities of cities today, I want to feel the essence of history, the grains of culture that the streets have retained from bygone epochs.

It is this elusive nature of travelling and wandering and being a part of and yet an outsider that I absolutely love and relish, to the extent that I finally became or stumbled upon becoming a travel journalist.

Now, you might well wonder why, when I love history and culture so much, I decided to write about Dubai. One thing is, I was moving to this country. And the other is, that though Dubai is such a 'new' city as it were, such an indulgent and pleasureful city with a history that nobody really knows and a people that have limitless spending power, I started to realise that I could not make a judgement that was founded solely on what I saw – high-rise buildings, artificiality and a fantasy city; but I had to see deeper than that – what has in fact made Dubai what it is and what makes it so special? Why indeed has Dubai become an enticement, a magnet for anyone and everyone?

The truth is, living in Dubai offers an awesome combination of all the city pleasures – fantastic restaurants and nightlife – and sun, beach and relaxation; it offers a blend of cultures and people, of interesting things to do, a variety of sports and watersports and a growing arts scene. The burgeoning economy that it is, allows for plentiful opportunities to do new things and start new ventures. And so it caters well for both young singles and couples as well as for families.

Meera Ashish

PART 1

Dubai and the UAE

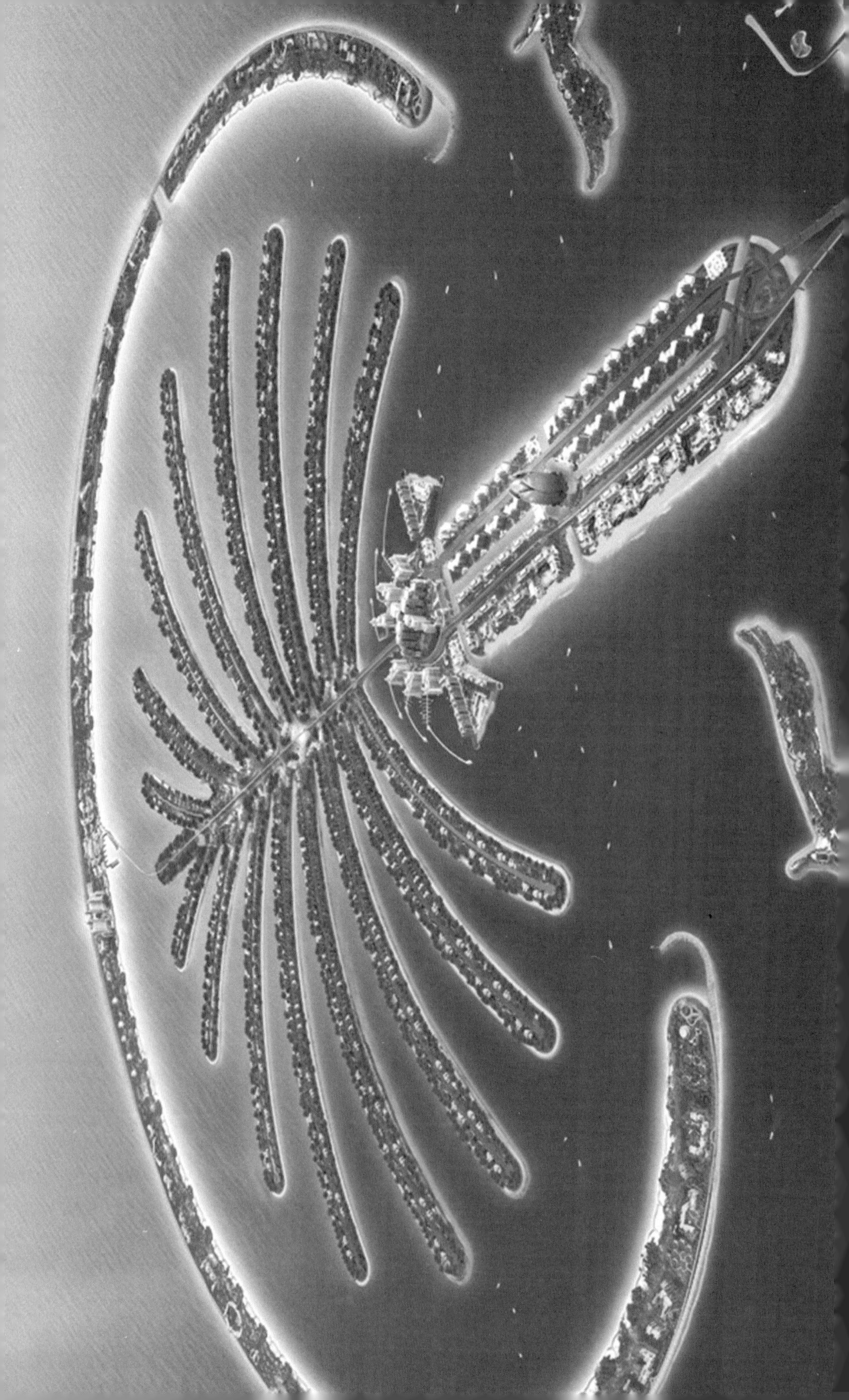

Chapter 1

Overview

A city which once started as a vibrant trading port, Dubai has now become an economic powerhouse, a gateway between East and West, a place where you have the best of sun, beach, leisure, work and nightlife.

There has been much in the media about Dubai's recent economic downturn, and while there are many moving out, there are also just as many staying put and others moving to Dubai. Apart from what Dubai has to offer, one of the best things about this city is its multicultural aspect. You will meet people from different parts of the world, make new friends and learn about different cultures. It is in fact the diverse people that make Dubai what it is.

GEOGRAPHY

Dubai is situated on the Arabian Gulf between Sharjah and Abu Dhabi. It lies in the northwest of the United Arab Emirates (UAE) and after Abu Dhabi, Dubai is the second largest and probably the most well-known city in the UAE.

Four-fifths of the UAE is desert and the neighbouring countries are Oman to the north and east, Saudi Arabia to the south and west and Qatar to the west.

Dubai has 60 km of natural coastline and the city is divided in two by the Creek, an inlet from the Gulf which runs through some of the oldest parts of Dubai and bisects the centre. North of the Creek is Deira, where you'll find the spice, fish and gold *souks*, while on the south side is Bur Dubai, an urban and more modern area. Most of the land is barren and sandy.

TIMEZONE

Dubai is four hours ahead of GMT in winter time and three hours ahead in summer time. There is no adjustment for summer-time in Dubai.

CLIMATE

With a sub-tropical climate, Dubai is usually hot, arid and desert-like. During the summer, from June/July till September/October, the average maximum temperature reaches above 48°C, with humidity averaging over 90% and sea temperatures over 32°C. Up in the Al Hajar mountains, temperatures are cooler.

Tip

Your car will get very hot, so keep it parked in shade and keep something to cover your front window.

In winter, temperatures average 26°C during the day, though nights can be rather cool, with an average minimum temperature between 10°C and 14°C, and less than 5°C deep in the desert or high in the mountains.

It rains sporadically mostly in February and March in the form of short, heavy showers. Being a desert, there are frequent sand- and dust-storms.

A word of caution

It might be boiling hot outside, but if you're going to be in an office or a mall, take a shawl, cardigan or jumper. The air conditioning is always on full blast!

It is also true to say that the weather is continuously changing. For the past two or three years, it's been surprisingly cold in December and January. There has sometimes been unexpected fog, especially in the mornings and more rainfall than anticipated.

POPULATION

Dubai's population was estimated at 1,422,000 in 2006. 80% of the population comprises expatriates.

The population of the UAE was estimated at 4,104,695 in 2006.

FLAG

The flag consists of three horizontal bands, green at the top, white in the middle and black at the bottom and then a vertical red band down the hoist side. The colours symbolise the ruling families of the Arab nations and their unity.

PRICES

Legal tender in Dubai is the UAE dirham (Dh). In October 2009 the exchange rate was approximately £0.17, €0.19 and US$0.27 to Dh1.

The following are approximate prices just to give you an idea of the day-to-day costs you'll incur whilst living in Dubai:

- in an average mid-range restaurant, a meal for an adult: Dhs70–100
- Subway sandwich: Dhs15
- grande latte from Starbucks: Dhs16
- pint of draught beer: Dhs25–35
- large bottle of mineral water from a supermarket: Dhs5
- loaf of white bread: Dhs2.50
- bag of potatoes (1kg): Dhs2
- bottle of Dettol soap (125g): Dhs3.95

- taxi from World Trade Centre Roundabout to Mall of the Emirates is Dhs25
- bus fare: Dhs2 with designated stops and timings
- 1 gallon of petrol: Dhs6.25 and to fill up a tank would cost approximately Dhs60
- cinema ticket: Dhs30
- Clothes prices are similar to the UK e.g. a dress from H&M will cost Dhs200–300 and sandals from Aldo or Nine West Dhs250–350.

IMPORTANT NUMBERS

Name	Number
Police	999
Ambulance	998
Fire	997
Rashid Hospital	04 3371111
Al Baraha Hospital	04 271000
Welcare Hospital	04 282 7788
American Hospital	04 3367777
Airport	04 2245252
Tourist Information Centre	04 2245252
Directory enquiries	181
Operator	100
Dubai Electricity & Water Authority (DEWA)	04 6019999
Road & Transport Authority (RTA)	04 2844444

Embassies				
Australia	04 5087100		France	04 3128400
UK	04 3094444		US	04 3116000
Canada	04 3145555		South Africa	04 3975222
India	04 3971222		Philippines	04 2544331

USEFUL WEBSITES FOR DUBAI

Website	Description
www.timeoutdubai.com	Event listings, new restaurants and bars, art coverage
www.dubai-eating.com	Up-to-date user reviews of Dubai's restaurants
www.dubizzle.com	Online marketplace of short-term lets
www.dubaidonkey.com	Busy listings website, also useful for finding short-term lets
www.dubailime.com	General information on and insights into the UAE
www.grapeshisha.com	Resource providing important information Dubai and UAE
www.expatwoman.com	Well organised site packed with information on everything
www.cityshoppingdubai.com	One-stop website for all shopping needs and wants plus a guide to every shop you can think of
www.quickdubai.com	Regional gift and home delivery service – you can order anything from skydiving to personal shopping
www.roomservice-uae.com	Choose from over 50 restaurants and place your order
www.brownbag.ae	Online shopping site
www.mymovedubai.com	Gives essential information for relocating in Dubai such as accommodation, banking, jobs, sports clubs and events
www.dubaicityguide.com	Gives complete information on everything in Dubai
www.dubai.ae	A government portal that provides basic information including visas and other procedures
www.godubai.com	A community website that provides tourist information
www.dubaiinfo.ae	A comprehensive guide on Dubai with information such as events, cinema times, airport information
www.dubaiparent.com	Basic information on Dubai which also includes support groups, fun activities and a kids section
www.indexuae.com	Search engine and web directory for the UAE

Interview with Rahim Hirji, founder of grapeshisha.com

What is the concept of grapeshisha.com?

The concept is to share information about the UAE, not biased, not pro, not against – just a balanced view from an insider's perspective. I think it has evolved to give those not familiar with Dubai and Abu Dhabi another view on what it is really like, the things that you need to consider when you travel or move to this part of the world. The concept is diverse – we help people get jobs, we provide data on rentals, we give cultural information and we also blog to provide a lens on what is going on in the UAE.

Why did you start grapeshisha.com?

When I moved to the UAE in 2003, there was an increasing thirst to find out more about what was going on in places like Dubai and whether the media stories were to be believed. I started an initial newsletter to a few friends and family just to let them know what life was like. These emails were forwarded around and my distribution list very quickly grew out of control. At some point I just decided to formalise this - and grapeshisha was born. It has since had various reincarnations and we maintain a blog that gives a quirky view on things related to Dubai and Abu Dhabi, and still have and update lots of general information on the site. Many people ask me why I chose grapeshisha as a name. I just happened to like it at the time.

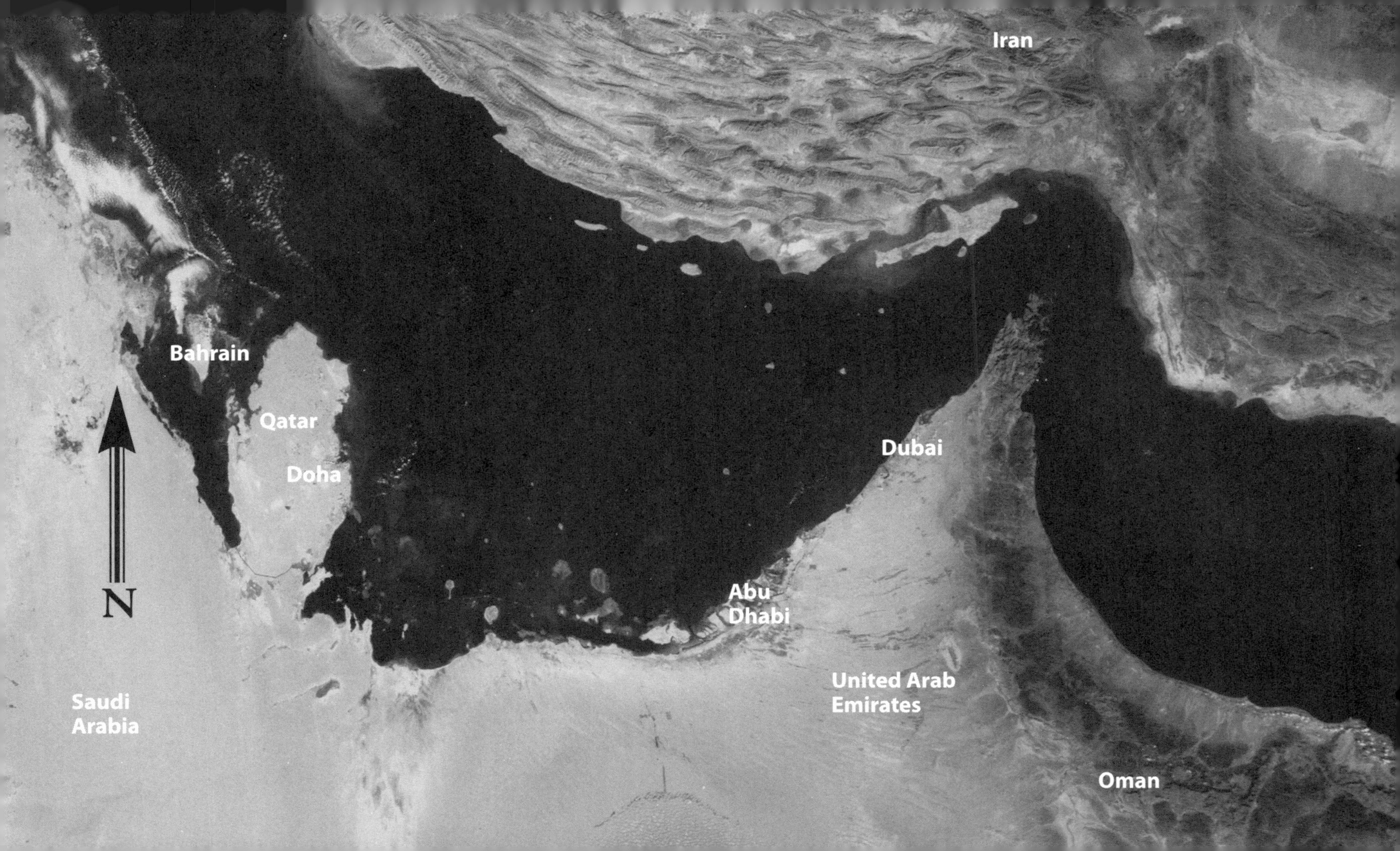

Iran
Bahrain
Qatar
Doha
Dubai
Abu
Dhabi
United Arab
Emirates
N
Saudi
Arabia
Oman

Sheikh Zayad Road 1980

Sheikh Zayad Road today

Chapter 2

History

With a fascinating history going back over 5000 years, Dubai never fails to inspire.

EARLY HISTORY AND ISLAM

Archaeological excavations in Hatta, Al Qusais and Jumeirah reveal that there was civilisation in Dubai around 3000BC. The history of Dubai is closely linked to the spread of Islam which first developed in Saudi Arabia in the 7th century. It quickly spread through military conquests to the Middle East and North Africa.

The old days

- The main *souk* in Deira used to be the largest market in the region. It was lined with narrow, covered passageways, selling commodities from around the world.
- Most of the locals lived in *barastis*, huts made from palm fronds.
- The highest points in the city were windtowers, used for ventilation, as well as the Al Fahidi Fort, built in 1799 and which now houses the Dubai museum.

PIRATE COAST

Centuries later, when the UAE was known as the Pirate Coast, the British became interested in the region for its important trading location en route to India. In 1820, the British managed to capture the Qawasim vessels and thus were able to control the activities of the pirates. The Sheikh of Dubai and other Sheikhs in the region also signed the 'General Maritime Peace Treaty' with the British government.

A General Treaty of Peace was agreed by the rulers of the nine sheikhdoms, which resulted in the area being called Trucial States or Trucial Coast instead of Pirate Coast. The role of the British was to provide these states with protection rather than rule them as a colony.

BANI YAS

In 1833, the Al Maktoum dynasty of the Bani Yas tribe left the settlement of Abu Dhabi and inhabited a small fishing village at the mouth of the Creek. The descendants of the Maktoum family continue to rule Dubai today.

TRADING

By the 1870s, Dubai had become the principal port of the Gulf coast and was attracting traders from Iran, India and around the Gulf. Sheikh Maktoum bin Hasher Al Maktoum, Dubai's ruler, signed a business deal with the British in 1894, providing full tax exemption for foreign traders. This meant they had an incentive to switch their base of operations from Iran and Sharjah to Dubai. Later on in the 1950s, Sheikh Rashid bin Saeed Al Maktoum ordered the creek to be dredged to deepen the channel and reinforce the banks. This provided access for larger vessels. During this period, the pearl industry helped Dubai to build trade relations. Pearls

Did you know?

Pearling might sound amazing, but there were many dangers involved for the divers, who were mainly slaves from East Africa. They had a rope around their waist, a turtle-shell peg on their nose and leather gloves for protection from sharp coral.

The biggest market for pearls was India, but later the UK and US also started buying pearls. See the great displays and understand more about pearling at Dubai Museum and Diving Village (see pp 137, 139).

continued to be the basis for Dubai's prosperity until the 1940s, when the development of Japanese cultured pearls led to a collapse in demand for natural pearls. It was then that trade in other products including gold grew, and Dubai became known as 'the city of merchants'.

OIL

Abu Dhabi discovered huge reserves of oil in 1958 and Dubai discovered oil in 1966. When the Emirates began to export oil, the economy completely transformed with a period of rapid development which formed the bedrock of the modern and diversified city we see today. The major projects that took place at that time were executed by Sheikh Rashid bin Saeed Al Maktoum, who ensured that the oil revenues were used to develop the infrastructure of Dubai. There has also been an influx of foreign workers in Dubai since then, which has continued to boost the economy.

UAE

In 1968, the British decided to end the General Maritime Peace Treaty and so withdrew from the Trucial States, along with Qatar and Bahrain. The nine sheikhdoms tried to merge, but Bahrain and Qatar decided to become independent states. The other states, Dubai, Abu Dhabi, Sharjah, Ajman, Fujairah and Umm Al Quwain, came together to form the United Arab Emirates (UAE) on 2nd December, 1971. Ras Al Khaimah joined the UAE in 1972.

PRESIDENT OF THE UAE

Ruler of Abu Dhabi, Sheikh Zayed bin Sultan Al Nahyan, became president of all the emirates. After his death in 2004, Sheikh Khalifa bin Zayed Al Mahyan took over the presidency. However, Dubai has always maintained a great degree of autonomy in decision making.

RULERS OF DUBAI

In 1990, Sheikh Maktoum bin Rashid Al Maktoum became the ruler of Dubai, after his father Sheikh Rashid bin Said Al Maktoum died. In 1995, his younger brother, Sheikh Mohammed bin Rashid Al Maktoum, also became crown prince, and in 2006, he succeeded as the ruler of Dubai after the death of Sheikh Maktoum bin Rashid Al Maktoum. Sheikh Mohammed bin Rashid Al Maktoum is the current ruler of Dubai and, like his elder brother, he is also the Vice President and the Prime Minister of the UAE.

TOURISM

Sheikh Maktoum bin Rashid Al Maktoum and his brother realised early in the 21st century that Dubai would soon run out of oil (oil accounts for less than 10% of Dubai's GDP) and thus devised a plan to diversify Dubai and attract tourism. His vision and decisive leadership accelerated the process of transformation. The Arabian Travel Market has become the largest travel and tourism exhibition in the region. And with Emirates Airlines, there are so many connection options that Dubai has become a convenient stopover and a significant hub.

MEGA CITY

Dubai has seen huge towers and architectural masterpieces rise at an unbelievable pace over recent years. The vision and ambition of the leaders of Dubai has, of course, made this possible. But it is also due to the efforts of the huge foreign workforce who have carried out the work, who were initially overworked, living in bad conditions and often unpaid for months. We have thankfully now seen an improvement and the government has taken action against unscrupulous employers and even set up a hotline for workers to report any concerns regarding wages and conditions.

PROPERTY MARKET

The real estate boom began in May 2002, when crown prince Sheikh Mohammed bin Rashid Al Maktoum, issued a decree allowing foreign nationals to buy and own freehold property in various areas of Dubai. This entirely changed the property market. The period also witnessed the announcement of Palm Jumeirah and other mega projects such as the Dubai International Financial Centre and Dubai Festival City.

Chapter 3

Culture and religion

Courtesy and hospitality, the most highly prized virtues of the Arab world, are qualities that you'll find in the friendly locals here.

When you arrive at your hotel, you'll most likely be welcomed with fresh Arabic coffee poured from a traditional long-spouted coffee pot. If you make some local friends, who will inevitably teach you more about the life and culture here, you will soon realise that the family is the most important institution in Arab society. This includes the immediate family of grandparents, uncles, aunts, cousins as well as other, more distant, relatives. There are also certain social norms and expectations that newcomers need to adhere to, such as not shaking hands with members of the opposite sex as per the Islamic tradition (see The law, pp 43–5), but these are things you will pick up once you start living in Dubai.

ISLAM

Islam is more than just a religion; it is deep-rooted in the life of the locals and governs day-to-day life in Dubai, from eating and drinking to what you wear. Hence the culture in Dubai is directly affected by the Islamic religion.

- Mosques are dotted throughout the city and you'll be able to hear the call for prayer five times a day. One of the largest and best known is the Jumeirah Mosque, a true example of Islamic architecture.

- The Islamic holy day is Friday.

Ramadan

- Ramadan takes place in the ninth month of the Islamic calendar. Dates are determined by the lunar calendar and it goes back about 11 days earlier each year. In 2009, Ramadan was from 21st August to 19th September. The exact timings for sunrise and sunset each day during Ramadan are published in all major daily newspapers.

- During the holy month of Ramadan, which commemorates the revelation of the Koran, Muslims are expected to fast and thus refrain from eating, drinking or smoking from dawn to dusk.

- Ramadan is a time of giving, of generosity in the community, remembering the blessings of Allah and of forgiveness. Ramadan is followed by the celebration of Eid Al-Fitr, which is celebrated for three days. By law, Muslim employees have shortened work days.

- It is expected for non-Muslims to be culturally sensitive and if you accidentally eat, drink or smoke in public, someone will probably ask you to stop.

Did you know?

- A fifth of the world's population fast during Ramadan.
- Ramadan begins at the sighting of the new moon and ends at the sighting of the next moon.
- A lot of Muslims read the entire Quran during this month.

- Almost all restaurants and cafés are closed during the day. However, hotel restaurants usually remain open with screened-off areas for guests, and grocery stores are open during the day. You are also encouraged to wear more conservative clothes during this month.

- At sunset, you'll find large Ramadan tents put up for the Iftar, the break of fast, with food and shisha. Hotels, restaurants and mosques hold Iftar feasts daily during this month and Muslims generally break their fasts by first eating a date. People of all nationalities and religions gather to enjoy these festivities, which go on into the early hours of the morning.

- Ramadan is a time to give back, so it's a good month to give time and money to charity. Charity is one of the five pillars of Islam, so it is essential for Muslims.

OTHER RELIGIONS

- Though the UAE is an Islamic country, followers of other religions are respected and allowed to practise their beliefs. There is a Hindu temple, Christian churches and a guru dwara for Sikhs. Religious festivals such as Christmas and Diwali are celebrated throughout Dubai.

- While Dubai has a very liberal attitude to religion, it is courteous to respect the religion of the country by dressing modestly.

- When holding a religious event, it is important to gain permission from the government of Dubai.

NATIONAL DRESS

- The national dress for men in Dubai is the *dishdasha* or *kandoura*, a white ankle-length, loosely fitted cotton garment adapted to the high temperatures of the region. They also cover their head for protection from the sun.

- Arab women in Dubai are usually dressed in a long-sleeved, full-length black *abayah* which often has glittering embellishments and stylish borders, as well as the *sheyla*, a casual headscarf. Some women also have their faces covered by a thin veil, known as a *gishwa*. They are very fond of jewellery as well as make-up and henna is widely used for the palms and soles of the feet for special occasions, such as weddings.

ARABIC NAMES

- First names are usually taken from an important person in the Quran. The first name is followed by *bin*, meaning son of or *bint* meaning daughter of. After this comes the name of the child's father. Then the last name is the person's family. For more prominent families *Al* comes before the last name, meaning 'the', for example, Sheikh Mohammed Bin Rashid Al Maktoum.

WOMEN

- It is often thought that women in the Middle East are suppressed and not allowed to work. However, women are not only respected in Islamic society, but also have equal educational opportunities as men, can practise the profession of their choice and have the same legal status as men. You'll find that most women wear the *abayah* and headscarf out of choice and respect for their traditions.

GENERAL CONDUCT

- Public displays of affection between a man and a woman are frowned upon and may be subject to arrest.

- Unlike some of the other more conservative Gulf States and neighbouring countries, Dubai has a liberal attitude towards women. Short skirts and tops in public and bikinis on the beach are permitted, though it is considerate and respectful to dress with some modesty.

- During Ramadan, it is expected that non-Muslims also refrain from eating, drinking and smoking in public (refer to Ramadan in this section). In addition, it is important for men and women to dress more conservatively in public.

LANGUAGE

- The official language in Dubai is Arabic and this is widely spoken. However, English is equally popular and road signs, shop signs and restaurant menus are generally written in both Arabic and English.

- Other commonly spoken languages in Dubai include Hindi, Farsi, Urdu, Malayalam and Bengali.

- Arabic is certainly not an easy language to learn, but it's very useful and handy to know a few Arabic words which you can drop into conversations with the locals.

Greetings	
Welcome	*Marhaba*
Good morning	*Sabah el khair*
Hello	*As-salam alaykum*
Good afternoon	*Masa el khair*
Response to hello	*Wa alaykum e-salam*
Good night	*Tisbah ala-kheir*
Goodbye	*Ma'a salama*

Small Talk	
How are you?	*Kaif al hal?*
I don't understand	*La afham*
Well (praise be to Allah)	*Al-hamduillah*
Where are you from?	*Inta min weyn?*
What's happening?	*Shu-ikhbaarak*
I am from England	*Ana min Ingliterra*
What's your name?	*Aysh ismuk*
No problem	*Mafi mushkil*
My name is	*Ismi*
Please	*Min fadhlik*
I don't know	*Ma adhri*
Thank you	*Shukran*
By God's grace	*Inshallah*
Congratulations	*Mabrook*
Excuse me	*Affwan*

Basics	
Yesterday	*Ams*
Maybe	*Mumkin*
Today	*Al youm*
Where is the toilet?	*Wain il hamam?*
Tomorrow	*Bukra, ghadan*
How much?	*Bekam?*
Yes	*Aiwa, na'am*
What is this?	*Shoo hada?*
No	*La*
Address	*Onwan*

GREETING

- Shaking hands is acceptable only between two men. It is generally considered unacceptable for a man to shake hands with a Muslim woman or a woman to shake hands with a Muslim man.

TIPPING

- Tipping in Dubai is similar to most parts of the world.

- Some restaurants include a service charge, but if not, a 10% tip is adequate.

FOOD AND DRINK

- Local cuisine: Arabic food in Dubai is based on Lebanese cuisine such as Arabic bread, *shawarmas* (best places for *shawarmas* on p 249), *falafel*, salad and pickles. You'll find this at any of the local restaurants.

- *Halal*: there are rules as to what a Muslim can and can't eat. The only kind of meat they can eat is *halal*, meat which has been slaughtered according to the Islamic *halal* method.

- Pork: pork and all pig products are taboo in Muslim culture. Therefore, while it is not illegal to consume pork in Dubai, the availability is limited. In restaurants, pork is placed in separate fridges and prepared with separate utensils.

- Arabic coffee and dates: guests are welcomed traditionally with coffee and fresh dates. The coffee is flavoured with cardamom and is poured from the long-spouted Arabic coffee pot into very small glass cups with no handles. Dates are one of the few crops that thrive in the Middle East.

- *Shisha*: the Arabic water pipe in which fruit flavoured tobacco is smoked, is very popular in Dubai and is available in cafés and restaurants. It's a relaxing thing to do on weekends and especially at Ramadan, when tents are erected in Dubai.

Did you know?

- Dates and camel milk were once the staple diet of the Bedouins.
- Camel milk has great benefits for health and well-being, and more people are now starting to drink it.

TRADITIONAL SPORT

- The sport of falconry is a traditional pastime and still practised today. It is the most valued traditional sport. Training the birds to hunt and to respond to commands requires skill. The hunting season is normally during winter and spring.

- Camel racing has, over the years, become a formal and proper sport, with camels brought in from as far as Saudi Arabia to compete. Camels have historically played an important role in the desert culture of the UAE by providing food, transportation and security to the Bedouins, as well as a means of entertainment with camel racing as a regular part of festivities. The camel racetrack in Dubai has now moved from Nad Al Sheba to Al Ain Road (past the Dubai Outlet Mall and right off the Al Lisali exit). Races usually take place between November and April on Thursday and Friday mornings. Contact the camel racing office on 04 3388170.

- The Arabs' love for horses is brought together at the world's richest horse race, the Dubai World Cup, which takes place in March.

Chapter 4

Festivals

The Dubai government has encouraged and promoted a number of events and festivals in its unceasing effort to create a buzz about the city and to encourage tourists.

There are new events cropping up each year. The March 2010 Emirates Airline International Festival of Literature is likely to become an annual event. And in 2013, Dubai will be hosting the swimming world championships. So take your pick and you'll have something new to see and experience each month.

JANUARY

Dubai Shopping Festival

www.mydsf.com

Dubai is famous for shopping, and to celebrate this, there is a month-long festival dedicated entirely to shopping. This annual feast of shopping attracts millions of tourists each year and usually runs from mid-January to mid-February. There are live music events, international theatre, fashion shows and kids' events going on in the malls as well as fireworks over the Creek and offers, raffles and competitions. For a round-the-world shopping experience, head to Global Village (see overleaf) and don't miss out on the newest Dubai Mall – the largest mall in the world.

Global Village

www.globalvillage.ae

Global Village usually runs from November to February, and is one part of Dubailand (on the Emirates Road) that has already come to life. Featuring 31 country pavilions, each of which showcases wares from crafts- and trades-people of those countries, as well as traditional snacks and meals. There's also some live entertainment at night. Global Village has gained popularity over the years and in 2008/2009 attracted more than 4.5 million visitors.

Dubai Marathon

www.dubaimarathon.org

Take part in one of the three races – there's a 3 km stroll for charity, a 10 km run for the moderately fit and, of course, the full marathon (26 miles) for the super-fit. With a prize fund of a million dollars, the marathon attracts some of the biggest names in long-distance running each year.

Dubai Racing Carnival

www.dubairacingclub.com

It's worth experiencing a race night at Nad Al Sheba, one of the world's leading racecourses, which also hosts the world's richest horse race in March every year (Dubai World Cup, see p 26). Race nights take place from October to April and there are usually six to seven races each evening.

FEBRUARY

Dubai International Jazz Festival

www.dubaijazzfest.com

This three-night event with performances from up-and-coming artists alongside international legends takes place in the week after the Shopping Festival at Dubai Media City and has been going on since 2003.

Dubai Desert Classic

www.dubaidesert.classic.com

With a line-up of international golfing legends to entertain you, this is the leading golf event in the Gulf region and is held on the first weekend of February at the Emirates Golf Club.

Dubai Tennis Championships

www.dubai tennischampionships.com

Held over two weeks in February and March, this is when some of the biggest tennis champions arrive in Dubai to compete in the men's, women's and doubles matches. It's an opportunity to see some of the best players in the world.

MARCH

Dubai Desert Rock

www.desertrockfestival.com

This annual live rock music event showcasing different styles and types of rock and metal music from around the world, started in 2004 as an idea to develop a large rock festival in the Middle East. As well as live music, extreme sports are also featured as a crowd attraction.

Art Dubai

www.artdubai.ae

This is the first contemporary art fair in Dubai, which began in 2007 and takes place annually at the glamorous Madinat Jumeirah in the second week of March. It's a great place for artists, dealers and gallery owners to mingle and, in 2009, it hosted nearly 70 international galleries.

Emirates Airline International Festival of Literature

www.eaifl.com

The first Literature Festival took place in February 2009 and was the first of this stature and size in the Middle East. It was a true success, having brought together 65 internationally-esteemed authors from 20 countries to speak to large audiences at the InterContinental Hotel in Festival City. The second festival took place from 10th–13th March 2010.

Dubai International Boat Show

www.boatshowdubai.com

Now in its 17th year, it has become the largest, most important event of its kind in the region and showcases boats from local and international builders alike along with the latest innovations in marine equipment, supplies and services. It usually takes place at the Dubai International Marine Club – Mina Seyahi in the second week of March.

Dubai World Cup

www.dubaiworldcup.com

It's a great social event that takes place at the end of the Dubai International Racing Carnival, and with a purse of $6million, it's the world's richest horse race. The Dubai World Cup has been held annually since 1996 at the Nad Al Sheba Racecourse and no betting is allowed. It's quite a fashion event where women dress up and sport spectacularly large hats. 2010 marked the first World Cup race to be held at the new and incredible Meydan racecourse.

APRIL

Dubai Fashion Week

www.dfw.ae

This usually takes place in April for the Autumn and Winter collection and in October for the Spring and Summer collection. It is the region's flagship fashion trade event and focuses on offering retail buyers, fashion professionals and the media an exclusive preview of the season's upcoming collections and trends. The Fashion Week attracts high-profile designers and buyers from across the entire region.

JUNE, JULY, AUGUST

Dubai Summer Surprises

www.mydsf.com

This festival, which simply comprises kids' entertainment, sales in shopping malls and a happy, yellow man called Modhesh, runs over the most sweaty, blistering summer months. The main venues for this event are the participating shopping malls as well as the Modhesh Fun City which is known as the region's largest indoor edutainment area. You'll find various activities and programmes to entertain and educate children.

OCTOBER

UAE Desert Challenge

www.uaedesertchallenge.com

This five-day desert rally starts in Abu Dhabi and finishes in Dubai. It attracts car, truck and motorbike riders and is the final race of the FIA Cross-Country Rally World Cup.

Desert Rhythm Festival

www.desertrhythmfestival.com

This festival brings together musical artists from around the world, uniting cultures through the beats of Arabic, Turkish, Latin, Urban and Soul, Caribbean, South African and Western music. Celebrations also include belly dancers, fire dancers and food from around the world.

NOVEMBER

Dubai Rugby Sevens

www.dubairugby7s.com

Part of the IRB World Sevens Series, Dubai Rugby Sevens takes place during the last weekend of November and features 16 international squads, a large number of amateur teams and live entertainment over three days. Something that started as a hobby has now expanded to be world-renowned and by 2008, Rugby Sevens moved to 'The Sevens', the Emirates' purpose built sporting venue.

DECEMBER

Dubai International Film Festival

www.dubaifilmfest.com

A non-profit cultural event featuring short films and documentaries from around the world, highlighting Dubai's multicultural nature. Cinema from the Arab countries and India is promoted, along with visits from the likes of George Clooney, Sharon Stone and Morgan Freeman.

You can buy tickets for major events and festivals at:

- Time Out Tickets – www.itp.net/tickets
- Box Office Middle East – www.boxofficeme.com.

NATIONAL HOLIDAYS

- New Year's Day – 1st January is a holiday in Dubai.
- Mouloud – The Birth of the Prophet is on 26th February.
- Leilat al-Meiraj – This is Ascension of the Prophet and in 2010 falls on 9th July.

- Eid Al-Fitr – This comes at the end of the Ramadan month and is the 'breaking of the fast'. It lasts for three days and in 2010 is on 11th September.

- Eid Al-Adha – This festival is part of the Hajj and lasts for four days. In 2010, it falls on 17th November.

- UAE National Day – This is always on 2nd December and is a public holiday.

- Islamic New Year – Al-Hijra, the Islamic New Year, is on 7th December in 2010.

- Ashura – This commemorates the death in battle of the Prophet's grandson, Imam Husain and falls on 16th December in 2010.

رئيس مجلس الادارة

Chapter 5

Economy

With such a dizzying array of mammoth developments and an unbelievable rate of urban expansion, Dubai was brought to global attention and started to become a huge attraction for investors, job seekers and anyone who wanted to be a part of this major transformation.

Dubai's economy has been one of the best performing in the Gulf region in recent years, with a yearly growth of 17.9% since 2001. It is also the most mature market in the UAE with real estate and construction representing about 30% of the GDP in 2007, according to HSBC.

Thoughts about the future of Dubai have always been divided. While many believed in continued and sustained growth, other analysts said that Dubai had expanded too far too fast and was headed for trouble. Of course, this wasn't something many could believe until the shock of recession, which only started taking its toll early in 2009.

Dubai has been hit pretty badly, especially the real estate market. However, towards the end of 2009 there was some balancing out as many companies decided to stick it out and just survive the year. 2010 is looking more optimistic. There are new businesses being set up and more jobs on offer. Despite Dubai's downturn, latest figures from the Dubai World Trade Centre have revealed a 12% increase in visitor volumes for exhibitions, conventions and conferences at its venues in 2009.

OVERALL

- Though Dubai's economy was built on the back of the oil industry, by 2000, the oil sector accounted for just 10% of the GDP. The visionary Sheikh Mohammed bin Rashid Al Maktoum realised that tourism was the way forward. This brought about increasing levels of investment and an unimaginable transformation of the city.

- Free trade zones, industry growth, transportation, farming, fisheries and communications are all areas that the government has developed in order to reduce the dependence on oil.

- The introduction of free trade zones – such as that at Jebel Ali – offering zero-tax incentives, have further attracted direct foreign investment.

- It is said that a quarter of the world's construction cranes are located in Dubai. A building boom has occurred: skyscraper after skyscraper has risen up in the desert; there's a pick and mix of vast malls. From a barren desert, Dubai has morphed into a bustling city.

- It is said that three out of four people in Dubai are tourists and approximately 7 million tourists visited Dubai in 2007. The overall contribution of tourism to Dubai's economy has risen by 30%, overtaking the contribution of the real estate, oil and construction services. By 2016, Dubai is expected to generate Dhs170.7 billion, according to WTTC (World Travel and Tourism Council).

LOCAL CURRENCY

- The monetary unit is the Dirham (Dhs), also known as the Arab Emirate Dirham (AED), and is divided into 100 fils.

- It has been held constant against the US Dollar since 1980 at a mid-rate of approximately $1 = Dhs3.67.

- Notes are in the following denominations: Dhs5, Dhs10, Dhs20, Dhs50, Dhs100, Dhs500 and Dhs1000. Coins are: Dhs1, 50fils and 25fils. While denominations on the notes are in Arabic and English, the coins are in Arabic only.

- The Dirham exchange rates as of November 2009 are:
  1 US dollar = Dhs3.70
  1 UK pound = Dhs5.88
  1 Euro = Dhs5.26.

BANKS

- There are many international banks in Dubai, with branches providing the usual commercial banking services. You can find a list of banks in the UAE at www.centralbank.ae/CommercialBanks.php.

- Most banks operate a six-day week and are open from 8am to 1pm Saturday to Thursday, although HSBC is open 8am to 3pm. All banks are closed on a Friday.

BUSINESS HOURS

- Most companies work from 8am to 5:30pm with an hour's lunch break. There are some which work from 8am to 1pm and then from 4pm to 7pm. Government offices are open from 7:30am to 2:30pm.

- Weekends are generally Friday and Saturday, though some companies are closed on Thursday afternoon and Friday.

Chapter 6

Projects

Dubai is home to some of most exciting, ambitious and extravagant projects in the world. Something that seems utterly impossible becomes a reality in this stunning city.

Living on the Palm now can seem surreal, but projects bigger and more unbelievable than this are in the making. Do bear in mind there are a number of projects that have been put on hold due to the current crisis and therefore completion dates no longer hold in those cases – which is why you won't find any completion dates in this section.

PALM

Built out in the sea, the ambitious Palm Islands have grabbed the world's attention. There are three Palm islands, two of which are not yet complete. All three are in the shape of a palm tree and are visible from space with the naked eye. Palm Jumeirah was the first to be built, and now has people living in the prestigious beachfront residences able to enjoy their own secluded areas. At the far end of the Palm is the recently opened and spectacular Atlantis hotel. All three islands will include a mixture of entertainment, residential and leisure areas.

WORLD

www.theworld.ae

A true icon in the making, The World is a collection of 300 private and resort islands in the shape of the world map. Announced in 2003 by Sheikh Mohammed bin Rashid Al Maktoum, these islands are sold by invitation to chosen individuals. The entire development will cover approximately 931 hectares and yachts will be the main mode of transport between the islands and to Dubai. Island reclamation was completed on schedule (January 2008) and construction is now on-going on the acquired islands.

Unbelievable

Over 320 million cubic metres of sand have been used to form the islands.

One island was offered at a price of $250 million!

THE UNIVERSE

In the shape of the solar system, the islands of the Universe will take the shape of the sun, moon and planets.

DUBAI MARINA

www.dubaimarina.ae

Built along a two-mile stretch of the shoreline, this man-made marina has created a waterfront community with apartment towers and villas set against the backdrop of water. The development can accommodate more than 120,000 people. With public walkways, great restaurants and cafés, and yatching and fishing available on your doorstep, the Marina creates a great living environment.

DUBAILAND

www.dubailand.ae

Covering 186 million square metres, an area twice the size of Disneyworld in Florida, Dubailand will comprise six areas with 50 themed leisure attractions and hotels. It is set to launch its first phase in October 2010. To date there are already 22 projects under development and some, such as Dubai Autodrome and Dubai Heritage, are already operational.

The following are some of the projects planned within Dubailand:

City of Arabia

Covering an area of 1.85 million square metres, this project will include the Mall of Arabia, the largest mall in the world, a massive indoor ski slope, a gaming arena, Restless Planet theme park along with residential homes, offices, schools, mosques, hotels and restaurants.

Dubai Sports City

Covering 5.25 million square metres, Dubai Sports City (www.dubaisportscity.ae) will include a wide range of sport and leisure facilities plus numerous residential areas such as Victory Heights and Gallery Villas. There will also be a cricket stadium with 25,000 seats, an outdoor stadium for football, rugby and athletics with a capacity of 60,000, and an indoor stadium for basketball, ice hockey, etc. Sports City will also be home to some world-class sporting academies as well as an 18-hole Ernie Els golf course.

Dubai Golf City

This will be one of the largest projects at Dubailand and will include world-class golf courses, a golf academy, a resort and spa, themed golf villages and a souk.

DOWNTOWN DUBAI

www.emaar.com

This 500 acre project with an urban-inspired concept, includes a number of residential, hotel, shopping and leisure developments. These include:

Burj Khalifa

www.burjkhalifa.ae

This awe-inspiring tallest tower is the epicentre of the new Downtown Dubai, comprising The Dubai Mall, Dubai Fountain, hotels, and residential and commercial areas. Launched on 4th January 2010 to an astounding display of fireworks and fountain dancing, Burj Khalifa is over 800 metres and 160 stories high, making it the tallest free-standing structure in the world. The lower 37 floors will be home to the world's first Armani Hotel.

Did you know?

The 700 private apartments covering 64 floors in Burj Khalifa were apparently bought within eight hours of going on sale.

Dubai Mall

The largest mall in the world, Dubai Mall includes more than 1200 retail stores, its very own huge Gold *Souk*, an Olympic-sized ice rink, a large cinema, the world's largest aquarium and a plethora of dining options (www.thedubaimall.com).

Old Town

Set around Burj Khalifa tower, Old Town (www.theoldtown.ae) has residential and retail facilities and its architecture depicts traditional Arabic design. This is the new hip place to live.

CULTURE VILLAGE

www.culturevillage.ae

This will be a world-class centre for culture and arts, featuring museums, exhibition halls, a *souk*, art galleries, academies for art, music, dance and other crafts, hotels and restaurants.

DUBAI PEARL

www.dubaipearl.com

The Dubai Pearl will be a mixed-use development, with office towers, luxury apartments, hotels, a shopping mall, art gallery and the Royal Hall, a large performing arts theatre. It will overlook the Palm Jumeirah and be situated beside the Dubai Media City. It is a $4billion development and covers an area of 17 million square feet.

DUBAI WATERFRONT

www.waterfront.ae

This will be the world's largest coastal development transforming 1.4 billion square feet of desert and sea into an international community, consisting of over 250 individual communities.

DUBAI PROMENADE

www.dubaipromenade.ae

Located between Dubai Marina and the seafront, Dubai Promenade will create a virtual peninsula along the Dubai shoreline, anchored by an awesome wheel-shaped five-star hotel, able to accommodate around 10,000 residents.

DISCOVERY GARDENS

www.discoverygardens-dubai.com

Located near Jebel Ali Free Zone, Discovery Gardens is a 26 million square foot development, which will provide affordable modern housing for almost 60,000 residents. Devoted to garden landscaping, the buildings will be grouped into six themes – Zen, Mediterranean, Contemporary, Cactus, Mogul and Mesoamerican.

DUBAI INTERNATIONAL AIRPORT

www.dubaiaiport.com

The new Terminal 3, which opened in October 2008, covers an area of 515,000 square metres located 20 metres beneath the taxiway area and is used exclusively by its official carrier, Emirates Airlines. It has six floors, 157 lifts, 97 escalators and 82 moving walkways. Terminal 3 is able to handle 43 million passengers a year.

Did you know?

The new terminal mega project required excavation of over 10 million cubic metres of land – that's enough to fill 4000 Olympic-size pools!

THE LAGOONS

www.lagoons.ae

These are seven artificial islands linked by bridges under construction by Dubai Creek. There will be luxury villas and apartments overlooking the creek with scenic yacht marinas and waterways. And for those living and working here, there will be over 50 shopping malls, spas and parks, as well as cultural attractions including a theatre, museum, arts centre and opera house.

HYDROPOLIS UNDERWATER HOTEL

www.hydropolis.com

This underwater luxury resort just off Jumeirah Beach is set to open sometime this year. It will cover an area of 260 hectares and will include a land station, a connecting tunnel to transport guests by train to the main area of the hotel, and a submarine leisure complex with 220 suites.

DUBAI MARITIME CITY

www.dubaimaritimecity.com

This is the world's first purpose-built maritime centre, a mammoth project in the Arabian Gulf which aims to become a maritime hub, integrating diverse sectors of the industry. The project abides by green construction concepts – buildings that consume less energy and thus generate less waste. There will be an Academic Quarter, a Maritime Centre, offices and residences.

﴿٥١﴾ قُل لَّن يُصِيبَنَآ إِلَّا مَا كَتَبَ ٱللَّهُ لَنَا هُوَ مَوْلَىٰنَا ۚ وَعَلَى ٱللَّهِ فَلْيَتَوَكَّلِ ٱلْمُؤْمِنُونَ

﴿٥٢﴾ قُلْ هَلْ تَرَبَّصُونَ بِنَآ إِلَّآ إِحْدَى ٱلْحُسْنَيَيْنِ ۖ وَنَحْنُ نَتَرَبَّصُ بِكُمْ أَن يُصِيبَكُمُ ٱللَّهُ بِعَذَابٍ مِّنْ عِندِهِۦٓ أَوْ بِأَيْدِينَا ۖ فَتَرَبَّصُوٓا۟ إِنَّا مَعَكُم مُّتَرَبِّصُونَ

﴿٥٣﴾ قُلْ أَنفِقُوا۟ طَوْعًا أَوْ كَرْهًا لَّن يُتَقَبَّلَ مِنكُمْ ۖ إِنَّكُمْ كُنتُمْ قَوْمًا فَٰسِقِينَ

﴿٥٤﴾ وَمَا مَنَعَهُمْ أَن تُقْبَلَ مِنْهُمْ نَفَقَٰتُهُمْ إِلَّآ أَنَّهُمْ كَفَرُوا۟ بِٱللَّهِ وَبِرَسُولِهِۦ وَلَا يَأْتُونَ ٱلصَّلَوٰةَ إِلَّا وَهُمْ كُسَالَىٰ وَلَا يُنفِقُونَ إِلَّا وَهُمْ كَٰرِهُونَ

فَلَا تُعْجِبْكَ أَمْوَٰلُهُمْ وَلَآ أَوْلَٰدُهُمْ ۚ

iself,
it

Cause)
ly : 1314
be
indeed
and wicked."

why
ns are not
at they reject
postle ;
e to prayer
stness ; and that
ntributions
unwillingly.

ir wealth
following in) sons 1315

In

56. They sw
That they a... but they
Of you ; but they
Of you : yet they
(To appear in th

57. If they could
A place to fle
Or caves, o
Or conceal
Turn stra
With an

58. And a
Who
Of
If
T

iting of the Unbelievers and that of the Believers are in di
for disaster to the Believers, but the Believers will either c
either case happy in the issue. The Believers expect puni
ity, either through their own instrumentality. or in s
evers would not like it in either case. Cf. vi. 158.

Hypocrites, who secretly plotted against Islam,
king some contribution to the Cause in order to gi
not acceptable, whether they seemed to gi
ience were in their hearts. Three reas
verse : (1) they did not believe ; (2) their
y their hearts were not behind the contr
nich does not proceed from a pure and sinc

If they appeared to be prosperous, with th
e not to be envied. In reality their wealth a
On this particular occasion this was proved to th
kened their understanding, and led to th
their fathers had fought against, mu
han their discomfiture in this

rs
an,
make
contri
se rebelli
ir rejecti
mere show
hing is acce
ull (metaph
emselves be
alth of the P
Their sons a
agrin of the fa

Chapter 7

The law

You need to have some idea of how the local laws operate – and make sure that you don't, albeit unwittingly, contravene any of them.

HOW THE LEGAL SYSTEM WORKS

The 1971 Constitution agreed by the various rulers of the Emirates stated that the highest legislative authority in the UAE should be the Supreme Council of Rulers. The President, therefore, approves all federal laws in the UAE. Local authorities in the various emirates can also issue their own decrees as laws applying only within their own region. Generally laws in Dubai do change quite often, so in case something should apply to your area of business or any other aspect of life, you should keep up-to-date.

SHARIA LAW

Sharia law is the oldest source of law in the UAE and the basis of the legal system. It is a collection of principles pertaining to public and private life for those living in Islamic countries. However, in Dubai, Sharia law is used only in the areas of inheritance, Family Law such as divorce and child custody, Succession Law and the Penal Law.

EXPATRIATES

For expatriates living in Dubai, the laws of their home countries will generally apply in personal matters of marriage and divorce. However, penalties for breaking the law in Dubai are severe. If convicted of a crime, you will receive a judicial sentence and immediate deportation.

A FEW THINGS YOU SHOULD NOTE

Dressing

Since you need to be dressed decently in any public places, beachwear should not be worn anywhere other than at the beach.

Public display of affection

You must have heard of cases where people, even tourists have been arrested for public displays of affection, as they are considered an offence to public decency. This includes kissing. So, whether you're married or not, it's something you should definitely be very careful about.

Traffic lights

Don't cross a red light. If you do, you could get sentenced to a maximum one-month detention and a small fine.

Drinking and driving

The UAE has a zero-tolerance policy to driving under the effect of alcohol.

Drugs

Whether you're consuming, holding, buying or selling drugs, this is considered a crime in Dubai.

Smoking

If you're caught smoking in any government facilities, offices, malls and shops, you'll be fined.

Insults

If you swear at or insult somebody or make an offensive gesture and they complain about this, this could lead to a fine and/or imprisonment.

Photography

You shouldn't take photos of people in public places, especially of women and families, without their permission.

Ramadan

During the month of Ramadan when Muslims fast from dawn to sunset, nobody is permitted to eat, drink or smoke in public areas. It is considered a public offence and is punishable by law.

Living together

Pre-marital sex and homosexuality are both illegal in Dubai. While landlords don't usually ask to see a marriage certificate, if you're found to be living with a member of the opposite sex who is not your relative or spouse, this is a punishable crime.

COURTS

- The Sharia courts deal with civil matters for Muslims in the UAE.

- The Civil Court deals with commercial matters and disputes such as debt recovery.

- The Criminal Court deals with criminal cases, which have initially been referred by police to the Public Prosecutor, who then decides to refer the matter to the Criminal Court.

- Most commercial matters are dealt with by either civil courts or permanently-established arbitration tribunals.

Chapter 8

The media

There is an abundance of newspapers and magazines based in Dubai. Dubai Media City (www.dubaimediacity.com) has rapidly emerged as a global media hub where many media-related businesses including Reuters, Bloomberg and MBC have offices.

There are many magazines published in Dubai, both weekly and monthly, which give an idea of what's on, the latest gossip, trends, topics and listings and so on. You can buy most of them from a bookshop.

MAGAZINES

- Automotive and transport: *Full Throttle, Wheels*
- Computers and IT: *Arabian Reseller News, Computer News Middle East, PC World Middle East*
- Business: *Forbes Arabia, Your Business*
- Entertainment, Gossip, Health and Beauty: *Ahlan!, E+, OK! Middle East, Aquarius, Connector, Harper's Bazaar*
- About Dubai and lifestyle: *Etc, Friday, TimeOut Dubai, What's On.*

NEWSPAPERS

Name	Type	Website
7days	Daily	www.7days.ae
Dubai Chronicle	Online	www.dubaichronicle.com
Emirates Business 24/7	Daily	www.business24-7.ae
Gulf News	Daily	www.gulfnews.com
Gulf Today	Daily	www.godubai.com/gulftoday
Khaleej Times	Daily	www.khaleejtimes.com
The National	Daily	www.thenational.ae
Xpress	Daily	www.xpress4me.com

PART 2

Moving to Dubai

Chapter 9

The move and formalities

You're in Dubai, an awesome place with sunshine, beach, good career prospects, tax-free salaries, of course, and the cut and thrust of day-to-day living! The red tape you have to cope with, trying to find accommodation and the processes you have to go through might seem a little tedious, but the sunshine, beaches and shopping will make it all the more worthwhile.

There are many reasons you would want to move to Dubai and, of course, just as many that would make you decide against it. It is up to you which outweighs which. Even after a year, it's easy to get bored with the artificiality of life in Dubai and all that surrounds you. But at the same time, Dubai is an experience, a totally different experience ... even if it is only for a short period of time. And in case you get bored, you can use your weekends to explore the other emirates and plan short getaways, go trekking and diving and get involved in a number of diverse activities.

As you will see in the sections to come, there is much more to this city than meets the eye. While the recent downturn may be a slight put-off, there are many who are looking at this as an opportunity. In some cases, property prices have more than halved, making this a good time to start investing. However, it has generally become more difficult to get jobs, primarily due to the soaring demand and thus growing competition.

10 reasons to move	10 reasons not to move
Be a part of what Dubai is becoming as the world watches with wonder at the latest incredible projects	It's all glitz and glamour, and excessively artificial. There's hardly any natural environment
No tax – well what more can be said about this?	It's an expensive city with a high cost of living
The weather – again, a bestseller	Offices, malls, buildings are all air-conditioned to such a degree you have to wear a jumper
Dubai has a great mix of cultures and people	The lower classes (e.g. builders, taxi drivers) are often discriminated against, made to work in poor conditions and are badly paid
Outdoor activities and beaches are great – something you can always enjoy at weekends and a real plus point for kids	In terms of culture, there are hardly any theatres, opera or ballets ... and you can't even walk anywhere
Shopping is fantastic. There are so many malls, you can even go mall-hopping	Shopping isn't cheap and you hardly get any sales
There are ample spas and restaurants, so you'll never wonder what to do with friends	It's pricey and you end up eating so much food, you get the 'Dubai belly'
Dubai's a liberal country – all religions are tolerated and there are mosques, churches and temples	It is still an Islamic country and therefore there are things you can't do. Ramadan becomes an especially difficult month
It's a safe place with a very low crime rate	Driving on the roads in Dubai is dangerous!

BEFORE YOU LEAVE

There's a lot to look forward to when moving to Dubai, but there's also a lot you'll need to get done before getting there and even once you've arrived. The more research you do before you leave, the easier the process will prove to be.

It is certainly better to get a job and *then* leave for Dubai. This way, your company will be your 'sponsor' and the process of getting a residency permit or visa will be much easier. It is also likely that your company will provide initial accommodation, for which they will pay. Of course, in the current global downturn, getting a job in

Dubai might be a little more difficult than hitherto, but this year, things are looking better and companies are recruiting again.

If you are planning to look for a job once you get to Dubai (see pp 76–8), it would be best to start emailing and calling recruitment companies in Dubai before you leave. There might also be some job agencies in your home country specialising in overseas recruitment.

If you have children, then you should start researching schools (see pp 235–42), narrowing down and then speaking to those on your shortlist. Some will have waiting lists so it's best to start early. It's also advisable to start looking into residential areas (see pp 98–117), depending on where you will be working.

Need to know

- Electricity – The electricity supply in Dubai is 220/240 volts at 50 cycles. Plug points are the same as in the UK.
- Water – The water in Dubai is desalinated and very safe to drink. However, most people prefer to buy bottled drinking water.

Documents you need

You will need qualification certificates and important documents, such as your marriage certificate and children's birth certificates, attested in your home country. Start this early, as it can take some time to sort everything out.

You will also need passport photocopies and passport photographs for many of the procedures when in Dubai. Make lots of copies so you don't need to worry about this later.

Your belongings

International shipping companies will transport goods to Dubai from anywhere in the world. It is possible to get a door-to-door service or to have goods delivered to the airport or Jebel Ali Port.

Tips

- List all the items in each box.
- Get more than one quote and compare.
- Give as much notice as possible to the relocation company.

Some helpful websites

www.compare-international-movers.com lists all the relevant companies and allows you to request quotations. Exact prices will depend on various factors including location, items shipped and weight.

www.weknowdubai.com/relocation-services/index.php lists all relocation companies from Dubai.

If you want to wait till you get to Dubai, furniture and clothes can be bought easily. You may find the cost of shipping particular goods very expensive, in which case it would be cheaper to buy them new on arrival. There are, of course, the high-end designer shops to source your requirements from, but there are also notice boards offering second-hand appliances and furniture for sale.

Pets

It is possible to import pets to Dubai, though it is a somewhat tedious and expensive process. Before deciding to bring your pet, you should consider the fact that in the summer months, it might become very hot for pets to be outdoors. Also, if you are living in an apartment, space might be a problem.

Pet Charities		
Name	**Location**	**Phone**
www.animal-home.com	online	04 3671749
Feline Friends	Jumeirah	0504510058
K9 Friends	Jumeirah	04 3474611

Pet Shops		
Name	**Location**	**Phone**
Animal World	Jumeirah Beach Rd	04 3444422
Petland UAE	Oasis Centre	04 3380171
Petshabitat	Barsha	04 3418085
Marina Treasures Pets	Barsha	04 3474666

Veterinarians		
Name	**Location**	**Phone**
Al Barsha Veterinary Clinic	Near Mall of Emirates	04 3408601
Al Safa Veterinary Clinic	Al Wasl Rd Jumeirah	04 3483799
European Veterinary Centre	Sheikh Zayed Rd	04 3439591
Jumeirah Vet Clinic	Jumeirah Rd	04 3942276
Veterinary Hospital	Al Quoz	04 3387726

If you decide to bring your pet, you will need to contact the airlines to find out if they allow animals. You will need to have your pet vaccinated and obtain a Health Certificate and a Vaccination Certificate.

Your pet will also need to wear a municipality ID tag, which will be registered to your mobile number, so that the police will know it is not a stray. You can find out more details on importing animals to other countries from the Ministry of Agriculture Fisheries and Food in the UK (+448459 334477). For more information on pets, check www.petdubai.com.

DOCUMENTS AND LICENCES

Essential documents

You will need a few essential documents for many of the procedures such as driving licence, health card, buying a car and the like.

The most important are:

- original passport

- passport photocopies

- passport-sized photographs.

It's also good to keep a copy of these at home, in a safe place, just in case.

Make a copy of all your certificates once in Dubai since you might have to show a copy of your labour contract, salary certificate and no objection certificate when renting a property, buying a car or opening a bank account.

Entry visa

It's important to get advice on visa requirements from the embassy in your home country. The requirements vary from country to country. It's also worth bearing in mind that rules and regulations often change without warning in Dubai, so it is advisable to recheck before leaving.

Citizens from many countries including USA, Australia, Canada, UK, many EU countries, Japan, Hong Kong and Malaysia automatically get visas upon arrival at the airport, valid for 60 days. This can also be renewed for a further 30 days for Dhs500 at the Department of Immigration and Naturalisation (04 3981010) in Karama.

After entering Dubai on a residency visa or an employment visa, you will need to complete procedures and become a resident within 60 days, though it will probably take far less time. It is acceptable to leave the country before obtaining the residency permit, as long as you have the entry visa stamped in your passport when you first arrive.

Health card

Once you have an employment visa or a work visa, you will need to apply for a health card. If employed, your company should take care of this paperwork and advise you where to go to take a medical test.

If applying yourself:

- Get an application form from Rashid Hospital (available in other hospitals, but

Rashid is where you will need to submit it)

- Take this to the health card section at Rashid Hospital
- You will also need your passport, passport copies, a copy of your visa, two passport photos and Dhs310 to cover the charge for the card
- You will now get a health card and a blank form for your medical test.

Medical test

The two most common hospitals at which to take your test are Maktoum Hospital and Al Baraha Hospital. You can also ask at Rashid Hospital where to go. To take the medical test, you will need:

- health card
- copy of the receipt for the health card
- the test form filled out in Arabic
- two passport photos.

What you need to do:

- Submit the forms, pay the fee of Dhs210 and wait your turn at the hospital
- You will take a blood test (which checks for HIV and hepatitis)
- After this, you might need to have an x-ray (check for tuberculosis)
- After the tests, collect a receipt, which will tell you when to collect your results
- If your tests are positive for HIV or hepatitis, you will be called back for another test and if the second test confirms this, you will be deported to your home country.

Residency permit

You can get your residency permit once you have your health card along with the medical test results. The permit is valid for three years and is easy to renew. You will need a residency permit to rent a property.

For employment

If you are sponsored for employment, your employer will handle the paperwork, which means you will not have to visit the Immigration Department yourself. You will need to give your passport, employment visa, medical test results, education certificates and three passport photos to whoever is dealing with the process. This will cost Dhs300 and could take up to 10 days. If you need your passport urgently, you can get your application processed on the same day for an extra Dhs100. Your company should pay these expenses.

Your education certificates also need to be verified by a solicitor in your home country.

Sponsoring family

As a resident in Dubai, you can sponsor family members. To sponsor your wife and children for an Entry Permit, you will need:

- A prepaid e-form application (Dhs110)
- A copy of the sponsor's passport
- A copy of the sponsored person's passport
- Marriage contract attested by UAE embassy in the country where the marriage took place, and by UAE Ministry of Foreign Affairs
- Salary certificate or employment contract in which the salary cannot be less than Dhs4000, or Dhs3000 plus accommodation.

It costs Dhs10 for ordinary delivery application and Dhs110 for an ordinary e-form application. For urgent delivery applications, you will need to pay an extra Dhs100 and Dhs10 at the typing offices or to the bank staff.

If you wish to sponsor parents and first-degree relatives, you will need all of the above, and in place of the marriage certificate, you will need proof of blood relationship.

Since these requirements could change at any time, it's worth checking at www.dnrd.gov.ae.

Labour card

You can apply for the labour card once you have a residency permit. It is also a legal requirement for working in Dubai. The card will feature your photo and details of your employer.

ID card

The Emirates Identity Authority (EIDA) is responsible for issuing electronic identity cards for the whole population, to verify and confirm the identity of each individual. This electronic means of identification is mandatory for all inhabitants over 15 years old of the United Arab Emirates, whether nationals or expatriates. The deadline for everyone having electronic ID cards is set at 1st January 2011. The idea is for the ID to eventually replace all other identification means such as labour permit, health card, driving licence, etc.

Process

- Fill in the pre-registration form at the typing centres within the registration centre or at a post office.

- It will cost Dhs40 or is free of charge from the website.

- Visit the registration centre with a pre-registration form (with 2D barcodes) and an original valid passport with valid residency permit.

- It will cost Dhs100 for registration fees against each valid year in your residency permit and Dhs20 for card delivery fees.

For more detailed information, please refer to: www.emiratesid.ae.

Opening a bank account

Opening a bank account in Dubai is straightforward and you will undergo a similar process in most countries. However, though bank staff are generally helpful and friendly, things can take much longer in Dubai, so do expect delays. Some banks can send out representatives to meet you at your office – so if you're busy, make sure you call in advance. It's also best to compare rates from various banks. You will need to have a minimum monthly balance Dhs5000 in most banks.

What you need

To open an account, you need to produce your original passport as well as a copy of your passport, including the page with the residence visa stamp, a no objection certificate from your employer stating your salary and a reference letter.

Credit card

Some banks will automatically offer you a credit card on opening an account. Others have policies whereby they can only issue you with a credit card once you've completed six months at your company.

Cheque book

A cheque book will not be given to you unless you have a valid residence visa. Please also note:

- It is a criminal offence to write a cheque if there are insufficient funds in the account. You can be arrested and be sent to prison for this

- The UAE Central Bank has ruled that if you issue three or more cheques which are dishonoured, you will no longer be able to operate a cheque account

- It is possible to issue a post dated cheque.

ATMs

Most banks, malls and supermarkets have ATM machines from which you can withdraw cash using your bank card. You can also make deposits and pay your bills without too much hassle.

Bank contact details		
Name	**Phone**	**Website**
Abu Dhabi Commercial Bank	8002030	www.adcb.com
Citibank	04 3114000	www.citigroup.com/uae
Commercial Bank of Dubai	800CBD (223)	www.cbd.ae
Emirates Bank	04 3160316	www.ebi.ae
First Gulf Bank	600525500	www.fgb.ae
HSBC	8004722	www.uae.hsbc.com
Lloyds TSB Bank	04 3422000	www.lloydstsb.ae
Mashreq Bank	04 4244444	www.mashreqbank.com
National Bank of Dubai	04 3100101	www.nbd.com
National Bank of Abu Dhabi	04 3433030	www.nbad.com
RAK Bank	04 2130000	www.rakbank.ae
Royal Bank of Canada	04 3313196	www.rbcprivatebanking.com/dubai
Royal Bank of Scotland	04 3086000	www.rbsinternational.com/offshore
Standard Chartered Bank	04 3138888	www.standardchartered.com/ae
United Arab Bank	04 2220181	www.uab.ae

Liquor licence

You cannot buy alcohol from supermarkets, but can get a liquor licence so that you can buy it from licensed shops. It is a criminal offence to have liquor in your home without a licence. In public, only hotel bars and restaurants are licensed to serve alcoholic drinks.

To get a liquor licence, you must be non-Muslim, at least 21 years old, a resident in Dubai and earn a minimum monthly salary of Dhs350.

To apply:

- Get an application form from the police station or one of the *MMI* or *A&E* stores (the two licensed liquor chains in Dubai)
- Fill this in and include your spouse's details if you want them to use it
- Get this form signed and stamped by your employer
- Return this form to the outlet with your passport copy, residence visa copy, two passport photos, your tenancy contract copy and your labour contract copy (issued by Ministry of Labour). If you are self-employed, then take a copy of your trade licence and proof of income each month. You will need to pay Dhs150
- The licence usually takes around 10 days to be processed and the store will contact you when it is ready
- Your licence will have a monthly limit placed on alcohol purchase which is at the discretion of the police and is based on your monthly salary. When you buy alcohol, you will be asked for your liquor licence so that they can deduct credit from it.

Chapter 10

Getting around

Up till very recently, taxis and driving have been the main method of getting around Dubai. But the new Metro has changed all that ...

Since 9th September 2009 (in fact, at 9 seconds past 9pm on 9/9/9, Sheikh Mohammed did the grand opening of the Metro and travelled on the Metro himself), the Metro has become an easier and quite a luxurious way to commute, with some stations open and others to open later.

DRIVING

Although the Metro has started operating, buying or hiring a car is still a good way to move around as it gives you flexibility. Driving in Dubai is on the right-hand side of the road and the driver's seat is on the left.

The infrastructure makes travelling by car quite easy. However, the roads are continuously changing, so it's important to check for updates every so often. One main highway, Sheikh Zayed Road, runs through Dubai; this highway connects it to the other emirates in the UAE.

Note

- Driving in the UAE is on the right.
- Wearing of seatbelts in the front seats is mandatory.
- There is a zero tolerance drink-drive policy.

TRAFFIC AND SAFETY

www.dubaipolice.gov.ae

Due to the number of cars on the road, traffic is a major issue in Dubai. The government is trying to tackle this problem by introducing new interchanges and highways as well as the world-class metro, completed at the end of 2009. A toll system has also been introduced on Sheikh Zayed Road (Dhs4 per gate) to deter people from using this road. Having said all this, Dubai is continually changing and traffic certainly eased in 2009.

Driving in Dubai is also dangerous due to the speeding cars on the roads. Overtaking and swerving from one side to the other is very common, especially on Sheikh Zayed Road, and many drivers are pretty aggressive. Dubai continues to have one of the highest death rates from road accidents in the world, per head of population. You just have to be wary and alert.

If you're driving around yourself, always pay more attention to your mirrors than you would normally do and be cautious and aware of your surroundings. Make sure you are also carrying the correct documentation and insurance with you.

From March 2008, the Unified Federal Traffic Law came into effect, with hefty penalties for serious traffic offences and black points against the driver's licence.

A few points to note:

- For driving dangerously, the fine is Dhs2000, 12 black points and 30 days vehicle confiscation

- For driving under the influence of alcohol, drugs or similar substances, the fine is decided by court, the driver gets 24 black points and 60 days vehicle confiscation

- Drink driving is considered a very serious offence in Dubai and can result in a prison sentence

- If you get 12 points, you will have to reapply for a licence
- If parking tickets appear on your windscreen, you will only have a week or two to pay. The amount will also increase if you don't pay within the time indicated on the back of the ticket
- More details of fines and traffic violations can be found on www.dubaipolice.gov.ae.

Driving School	Telephone	Website
Al Ahli Driving School	04 3411500	www.alahlidubai.com
Belhasa Driving School	04 3243535	www.bdc.ae
Dubai Driving Centre	04 3455855	www.dcds.ae
Emirates Driving Institute	04 2631100	www.edi-uae.com
Galadari Driving School	04 3350532	www.gmdc.ae

Speed limits

- Usually 60–80 kph in and around town
- 100–120 kph on main roads
- The speed limit is clearly indicated on road signs.

If involved in a serious accident, dial 999 in emergency, or call the police if not so serious:

- Deira: 04 2660555
- Bur Dubai: 04 3981111
- Sharjah: 06 5381111
- You can find the phone numbers of police stations in the UAE from Dubai Traffic Police Information Line: 04 2685555, www.dubaipolice.gov.ae.

Some useful numbers:

- fines, violations and payments: 8007777 (toll free)
- Dubai police operator: 04 2292222 (24 hrs)
- security services: 04 2013430, 04 2013429 (24 hrs)
- traffic services: 04 2694444 (24 hrs).

PETROL

Petrol is very cheap in Dubai. The approximate cost for a litre of unleaded petrol is Dhs1.69 per litre and for diesel, Dhs2.56 per litre. Fuel is sold by the US gallon (3.99 litres).

HIRING A CAR

When you first arrive in Dubai, it's easy to hire a car while you settle in and obtain your residency visa. All you need is a valid international driving licence, a credit card, your passport and two photographs.

If you are under 21, and in some cases under 25, some companies may refuse to rent you a car. It is also necessary to have a credit or debit card so that the company can secure a deposit at the time of rental.

There are both local and international car hire companies and rates vary from US$55 (e.g. Honda) to $155 for a 4x4 and $175 for a luxury car (e.g. Mercedes). You can find a list of companies on http://weknowdubai.com/car-rental-companies/2.html.

Most rental companies will deliver and collect the car from your apartment. Always keep dirham coins handy for parking. When hiring, also ensure the car has a Salik sticker which allows you to pass through toll booths without having to stop to pay: charges are deducted automatically (see p 69).

DRIVING LICENCE

Once you have your residence permit, you will need to obtain a UAE driving licence. It's a very simple process for most Western expatriates.

For the countries shown in the following list, it is possible to transfer your licence without taking any tests or examinations. You need a residency visa and need to be at least 18 years of age.

Australia
Austria
Belgium
Canada
Czech Republic
Cyprus
Denmark
Finland
France
Germany
Greece
Holland
Iceland
Iran
Ireland
Italy
Japan
Luxembourg
New Zealand
Norway
Poland
Portugal
Singapore
Slovakia
South Africa
South Korea
Spain
Sweden
Switzerland
Turkey
UK
USA

You need to go to the Traffic Police with your existing licence, your passport, an eye test certificate and Dhs110. You will get your licence immediately.

For more information, contact the Dubai Department of Traffic at 04 2694444.

BUYING A NEW CAR

Almost all international manufacturers have distributors in Dubai and banks also provide financing at competitive interest rates. Car prices are generally lower than in other countries and with the wide variety of models on offer along with low petrol prices, buying a car can be quite fun. You need a UAE driving licence, along with your residency visa, passport and photocopies of all these. Most of the insurance policies will also cover multiple drivers.

BUYING A USED CAR

There are a number of second-hand car dealers selling good quality cars. Some expatriates choose to buy used cars as many have only been driven for a few months and are then sold at a much lower price than when they were new. You can find some great bargains! Have a look on supermarket notice boards, online forums and in the classified section of local newspapers (*Gulf News* and *Khaleej Times*).

Otherwise, head to 4x4 Motors (www.4x4motors.com), one of the biggest used-car dealers in Dubai or to Automall (www.automalluae.com). You can also buy at auctions such as Al Awir (www.goldenbellauctions.com), one of the largest auction houses.

Tip

A lot of Western expatriates have large 4x4 vehicles as they're handy if you're going to drive in the desert. Bigger cars are also more secure.

CAR REGISTRATION

Once you have bought a car, you will need to register it with the Dubai Traffic Police in order to obtain a licence plate. If you have bought a new car from a dealer, the dealer will register the car for you and in some cases, second-hand car dealers may also register the car.

PARKING CARDS

Road and Transport Authority: 8009090, www.rta.ae

It's best to get a pre-paid parking card. You can either buy a pay-as-you-go card from the post office or certain petrol stations, or a card with an unlimited amount over a period of time from Dubai Municipality. This is much better than carrying coins with you all the time.

TAXIS

www.dubaitransport.gov.ae

Direct booking (Dubai Transport Corporation): 04 2080808

Taxis are very convenient and the most common way of getting around Dubai, but it is sometimes difficult to get one. At malls, there are often long queues as well as at hotels. Taxis run on meters and there is therefore no chance of haggling over fares.

The fare starts at Dhs3 for a pick-up (Dhs3.50 from 10pm to 6am), followed by Dhs1.80 per kilometre. A taxi from Mall of the Emirates to Deira City Centre is approximately Dhs50. The passenger will also need to pay Dhs4 for Salik.

WATER TAXIS

Travelling across the creek is pretty easy. Just take the *abra* (Dhs1 each way) or water taxi between Dubai and Deira. The fee is approximately Dhs2. This is an experience in itself, so do try it out. You can also enjoy a 45-minute trip along the Creek for Dhs25 (starts at Shindagha station, by the heritage village).

SALIK

www.salik.ae

Dubai has an electronic toll system called Salik, which deducts a toll of Dhs4 from your prepaid toll account each time your vehicle passes through a Salik tolling point, using advanced technology.

You can register for a Salik tag at any of the Salik outlets (petrol stations and selected branches of Dubai Islamic Bank and Emirate Bank). It will cost Dhs100 for issuing the tag, including Dhs50 credit and to register, you will need a copy of the car registration card and a copy of the trade licence. You can find out more and top up you Salik credit at www.salik.ae.

METRO

www.dubaimetro.eu

When completed, Dubai Metro will have a total of 70 kilometres (43 miles) of lines, and 47 stations, making it the longest fully automated rail system in the world.

The Metro was launched on 09/09/09 with ten stations operational. For more information, check www.rta.ae or www.gulfnews.com. This has already begun to alleviate traffic and congestion in the city. Trains include first class and women-and-children-only sections.

In April 2010, seven new stations opened on the Red Line and the number of trains increased from 12 to 20. So by the time you read this, the metro will be even quicker and better.

Currently opening times are 6am to 11pm Saturday to Thursday and 2pm to midnight Friday, but they are being reviewed and may well change in the near future, so keep checking.

The Red Line runs from Rashidiva to Jebel Ali passing the American University of Dubai while The Green Line will run from Al Ittihad Square to Rashidiya bus station through Deira City Centre and Dubai Airport Terminals 1 and 3.

Metro fares are fairly cheap, from 80fils to Dhs6.50. You can also get permanent Nol cards which can be topped up.

Did you know?

- There are 47 stations in total (more on extension lines).
- The total length of the project is a whopping 74.6 km.
- Designed to carry around 1.2 million passengers a day.
- The entire Metro has no drivers!

CYCLING

Although this is an efficient way of commuting, most people still travel by car and bikes are generally used by those on lower incomes. The main reasons for not cycling are the extreme heat in the summer months, which will leave you sweating within ten minutes of cycling anywhere and the careless drivers who don't pay much attention to anything on the roads.

BUSES

Road and Transport Authority – www.rta.ae

There are over 60 bus routes through the main areas of Dubai. In order to encourage more people to use the bus, there will soon better timetables and route plans, as well as air-conditioned bus stops. Buses are air-conditioned, but generally overcrowded. They are regular, start between 5am and 6am and keep going until around 11pm. Fares are cheap, between Dhs1 and Dhs3 per journey, paid when boarding.

AIRLINES

Being such an accessible city, Dubai has become a real hub and transit point. Most large cities have direct flights to Dubai. Over 110 airlines operate to and from over 160 destinations at the Dubai International Airport. Emirates, Dubai's own award-winning national airline, is based here and operates flights to over 90 destinations.

Dubai International Airport

Flight information – 04 2166666, www.dubaiairport.com

The fantastic new US$4.5 billion Terminal 3 opened in October 2008. This spacious terminal has been built for easier passenger flow and to accommodate the increasing number of passengers every year.

Covering an area of 515,000 square metres, the new terminal is used exclusively by its official carrier, Emirates Airlines, and has six floors, 157 lifts, 97 escalators and 82 moving walkways. It also boasts 220 check-in counters.

And you'll be wowed by the facilities on offer – an airport hotel with a gym, pool and spa, Timeless Spas in the first and business class lounges, Starbucks, Costa, Paul and more – and, of course, a large duty free area.

At Dubai International Airport, there is also a dedicated desk for passengers with special needs.

Most airlines operate from Dubai airport, but Etihad operates from Abu Dhabi Airport and Air Arabia from Sharjah Airport.

Flydubai, owned by the government of Dubai, has recently become Dubai's first low cost airline, operating from Terminal 2. It is less expensive than Emirates.

The main airlines serving Dubai are:

Airlines	**Enquiries**	**Website**
Alitalia	04 2242257	www.alitalia.com
Air Arabia	06 5580000	www.airarabia.com
Air France	04 6025400	www.airfrance.ae
British Airways	8004413322	www.ba.com
Cathay Pacific	04 2042888	www.cathaypacific.com
Emirates Airlines	04 2144444	www.emirates.com
Etihad Airways	02 5058000	www.etihadairways.com
Gulf Air	04 2713111	www.gulfairco.com
Indian Airlines	04 2216789	www.indianairlines.in
KLM	04 6025444	www.klm.com
Lufthansa	04 3432121	www.lufthansa.com
Qatar Airways	04 2292229	www.qatarairways.com
Swiss Intl Airlines	04 2945051	www.swiss.com/uae
United Airlines	80004415492	www.united.com
Virgin Atlantic	04 4060600	www.virgin-atlantic.com

TRAVEL AGENTS

	Telephone	Area	Website
Airlink International	04 2821050	Dubai Internet City	www.airlinktmc.com
Al Futtaim Travels	04 3410237	Maktoum St, Deira	www.futtaim.com
Al Naboodah Travel	04 2940099	Al Ittihad St, Deira	www.uaetraveler.com
Al Tayer Travel	04 2236000	Sh Rashid Bldg, Maktoum St	www.altayer-travel.com
BCD Travel	04 2977997	Al Rigga Rd, Deira	www.bcdtravel.ae
Emirates Holidays	8005252		www.emirates-holidays.com
Kanoo Travel	04 3341222	Al Karama	www.kanootravel.com
Net Tours Group	04 2666655	Al Bakhit Centre, Deira	www.nettoursdubai.com
Orient Travel	04 3433332	Emarat Atrium, Sheikh Zayed Rd	www.orienttravels.com
White Sands	04 2826800	Saleh Bin Lehaj Bldg, Garhoud	www.whitesandstours.ae

Chapter 11

Working in Dubai

The exotic yet cosmopolitan destination that Dubai is, makes it a fun and ideal place to work. Dubai has plentiful opportunities, a high standard of living and, of course, a fun lifestyle, which pulls so many expats to work here each year.

With the increasing number of expats, the competition only became more fierce and getting a job in Dubai is not as simple as it once was. One thing about Dubai is that things are continually changing, so even by the time you read this, the situation in the job market will probably have changed. While Dubai has clearly gone through a dip, it seems the worst is over and more jobs are starting to emerge.

Dubai is certainly a glamorous place to work and the tax-free salaries are quite an attraction, but the cost of living is on the rise. The past few years have seen a massive rise in property prices, so living in Dubai has become all the more expensive. However, since mid-2008, property and rental prices have suddenly dropped, so this might be just the time to be living, renting or buying in Dubai.

One main difference between working in Dubai and working elsewhere is that your residence permit is sponsored by your employer and if you leave the company or are made redundant, then your permit will be cancelled and your next employer will need to get a new one. If you are moving to Dubai without a job, then getting a residence permit involves a lot of paperwork (see pp 58–9). So it's definitely better to secure a job before arriving in Dubai.

However, coming to Dubai on a visit visa, meeting recruitment companies and attending interviews is a good option. It always makes a difference when employers can meet candidates face to face.

BENEFITS

The benefits that you get as an employee in your home country may not apply in Dubai. If you're working in an international company, then you may get the same benefits as those in the country of their head office.

The benefit of a tax-free salary still stands and that is, of course, the main attraction for those moving to Dubai. However, needless to say, living in Dubai is not cheap and while rentals and property prices have gone down, they won't stay down forever.

FINDING A JOB

While the ideal situation is to be transferred by your company to Dubai, or to have landed a job in Dubai while still in your home country, it often doesn't work out like that.

You should start by carrying out some research on jobs in Dubai while still in your home country, perhaps even speaking to recruitment consultants and looking through the various websites on Dubai, listed in this section.

You should eventually head out to Dubai for a few weeks so that you're able to meet people and be available for interview. If you have already registered with recruitment consultants before arriving in Dubai, you'll have a head start and the process will be more efficient.

Recruitment consultancies

There are many recruitment consultancies and headhunters who could assist you in the process. It's just a case of calling one after the other, telling them what you're looking for and being available for interview whenever they call. The following are some reputable recruitment companies you could contact:

Clarendon Parker
www.clarendonparker.com
04 3910460
info@clarendonparker.com

Charterhouse
www.charterhouseme.ae
04 3723500
info@charterhouse.ae

Bac
www.bacme.com
04 3375747

Budge Recruitment
www.budgerecruitment.com
04 3748101
middleeast@budgerecruitment.com

Hays
www.hays.ae
04 3612882
dubai@hays.com

IQ Selection
www.iqselection.com
04 3244094
cv@iQselection.com

Kershaw Leonard
www.kershawleonard.net
04 3434606
kershawleonard@kershawleonard.net

Classifieds

You should read the Classifieds section of the local newspapers (mostly *Gulf News* and *Khaleej Times*).

Online

You should also be searching online. There are numerous websites which list vacant positions:

- www.bayt.com
- www.careerjunctionme.com
- www.careermideast.com
- www.gulftalent.com
- www.monstergulf.com

- www.naukrigulf.com
- www.uaedubaijobs.com

Networking

In Dubai, networking and meeting the right people is very important. Just through one reference, you may land up in a brilliant job. Speak to people, go to any parties you're invited to, go to fairs and events and read all the newspapers to find out what's going on where each week.

Join Pink Slip Dubai, a unique networking group that facilitates job seekers and career changers to meet with top recruiters and employers in the city. They have monthly networking events designed to bring together the right talent with recruiters and employers seeking such individuals.

STARTING WORK

Once you have secured a position, you will need to sign a contract which, among other things, outlines your salary, job title and provides a description of what you do and indicates length of contract.

When speaking to your potential employer about your pay package, you should try and negotiate as much as you can and get a good package.

Packages will, of course, vary from employer to employer, but you might want to discuss days off, housing allowance, school fees if you have children, transportation, medical fees and flights back home, which should be once a year, though by law, the company must provide you with a ticket once every two years.

There is quite a bit of paperwork which needs to be done when you're starting work, but most of this should be done by your company's PRO (Public Relations Officer). This includes getting a visa, a health card and a labour card (see The move and formalities, pp 51–62).

Interview with Rabih Omran

Living in Dubai for 3 years, originally from Lebanon

How have you found your time in Dubai?

I was actually studying in France when I was picked by Acer group, the third largest computer vendor in the world, to work in Dubai. The first year was amazing – professionally, it is very rich. The economy was moving really fast, so you got responsibilities very fast.

How has Dubai changed recently?

There have been many people made redundant – cutting expenses and being cost effective is the main thing. You can still get a job but in a recession they are looking for people who have more experience – they will lose time training those that are less experienced. They are able to be picky and therefore there is more competition to get that job you want. But from now, Dubai will be more about real business than speculation.

What is the best thing about Dubai?

The experience you get in such a short time and for me it was the opportunity to travel all over the region.

What is the most important thing about working here?

Networking is extremely important when working in Dubai because if you know the right people, you get business.

How do you change jobs?

It's not that hard in reality. Just looking for a job, interviewing, giving some notice and then leaving. The turnover rate in companies is very high but it is, of course, harder to find a job at the moment.

Interview with Rajat Arora and Palak Bhati

Living in Dubai for 2 years, originally from Delhi

What do you do in Dubai?

We both went to the top fashion school in India and are now fashion designers in Dubai.

How is the fashion scene in Dubai?

People here have a high spending power but less individuality. The access to unlimited brands and mall culture, leave most of the youth blinded with already tried and tested ideas. Also Dubai works with a maximalist approach rather than a minimalist one. The boutique culture is very private and extremely expensive. There are no fashion streets/vintage stores where people could buy random things, mix it with old and new and give their outfits a personal touch. The marble lobby of the mall has replaced the 'on foot' street vendors, artists, craftsmen sitting and selling on the streets. It's comical to see thousands of boys wearing the same Zara t-shirts, looking like clones of each other, the day after the new collection comes out.

Are there many opportunities for people who want to get into fashion here?

Bringing newness into design here is very difficult. But because there is a lot of money here, the recession is not affecting sales, which is great. There are fashion jobs here but only service-orientated, not so much design-orientated.

What is the best thing about working in Dubai?

Because people are so ignorant about what background you're from, what experience you have, this can really be used to your advantage and there are more opportunities to easily switch job profiles. Switching jobs on the other hand is difficult, since the reins of your visa status/passport are in the employer's hands. The law of imposing an 'immigration ban' upon leaving an employer prohibits for the talent to flow around and reach its ideal destination.

BUSINESS CULTURE

- In meetings, you may be offered Arabic mint tea or coffee. It's generally considered rude to refuse this, so even if you just take a sip, it's better than saying no.

- If you're a man, don't shake a woman's hand unless she offers it and if you're a woman, don't shake a man's hand.

- Friday is the Muslim day of prayer and rest. You should therefore avoid meeting or calling any of your local clients of partners.

- Don't offend or put down a colleague or client in front of anyone.

- During a business lunch, don't order alcohol.

- It's advisable to have your business card translated into Arabic, on one side.

SETTING UP A BUSINESS

Dubai's strategic location between continents makes it a real hub for trading activity. It is therefore an ideal base for doing business in the Middle East and other regions. Dubai offers freedom of capital movement, has a developed financial sector and excellent facilities. The Jebel Ali Free Zone, Dubai Airport Free Zone and the Dubai International Financial Centre allow overseas companies to set up their own ventures, with some great incentives such as exemption from import duties.

Your sponsor

The most common way to do business in Dubai is by setting up a Limited Liability Company (LLC). In this case, you will need a UAE National as your sponsor, unless you want to be in a free zone. Try and find a sponsor with a good network, as influence is very useful when doing business. Relationships are given great importance in business and *wastah* or favours are very much a part of business life here.

Licensing

The basic requirement for all businesses in Dubai is one of the following three categories of licences, issued by the Dubai Economic Development:

- Commercial licences covering all kinds of trading activity;
- Professional licences covering professions, services, craftsmen and artisans;
- Industrial licences for establishing industrial or manufacturing activity.

All sponsors have fees and it may also be necessary to give them a percentage of profit. However, in most cases, it is normally settled with an annual flat fee which is typically paid 12 months in advance. Now you can register your business and get your trade licence. Again, as with everything else, your documents will have to be in English and Arabic. Your sponsor will help at this stage. The initial and minimum share capital must be Dhs300,000. All the initial share capital must also be fully paid prior to the LLC being formed. Public subscription for raising capital is not permitted. You will need to appoint an auditor who must be accredited in the UAE.

FREE ZONE

The Free Zones have been set up to encourage investment, and companies operating in any of the Free Zones are treated as offshore companies. In order to operate in the Free Zones, you need a Trading Licence, an Industrial Licence and a National Industrial Licence. If you choose to set up in a Free Zone, then you will own the company 100%. If you import any goods into Dubai, you won't need to pay the 5% import duty.

Interview with Penka Pol

Living in Dubai for one year, originally from Belgium

How has the downturn affected you?

I work in Investment and Business Development. Business has slowed down and we have laid off a few people but are still trying to survive. We need to be smarter and are trying to figure out cash flow positions.

What do you think of what's going on?

It's interesting to see this whole readjustment. I'm going to stay put for the next year – where else are you going to get a job right now anyway?

What about your friends?

I have friends who have lost their jobs. Some went traveling and others are sticking it out.

Interview with Zena Habi

Living in Dubai for 5 years, originally from Jordan

What made you come to Dubai?

I moved to Dubai with family, looking for a new experience in the fitness field. I helped to set up Fitness 02, a registered sports services company in Dubai and am now also the face of Reebok in the Region as well as the new 'Reebok Fitness Expert'.

Why did you decide to start Fitness02 and did it take long to get it going?

We decided to start Fitness O2 because after spending years in personal training you feel like it's the time to take it to the next step, and we felt that the market was ready for a different way of exercising, like outdoor Bootcamps. The process was not easy for us because we did not know who to ask or where to go at the beginning, but the process itself was not difficult.

How did you market yourself?

At first, we didn't have a budget for marketing, so it was through e-mails to friends, word of mouth and free media spreads.

Have you seen any differences in the past six months due to the recession?

Sure, we saw some difference, but I think that our field 'fitness' was not affected as much as some other fields, like real estate. People kept on exercising even with the bad economic situation.

Interview with Rahim Hirji

Founder of grapeshisha.com

How useful are websites when finding a job in Dubai?

The problem with websites is that people make lots of general assumptions about Dubai before they have sometimes even visited the place. Some people even commit to working in the UAE without knowing what it is really like because they think they are getting a better deal than what they are currently doing. And Dubai has been painted as one of two extremes: it's either the glitz and glamour or it's the plight of the migrant labourers. In reality what the internet and media have painted is not a full picture and that's when people need advice through websites, forums or people they know in Dubai. With grapeshisha, we help point people in the right direction.

What's the best way to find a job in Dubai?

The quandary of how to get a job in Dubai is an age-old query. The ideal route is to be lucky enough to get placed by current employer as a transfer. That rarely happens though. The next best approach is by placing your resumé/cv with the relevant agencies, but in reality, this could be a very long process and you are never going to get a job in another country by tapping away at a laptop – and so, if you are serious, it is best to get the real lay of the land and get on a plane for a couple of weeks and speak to as many people as possible. Through meeting with multiple contacts and contacts of contacts, you have a good chance of creating some leads of your own.

What should you consider when looking for a job in Dubai?

It's important to have a balanced view on getting a job and comparing it to your current position. What people often forget is to calculate their cost of living. You can get very real rental levels and we also provide information on cost of living so that people can calculate how much it will cost versus how much they will earn. Going through this very simple process will save a lot of time and can even help determine the minimum you would need to be paid to make this worthwhile. Another point to note is that many people look at Dubai as a long-term move. However, Dubai is a transient place and many people struggle to stay past five years. That's not to stay it doesn't happen, but you need to be aware of this before you start committing to a longer-term plan.

What is the working culture like?

It all really depends where you are working. You could be working at one of the outward facing government institutions or one of the multinationals where the work ethic is very much the same as it is in the West. But you may indeed end up working for an Arab institution which may be a little more laid back. Companies will place priorities on different criteria than you may be used to, but if you are aware of those hurdles, then you'll very quickly figure out the best approach depending on the scenario. Also, Dubai is a very multicultural place – and you are likely to be working with a team who all come from different parts of the world: Levantine Arabs, Gulf Arabs, people from the Indian subcontinent, Westerners, Russians, etc. If you can't deal with people of different nationalities, then Dubai is not for you!

Chapter 12

Accommodation

First things first – prices are down and this is, therefore, the perfect time to be living here. For anyone who has cash and liquidity, you can find some of the best deals that have ever been available in Dubai.

An example of the extreme drop in prices is the apartments in Burj Khalifa (tallest building in the world) which were, in August 2009, selling for Dhs3500–4000 per square foot compared with Dhs8080 per square foot in summer of 2008. However, Dubai changes quickly – very quickly! So by the time you're reading this book, chances are prices will have changed a bit. And they're not going to stay down forever. All prices given are indicative and per annum.

HOW TO FIND ACCOMMODATION

Most international companies provide accommodation for their staff. If you have to find your own accommodation, your sponsor will, of course, be able to help. It's also worth speaking to colleagues about commuting to work and their own experiences.

It's not difficult to find an apartment or house to buy or rent in Dubai. There are new properties constantly going up and many residential developments.

Things to consider:

- villa or apartment?

- location
- access to work
- size of rooms
- number of bedrooms
- traffic in the area
- noise in the area.

Ways to find properties

The first step in finding accommodation in Dubai, no matter if it's to rent or to buy, is to contact a real estate agency. Even if you take the time to find information on the internet, in magazines or on supermarket noticeboards, you will most probably still run into a real estate agent as very few people take the trouble to list their own properties. The largest real estate agencies are:

- Better Homes, www.bhomes.com
- Landmark Properties, www.landmark-dubai.com
- Damac Properties, www.damacproperties.com
- Emaar Properties, www.emaar.co.ae
- Gowealthy, www.gowealthy.com
- Engel and Volkers, www.engelvolkers.ae
- Nakheel Properties, www.nakheel.com.

How to find out more:

- Word of mouth, recommendation from friends, colleagues
- Speak to anyone you meet
- Visit compounds by yourself, and ask for the office of the company running it. They are often based inside the compounds. Ask for availability and pricing.

VILLA OR APARTMENT

Villas

Generally, properties in Dubai are larger and more spacious than the equivalent in Europe and the UK. Beautiful villas are most people's dream home, but they certainly aren't cheap. Villas within a compound may have shared facilities like a pool and gym or even an individual pool.

Apartments

The kinds of features and amenities available in apartment buildings vary greatly, from en-suite bathrooms, balconies and car parking to a laundry facility and a gym and pool inside the building. It's for you to decide what you want. In most buildings, there will be 24-hour security, but it is still worth checking this. The newer buildings usually also have central air conditioning.

Sharing

Those with lower budgets might want to consider sharing an apartment or villa, as the rent will be lower and you might find better accommodation for the price you're willing to pay. The best way to find something is in the property classified advertisements in local newspapers as well as on supermarket noticeboards.

Hotel apartments

These are a good option for lengthy business and tourist trips as they prove to be cheaper than staying in hotels. They are rented on a daily, weekly, monthly or yearly basis and are ideal if you want something furnished, serviced and temporary. It is most popular for people on short-term contracts as well as those coming into Dubai for the first time. Hotel apartments are usually fully furnished, with everything from beds and linen to plates and kitchen utensils as well as a cleaning service. Of course, if your apartment is within a hotel, you will probably also have access to all the hotel sports and spa facilities as well as great restaurants within your complex.

Hotel apartment	Rate/night (in Dhs)	Area	Contact	Website
Standard				
Chelsea Gardens Hotel Apts	480	Al Barsha	04 4377321	www.chelseagardens dubai.com
Golden Tulip Suites	780	Sheikh Zayed Rd	04 3417474	www.goldentulip suites-dubai.com
London Creek Hotel Apts	450	Dubai Airport	04 3555444	www.londoncreek. com
Waterfront Hotel Apts	450	Dubai Airport	04 3979959	www.mincapartmen ts.com
Deluxe				
Al Barsha Hotel Apts	850	Al Barsha	04 3416111	www.mincapartmen ts.com
Chelsea Tower Dubai Apts	780	Sheikh Zayed Rd	04 3434347	www.chelseatowerd ubai.com
City Centre Residence	850	Deira	04 2941222	www.sofitel.ae
Coral Boutique Hotel Apts	750	Sheikh Zayed Rd	04 3409040	www.coral-boutique hotel.com
Deira Suites Deluxe Hotel Suites	600	Deira	04 2225353	www.deirasuites.com
Dusit Residence Dubai Marina	1080	Dubai Marina	04 4259900	www.dusit.com
Emirates Concorde Residence	700	Bur Dubai	04 2230003	www.emirates concorde.com
Flora Creek Hotel Apts	840	Deira	04 2943232	www.florahospitality .com
Grand Midwest Hotel Apts	400	Bur Dubai	04 3511114	www.grandmidwest. com

Imperial Residence Hotel Apts	350	Bur Dubai	04 3553555	www.imperialsuites hotel.com
Kirklees 2 Hotel Apts	600	Bur Dubai	04 3514949	www.kirklees2dubai .com
Le Meridien Al Sondos Suites	900	Deira	04 2145040	www.lemeridien.com
London Crown 1 Hotel Apts	580	Bur Dubai	04 3511119	www.virtualtours.ae /londoncrown
Marriott Executive Apts	1515	Deira	04 2131000	www.marriott.com
Oasis Beach Tower	1880	Dubai Marina	04 3994444	www.oasisbeach tower.com
Pearl Coast Premier Hotel Apts	600	Sheikh Zayed Rd	04 4289999	www.pearlcoast. dusit.com
Pearl Residence Hotel Apts	450	Bur Dubai	04 3558111	www.pearlresidence. com
Splendid Hotel Apts	600	Bur Dubai	04 3360004	www.splendidhotela partmentsdubai.com
The Baron Hotel Apts	550	Sheikh Zayed Rd	04 3232777	www.thebaron hotels.com
The Harbour Hotel and Residence	1200	Dubai Marina	04 3194000	www.emirateshotels resorts.com

Please note that rates are current as of February 2010 and are subject to change.

RENTING

You'll find furnished and unfurnished apartments, and costs will vary greatly. It will also cost more to be living in certain areas such as Jumeirah. Before anything, determine how much you want to spend.

Lease

The lease provides protection for both the landlord and the tenant. Make sure you check everything, go through the contract and have everything in writing. Always keep copies of receipts, contracts and any other documents.

Questions you may want to ask:

- Length of lease? Try to negotiate a fixed rate for two or three years
- Can I have room-mates?
- Utility cost included in price?
- Can I make any changes?
- Deposit size?
- When can I move in?

Other costs

When you rent, there will be some extra costs:

- 5% commission to the agent
- 5% as refundable deposit
- Utility costs (which may or may not be included in the contract)
- Municipality charges
- There is also a water and electricity deposit (anything from Dhs1000 for apartments and Dhs2000 for villas) paid to Dubai Electricity and Water Authority (DEWA).

Payment

Initially, the payment terms were one, two or a maximum of three cheques paid through the year, but the option of paying in 12 cheques has recently (due to the recession) been introduced. The number of cheques will need to be mutually agreed on. Of course, if you can pay the whole year up front, use that to try and reduce the rent.

Procedures for renting a property

When renting a property, you can follow the first four steps from Procedure for Buying a property, overleaf, after which a tenancy agreement will be drawn up between you and the landlord usually for a period of one year, unless otherwise mutually agreed.

Checking the apartment

It is important that you check the apartment yourself. Things to inspect:

- Is everything clean both in the building and by the swimming pool or gym?
- Are there any cracks in the walls or stains on the roof?
- Does the floor look new?
- Are all the light switches working?
- Is the flush in the toilet working?
- Is the water in the shower flowing properly?

Rent disputes

In case you have a rent dispute with your landlord, the Rent Committee will be able to help you. You need to go to the Dubai Municipality building in Deira, opposite the Sheraton Hotel (04 2063917). More often than not, the Rent Committee finds in favour of the tenant.

BUYING

As of 2002, when foreign nationals were first able to purchase freehold property, Dubai became the new international property destination and the property boom began. And with the variety and quantity of property available on the real estate market, people were truly spoilt for choice. Many bought in order to resell on the secondary market or let the property. Prices have been on the rise in the ensuing years.

Procedures for buying a property

Information in this section provided by Ahuti Chug, Trio Properties, RERA Registered Agent (+971 508595449).

1 Identify the area in which you want to live, depending on where you work and where you would need to commute to everyday. At this stage seek the advice of a real estate agent if required.

2 Choose three real estate agents for the sake of comparison and seek their advice:

- to help to narrow down areas you might want to live
- on the type of property required if you are not sure (apartment, townhouse or villa)
- on what type of property you will be able to buy within your budget.

You should confirm that the agents you deal with are RERA (Real Estate Regulation Authority) approved brokers. You have the right to demand to see their ID.

3 According to your requirements, compare various projects, developers and types of property in order to gain more knowledge and insight into what you are buying and with the help of an agent, arrange viewings to see what is available out there.

4 Once you have identified exactly what you are looking for, compare property prices given by the agents you have chosen.

5 Upon identifying your choice of property, put down a holding deposit and the agent will help to prepare a Memorandum of Understanding (MOU) between the seller and yourself to bind in selling you the property and giving you a specified time for the transfer of the property.

6 If you are a cash buyer, the process is much quicker. However, if you are a finance buyer, make sure you have your pre-approvals in place to be certain that you will not be rejected by your respective bank after placing a deposit.

7 The transfer on a ready property will take place at the Lands Department and a Title Deed will be issued for this. The fees are approximately 2% on the selling price of the property which the agent will thoroughly explain. The Lands Department is a government body which controls and lays out the rules and regulations for Dubai Real Estate (www.dubailand.gov.ae).

8 If you are purchasing an off-plan property, the transfer may take place at the developer's office, where you will need to pay a minimum of Dhs3000–5000 as the administrative fee and will be issued a PSA in your name which you can later register at the Lands Department.

9 Upon successful transfer of your property, the agent should be paid a commission (usually 1–2%) for their work and professional advice. While in other countries, a lawyer is required to conduct the transaction, in Dubai, a RERA registered Real Estate agent can fulfil all documentation and other requirements to safeguard your interest.

10 For further information on real estate regulations, please visit www.rpdubai.com.

Prices

Rental costs and property prices have shot up in recent years. However, due to the recent global economic crisis, prices are now falling and constantly fluctuating. Rental and buying prices are given in the Areas to Live section (p 102). These prices were taken in August 2009.

UTILITIES AND SERVICES

Electricity and water

Dubai Electricity and Water Authority (DEWA) is the sole provider of water and electricity. When you first move into your new accommodation, you'll need to pay a deposit of Dhs1000 along with your tenancy contract and your passport copy.

This process takes approximately three days to complete. Bills are then calculated by meter readings and the easiest way to pay them is to set up an online account. Alternatively, you can pay at a DEWA office.

The electricity supply in Dubai is 220/240 volts at 50 cycles. Plug points are the same as in the UK with three pins. The local tap water is safe to drink, but most people have bottled mineral water.

Telecommunications

Etisalat (www.etisalat.ae) and du (www.du.ae) are the two operators in the UAE. Sim cards can be bought on arrival at the airport, for which you will need to show your passport. The call rates to other countries are fairly high.

If you opt to get a contract rather than pay as you go, then you can set up a direct debit to pay your bill or pay by cash at one of the etisalat or du branches or through a payment machine which you'll find in a mall. Dubai also has broadband and wireless connectivity available in most areas. Etisalat has a wireless roaming facility for subscribers.

The international dialing code for Dubai is +971. This is followed by the landline code 04 (delete the initial 0 if dialling from outside Dubai) or mobile code 50, followed by the number. All local calls from landline to landline in Dubai are free. When calling a landline from a mobile phone, add 04 before the number (all telephone numbers in this guide book are written with 04 prior to the number). When calling a mobile phone, add 050 before the number.

Domestic help

You'll be relieved to find how much, or how little you have to pay to get a full-time maid in Dubai. Most villas and larger apartments come with a maid's room, so having a live-in maid to clean and look after the kids as well as cook, is very possible, especially when it costs around Dhs1500 per month. If you think this is too cheap, you can certainly pay more, but this is the normal rate in Dubai. You will find that most maids are from the Philippines, India or Sri Lanka.

If your maid is living at home with you, you will need to sponsor her on a full domestic worker's visa. For more details, check www.dnrd.gov.ae. If you want a maid part-time, it's best to go through a reputable company. You will need to pay her around Dhs20–35 per hour.

Name	Telephone
City Sky Maid	04 3324600
Dialamaid	800 5151
Euro Clean	04 3338766
Focus Cleaning	04 3316006
Home Helpers	04 3555100
Molly Maid	04 3397799
Ready Maids	04 2800670

Rubbish and recycling

There's a good rubbish disposal system in Dubai and skips are regularly emptied. If you live in an apartment, there will generally be a rubbish chute available on each floor and if in a villa, you'll have a skip on your street. Recycling in Dubai is getting better, but the UAE does have one of the world's highest levels of domestic waste. There are recycling points around the city for paper, cans and glass bottles. To find out more, visit www.recycle-dubai.com.

Postal services

www.emiratespost.com

Dubai has no house-address based postal delivery service. Instead, mail is sent to a PO BOX in one of the 27 post office locations around Dubai (the post office at the Airport is open 24 hours a day), from where it has to be collected. Most people prefer their mail to be sent to their place of employment which can accept deliveries. If you want to open your own PO BOX, you will need two copies of your residence visa and passport, two passport-sized photos and you'll need to pay a small fee.

The Emirates Post subsidiary, Empost (600565555, www.empostuae.com), has grown as a local courier providing domestic and international express delivery.

The speed of the mail service varies and therefore you should allow at least a week for a letter to be delivered to another country.

DHL (800 4004, www.dhl.com), FedEx (04 3314216, www.fedex.com) and TNT (800 4333, www.tnt.com) will provide you with quicker services. These options are available at the post office, but you will need to pay extra.

AREAS TO LIVE

Whilst Dubai isn't that big a city, the traffic situation means that location does make a big difference. It is also important that the neighbourhood you choose to live in is well suited to your needs and those of your family. And, of course, think about the distance and time from your work place or schools. How big an issue for you is a long commute every day? Traffic has gradually got worse, and especially during peak times it can become very slow moving. Would this become an issue on a daily basis? All of this should therefore be taken into consideration when renting.

This section will give you a clearer picture of the different areas and types of accommodation available in Dubai. The areas are given in alphabetical order.

The price indications given for each area are as of August 2009. Prices do fluctuate a great deal and it is therefore best to find out updated prices once in Dubai.

Al Barsha

Location and accommodation

This is a peaceful area, popular with families. It is mainly made up of stand-alone villas and apartments. Al Barsha is split into two areas. The main area has large villas with gardens while Al Barsha 1 has mostly apartments. It's also a stone's throw away from Mall of the Emirates.

Drive time to

Mall of the Emirates – 5 mins
Trade Centre – 20 mins
Airport – 40 mins

What's nearby

Hospitals: The nearest emergency hospital is Rashid Hospital.

Schools: Dubai American Academy and Al Mawakeb are in Al Barsha. Other schools in nearby areas include Wellington International School off Sheikh Zayed Road, JESS in Arabian Ranches and Dubai College in Al Sufouh. Al Noor Centre for Special Needs Children is also in the area.

Leisure: Mall of the Emirates, The Marina, Madinat Jumeirah and Umm Suqeim are all close by. Large supermarkets like Lulu and Choithram are also on your doorstep.

Cons

The only downside is that there are visible overhead power lines through Al Barsha.

Approximate rental for a 2-bedroom apartment is between Dhs70,000 and 90,000.

Al Qusais

Location and accommodation

If you're looking for cheap accommodation, Al Qusais has affordable options and is also relatively quiet. You can get studio to 4-bedroom apartments, but if you're looking for a villa, this is not the place.

Drive time to

Mall of the Emirates – 40 mins
Trade Centre – 20 mins
Airport – 10–15 mins

What's nearby

Hospitals: Zulekha Hospital

Schools: Al Ittihad Private School, The Sheffield Private School, Dubai Scholars Private School and The Westminster School are all nearby.

Leisure: You're near Deira and Sharjah. There are some large supermarkets such as Lulu and Union Co-Op close by, as well as the Al Bustan Centre.

Cons

Traffic within the area is not a problem, but the Sharjah-Dubai routes can get extremely congested during rush-hour times.

Approximate rental for a 2-bedroom apartment is between Dhs55,000 and 65,000.

Al Safa and Al Wasl

Location and accommodation

This area has a wide range of mainly large villas. The large, open spaces and parks are quite an attraction for families with children. You will need a car to go anywhere, but schools and entertainment are very close. Since there aren't many people walking on the streets, you'll be able to take your dog for a walk. This is also the parallel road to the popular Jumeirah Beach Road, and therefore you have cafés, restaurants and the beach on your doorstep.

Drive time to

Mall of the Emirates – 5–10 mins
Trade Centre –10–15 mins
Airport – 20 mins

What's nearby

Hospitals: Iranian Hospital located in Satwa is nearby. Al Wasl Road and Jumeirah Road have a number of medical centres and dentists. Al Safa Clinic is a government clinic on Al Attar Road, also nearby.

Schools: Jumeirah English Speaking School, The English College, Emirates English Speaking School, Jumeirah College and Jumeirah Primary School are all very close by as are The Palm Nursery and Kangaroo Kids.

Leisure: Various supermarkets like Spinneys, Choithrams, Union Co-op, Park n Shop are very close by. The Mazaya Centre is in Al Wasl and has various shops including Spinneys supermarket and Homes R Us. Mercato Mall on Beach Road is also not very far away. Safa Park is a well known and popular park.

Cons

You'll need to be a little careful as thieves can make the most of an open window. You will also need a car to get anywhere, but distances are short.

Approximate rental for a 3-bedroom villa is between Dhs140,000 and 160,000; and for a 5-bedroom villa is between Dhs220,000 and 260,000.

Arabian Ranches

Location and accommodation

Arabian Ranches is pretty luxurious with lush green surroundings and the Arabian Ranches Golf Course. It is located away from the centre of town, off the Emirates Road. There are mainly 2- and 4-bedroom, stunning villas as well as town houses. There are also some good schools in the vicinity. This is the new up-and-coming area with Dubailand development nearby.

Drive time to

Mall of the Emirates –15–20 mins
Trade Centre – 25–30 mins
Airport – 25–30 mins

What's nearby

Hospitals: There are no medical facilities close by. The nearest government medical centre is in Umm Suqeim and a private centre is in Al Barsha. The closest hospitals are in Oud Metha.

Schools: Jumeirah English Speaking School is the only school in the vicinity. Otherwise, Al Barsha and Emirates Hills aren't too far away.

Leisure: The Village Community Centre, with a supermarket, chemist, bookshop, petshop, laundry, bank as well as some cafés, is located on the estate.

Cons

You will have to commute quite a lot to get anywhere.

Approximate rental for a 3-bedroom villa is between Dhs130,000 and 170,000; and for a 5-bedroom villa is between Dhs250,000 and 320,000.

Bur Dubai and Al Mankhool

Location and accommodation

This area comprises a mixture of apartments and villas close to many restaurants and the Indian Mina Bazaar. It has a very lively, city atmosphere and there's nothing that's not a short ride away. All the main banks are also located in Bur Dubai and the main metro station will soon be open here. The Bur Dubai apartment buildings generally include swimming pools and gyms. You'll also find many serviced hotel apartments in this area. Most of the people who live here are from India.

Drive time to

Mall of the Emirates – 20 mins
Trade Centre –10 mins
Airport – 10 mins

What's nearby

Hospitals: Rashid Hospital and American Hospital are both very close.

Schools: Dubai English Speaking School is around 15 minutes by car.

Leisure: You have various supermarkets very nearby including Spinneys, Union Co-Op and Carrefour. The fantastic Burjuman Mall is also right here. Don't forget the *souk* in Bur Dubai – a taste of real Dubai. And in Mina Bazaar, you'll find Indian tailors, gold, textiles and more.

Cons

There is a crowded, busy atmosphere and not maintained as well as other areas.

Approximate rental for a 2-bedroom apartment is between Dhs90,000 and 110,000.

Deira

Location and accommodation

Deira is great for singles. You have Dubai Creek and the *souks* right on your doorstep so it's a great atmosphere. There is old villa accommodation, but it's mostly all apartments and while prices vary, it's generally on the cheaper side for Dubai.

Drive time to

Mall of the Emirates – 30 mins
Trade Centre – 20 mins
Airport – 5–10 mins

What's nearby

Hospitals: Dubai Hospital is nearby and the Rashid Hospital is the closest emergency hospital.

Schools: There aren't any schools in the area and this place is mainly for singles.

Leisure: With some great hotels on your doorstep, there are good dining options and clubs. Mamzar Park is nearby and has great views that you can enjoy while walking.

Cons

There's a lot of traffic and parking is very difficult. There aren't any good schools in the area, so it's not great for families.

Approximate rental for a 1-bedroom apartment will range from Dhs40,000 to 50,000; and for a 2-bedroom apartment from Dhs60,000 to 70,000.

Discovery Gardens

Location and accommodation

Inspired by garden living and with beautifully manicured lawns, Discovery Gardens is a great place if you're looking to rent a 1-bedroom flat. There are more than 26,000 studios, 1- and 2-bedroom apartments and 200 retail shops. With big building works complete in 2008, it's ready to be lived in and with Ibn Battuta nearby, and the Marina not too far, you have access to everything.

Drive time to

Mall of the Emirates – 15 mins
Trade Centre – 20–25 mins
Airport – 30–40 mins

What's nearby

Hospitals: The Jebel Ali Clinic is the nearest government health clinic. The nearest hospital with a 24-hour medical centre is Cedars Jebel Ali Hospital and the nearest government hospital with A&E is Rashid Hospital.

Schools: Jebel Ali Primary School and Winchester School are local.

Leisure: Ibn Battuta Mall is very close by and has a large cinema. Discovery Gardens also has many swimming pools, a football pitch, cycling and jogging trails and tennis, basketball and volleyball courts.

Cons

This area is a little away from town and if work is on the other side of Dubai, then traffic might prove to be a problem.

Approximate rental for a 1-bedroom apartment is between Dhs55,000 and 65,000.

Downtown Dubai

Location and accommodation

This is Dubai's newest residential area with Arabian style buildings and streets. You'll find mostly apartments such as the Old Town, Burj Residences and Southridge, with great views of the world's tallest building at its heart. There is a real sense of community here with children's play areas, coffee shops, *souks* and swimming pools. You can easily get around on foot and have The Address Hotel, Dubai Mall and The Palace Hotel all on your doorstep. This really is the place to live and is a very central location in between old and new Dubai.

Drive time to

Mall of the Emirates – 10 mins
Trade Centre – 5 mins
Airport – 15 mins

What's nearby

Hospitals: Jumeirah Road, which has a number of medical centres and dentists, isn't too far. The closest hospitals are Medcare Hospital opposite Safa Park and the Iranian Hospital on Al Wasl Road.

Schools: The primary and secondary schools in Jumeirah are just a short drive away. In Downtown Dubai, there's the new Old Town Nursery, a part of Raffles International School and Kangaroo Kids' nursery.

Leisure: Dubai Mall, the largest shopping mall in the world, is on your doorstep. Souk Al Bahar has some nice little boutiques and good restaurants. For supermarkets, there's a new Waitrose in Dubai Mall as well as Organic Foods and Café and several branches of Spinneys. Once it's open, the Lake Walk promenade outside the residences will be like The Walk at Jumeirah Beach Residence.

Cons

With The Dubai Mall on your doorstep, there is bound to be some activity and a fair bit of traffic at peak times.

Approximate rental for a 2-bedroom apartment is between Dhs115,000 and 155,000; and for a studio apartment is between Dhs55,000 and 65,000.

Dubai Marina and Jumeirah Beach Residence (JBR)

Location and accommodation

This is a glamorous and much sought-after area, with accessibility to everything at the famous Marina Walk and the Walk at JBR, lined with coffee shops and restaurants. If you like the beach and open spaces and if you're quite the social animal, this is definitely the place to be. There are a variety of apartments available here and with rents down, it's more affordable now.

Drive time to

Mall of the Emirates – 5–10 mins
Trade Centre – 25 mins
Airport – 30–40 mins

What's nearby

Hospitals: The nearest government hospital is Rashid. The Neuro Spinal Hospital opposite Jumeirah Beach Park has 24-hour A&E.

Schools: In Al Sufouh, there is Dubai College, Wellington International School and the International School of Choueifat. There is also the American University of Dubai within Knowledge Village.

Leisure: The Marina is a real hotspot with the best bars and restaurants, a golf course and beach clubs. There's a Spinneys supermarket on Marina Walk as well as a pharmacy. Ibn Battuta, Madinat Jumeirah and Mall of the Emirates are just a few kilometres away.

Cons

The opening of The Walk has led to increased traffic at the weekends. However, three bridges are being built which will take care of this congestion. The ongoing construction in the Marina and around Jumeirah Beach Residence creates extra noise and is also a cause of traffic.

Approximate rental for a 2-bedroom apartment is between Dhs105,000 and 135,000.

Emirates Hills

Location and accommodation

This is a relaxed and up-market area with green surroundings, beautiful lakes, gardens, pools, and shared public spaces. It is made up of The Springs (town houses), The Lakes (town houses), The Meadows (family detached villas) and The Greens (low-rise apartments). It's popular with families and makes a great escape from the city. It's good for those working in Media and Internet Cities as well as in Jebel Ali Free Zone, but isn't too far if you work in the city either. Emirates Hills also houses one of the best golf courses here.

Drive time to

Mall of the Emirates – 5–10 mins
Trade Centre – 15–20 mins
Airport – 25–30 mins

What's nearby

Hospitals: Medical facilities are not easily accessible, though there is a private medical centre in Al Barsha and a government clinic in Jebel Ali.

Schools: Emirates School, Dubai British School, Regent School and Dubai International Academy are all close. However, waiting lists tend to be long, so it's best to sign up well in advance.

Leisure: Mall of the Emirates and Ibn Battuta are pretty close, and for great restaurants, the Marina isn't far at all. The estates in Emirates Hills have a recreation area and swimming pool, so it's fantastic for the kids.

Cons

There is a new six-lane highway which has increased traffic and noise in the area. There is also an increasing insect population in some parts.

Approximate rental for a 2-bedroom villa in Springs is between Dhs90,000 and 120,000; for a 3-bedroom villa in Meadows is between Dhs170,000 to 210,000; for a 1-bedroom apartment in Greens is between Dhs60,000 and 90,000.

Garhoud

Location and accommodation

Just minutes from the airport, Garhoud is well-located with great shopping options, schools and private medical centres all close by. There is a range of accommodation from compound villas with gardens to modern houses and apartments, as well as lots of grassy areas for walking, jogging and cycling. Being so close to the airport, Garhoud is also very popular with airline staff.

Drive time to

Mall of the Emirates – 30 mins
Trade Centre – 10 mins
Airport – approx 5 mins

What's nearby

Hospitals: Welcare Hospital is a private hospital (which also has a massage centre and beauty salons). The government hospital, Al Wasi and Rashid, are not too far away.

Schools: Deira International School, American School of Dubai and Cambridge International School. Yellow Brick Road Nursery and Montessori Nursery are also nearby.

Leisure: There is a park with a skate ramp and sandy football pitch in Garhoud. Century Village, Dubai Creek, Aviation Club and Deira City Centre are also nearby.

Cons

Rush hour traffic on Garhoud Bridge can be a real problem. There might also be some aircraft noise.

Approximate rental for a 2-bedroom apartment is between Dhs80,000 and 100,000.

Green Community

Location and accommodation

Based in the desert, Green Community is peaceful and quiet and of course, green! It has mostly villas, but it's a little far out unless you work in the Jebel Ali Free Zone. It's a lovely environment for families. Property in Green Community is not 100% freehold – it is on a 99-year leasehold.

Drive time to

Mall of the Emirates – 5–10 mins
Trade Centre –15 mins
Airport – 20–25 mins

What's nearby

Hospitals: The Green Community Medical Centre (04 8853225) is a private clinic inside the Market shopping centre. The nearest government clinic is in Jebel Ali.

Schools: The Children's Garden (04 3498806) is a primary school offering a bilingual curriculum (English/German and English/French). Jebel Ali and Emirates Hills also have a number of primary and secondary schools.

Leisure: The Market is the nearest shopping centre, with a pharmacy, supermarket and many more shops. Ibn Battuta mall isn't too far either. There are also brilliant golf facilities nearby at Emirates Hills, Jebel Ali and Arabian Ranches.

Cons

It's pretty far from most areas in Dubai. So it's great if you're working in the area, but if not, the distances and traffic are a little crazy.

Approximate rental for a 2-bedroom apartment is between Dhs90,000 and 120,000.

International City

Location and accommodation

This 800-hectare development is the cheapest freehold property available in Dubai which comprises low budget studios and 1-bedroom apartments. There are ten themed residential communities including China, England, Italy, Spain, Morocco and others with over 20,000 apartments.

Drive time to

Mall of the Emirates – 45 mins
Trade Centre – 35 mins
Airport – 25–35 mins

What's nearby

Hospitals: Welcare Hospital, the nearest hospital, is around 10kms away. The nearest hospital with A&E is Rashid Hospital.

Schools: There are no schools in the vicinity, but the nearest is about 10–15 minutes away in Mirdif.

Leisure: Dragon Mart, a mammoth shopping complex selling Chinese products is right here. Dubai Festival City is just a 10-minute drive away. You've also got Al Warsan Lake, a freshwater wetland home to 200 species of birds.

Cons

You're quite far from central Dubai and there are also no medical facilities or good schools within the vicinity.

Approximate rental for a 1-bedroom apartment is between Dhs35,000 and 45,000.

Jumeirah

Location and accommodation

One of the most exclusive areas in Dubai, Jumeirah offers access to the beach, fantastic leisure facilities with some of the best hotels based along Jumeirah beach and the best selection of restaurants. It's a coastal residential area and to be living in Jumeirah is something of a style statement. There's a mixture of independent villas and villas in compounds with shared facilities. Prices here are on their way down.

Drive time to

Mall of the Emirates – 5–10 mins
Trade Centre – 25 mins
Airport – 30–40 mins

What's nearby

Hospitals: Al Safa Clinic (04 394 3468) is the nearest government health clinic. Emirates Hospital, opposite Jumeirah Beach Park, has a 24-hour walk-in clinic, but does not take emergency cases. The Neuro-Spinal Hospital is also on Jumeirah Beach Road.

Schools: There are many nurseries in the area, as well as Jumeirah Primary School, Jumeirah College and Jumeirah English Speaking School.

Leisure: Mercato is the nearest mall and also has a cinema. There are many supermarkets in Jumeirah. You will also find art galleries and boutiques in this area. Madinat Jumeirah and Mall of the Emirates aren't too far. There are restaurants and cafés dotted around the shopping centres along Beach Road and of course, plenty of beach.

Cons

The cost of living here has always been the number one problem, but with falling prices, it's more affordable now. There is also construction noise and heavy traffic.

Approximate rental for a 3-bedroom villa is between Dhs160,000 and 200,000; and for a 5-bedroom villa is between Dhs240,000 and 300,000.

Jumeirah Islands, upcoming Jumeirah Park and Jumeirah Village

Location and accommodation

Very close to the famous Ibn Battuta Mall, Jumeirah Islands has luxurious 4- and 6-bedroom family villas set in 300 hectares of land. If you like community living, greenery and peaceful surroundings, this is the place. The villas are arranged in 50 clusters of 16 villas each. There are also the new residential areas of Jumeirah Park and Jumeirah Village coming up, which will comprise villas and townhouses as well as apartments.

Drive time to

Mall of the Emirates – 5–10 mins
Trade Centre – 25 mins
Airport – 30–40 mins

What's nearby

Hospitals: The nearest hospital with 24-hour emergency service is Jebel Ali Hospital (private).

Schools: Dubai British School, Dubai International Academy and The American University of Dubai are all nearby.

Leisure: Ibn Battuta is the closest mall, with a large cinema, many restaurants and a hypermarket.

Cons

You're a little away from the main city, which is a problem if you work in the city or your kids go to school on the other side. You also don't have large supermarkets, convenience stores and other such facilities so close by.

Approximate rental for a 5-bedroom villa is between Dhs300,000 and 320,000.

Karama and Oud Metha

Location and accommodation

You'll find lots of affordable apartments and it's very densely populated with a lively Indian scene, but it can get very congested at times. There are also many supermarkets, corner shops and restaurants.

Drive time to

Mall of the Emirates – 15–20 minutes
Trade Centre – 10 mins
Airport – 5–10 mins

What's nearby

Hospitals: Rashid Hospital, with an emergency section, is right here and Al Wasl Hospital is around 15 minutes away. American Hospital (private) is also just 10–15 minutes away.

Schools: There aren't any good options in Karama itself, but Dubai English Speaking School, St. Mary Catholic School and Our Own English High School, all in Oud Metha, are only 10–15 minutes away.

Leisure: You've got plenty of shops, places to eat and you can walk just about everywhere.

Cons

This area is very busy and can get congested. It's certainly not the most relaxing place to live. Parking is also a nightmare.

Approximate rental for a 2-bedroom apartment is between Dhs90,000 and 110,000.

Mirdif

Location and accommodation

Mirdif has expanded, there's a lot more that's available here and there are quite a few affordable villas that have popped up. It's a great option for those working in Deira or Garhoud. You'll find a range of options from stand-alone, older villas to newer villas in compounds. You can lease, buy or rent. There are international schools, healthcare and sports facilities and shopping malls. Al Mushrif Park is on your doorstep, so you have some grassland and a place to take the kids. With International City nearby, the shopping options are great.

Drive time to

Mall of the Emirates – 35 mins
Trade Centre – 25 mins
Airport – 20 mins

What's nearby

Hospitals: Welcare Clinic is close by. The nearest hospital with A&E is Rashid Hospital.

Schools: The American Academy for Girls and the Royal Dubai School are both close by.

Leisure: Uptown Mirdif, The Mirdif City Centre mall, opening soon, will include more than 400 shops including a Carrefour hypermarket.

Cons

With the airport quite close by, there might be a bit of noise. Mirdif is also open and therefore theft is more likely. However, it's just a case of being more careful and closing doors and windows.

Approximate rental for a 3-bedroom villa is between Dhs140,000 and 160,000.

Palm

Location and accommodation

This is the latest and most glamorous place to stay and prices are no longer unreasonable. With your own private beach and pool on a palm-shaped independent island, it really is a holiday home. The trunk of the Palm has apartments and the fronds have town houses and villas. With the famous Atlantis hotel down the road, and not far from Mall of the Emirates and Marina, everything is pretty much accessible.

Drive time to

Mall of the Emirates – 5–10 mins
Trade Centre – 25 mins
Airport – 30–40 mins

What's nearby

Hospitals: The nearest government hospital is Rashid Hospital, 30 minutes away. The nearest hospital with 24-hour emergency service is Jebel Ali Hospital, 15 minutes away.

Schools: The British University, Dubai College, American University in Dubai, Wellington International School and International School of Choueifat are all around 10–15 minutes away.

Leisure: The Walk at JBR, Madinat Jumeirah, Mercato Mall, Mall of Emirates and Emirates Golf Club are all nearby. Of course, living on the Palm, you have the beach on your doorstep and the Atlantis Hotel down the road.

Approximate rental for a 5-bedroom villa is between Dhs340,000 and 400,000; and for a 2-bedroom apartment is between Dhs130,000 and 170,000.

Satwa

Location and accommodation

This area has a very lively atmosphere and has a range of accommodation, which makes it great for young people, especially if you don't want to be splashing out on accommodation and if you want to share. You will be able to find single rooms or small apartments as well as some old villas. Watch out, though, as Satwa is soon going to be demolished and reconstructed.

Drive time to

Mall of the Emirates – 20 mins
Trade Centre – 10 mins
Airport – 15 mins

What's nearby

Hospitals: Iranian Hospital, which has A&E, is on Al Wasl Road in Satwa. Rashid Hospital is also close.

Schools: Satwa doesn't have any good schools, but Jumeirah isn't too far away and you'll find a whole host of schools there (e.g. Jumeirah English Speaking School, etc.).

Leisure: Satwa has many shops and small supermarkets, and Spinneys on Beach Road is also not too far. Diyafah Street has various shops where you can find clothes, textiles, tailors and much more. Living in Satwa, you also have some great food on your doorstep – Rydges Plaza has good Mexican, American and Italian restaurants and Diyafah Street is also home to many restaurants.

Cons

Traffic and the constant business of this area is the main issue. There have been cases of petty theft and break-ins but, again, it's a case of being slightly more wary.

Approximate rental for a 2-bedroom apartment is between Dhs65,000 and 85,000.

Sheikh Zayed Road

Location and accommodation

This area is home to some of the largest and funkiest towers in Dubai, the bridge between old and new Dubai. It's a real showcase of the dramatic change the city has undergone. You'll find some great luxury apartments and offices. While rentals have recently decreased, this area is still on the expensive side for Dubai. You also have a good range of entertainment options on your doorstep.

Drive time to

Mall of the Emirates –10–15 mins
Trade Centre – 2 mins
Airport – 10 mins

What's nearby

Hospitals: The closest hospitals are Rashid and the Iranian Hospital on Al Wasl Road.

Schools: The primary and secondary schools in Jumeirah are just a short drive away, traffic permitting. Burj Khalifa is also close by, has two nurseries and a part of Raffles International School.

Leisure: This road is continually buzzing with an array of great eateries along both sides of Sheikh Zayed Road. There are various hotels as well as the Emirates Towers Boulevard. Various small supermarkets are dotted around. Downtown Dubai, housing the world's largest mall, is also very close by, so you're quite centrally located.

Cons

Sheikh Zayed Road gets crazily busy and noisy, and the traffic at peak times is just as maddening. The high rents are also a put-off.

Approximate rental for a 2-bedroom apartment is between Dhs120,000 and 160,000.

Umm Suqueim

Location and accommodation

With nearby beach access, the best hotels like Burj Al Arab and other malls close by, this is quite popular with expat families. There are more villas and some old-style mansions. Scrubland for dog walking is nearby. Entertainment options such as The Walk at JBR and Marina are also close by.

Drive time to

Mall of the Emirates – 5 mins
Trade Centre – 10–15 mins
Airport – 15–20 mins

What's nearby

Hospitals: Neuro Spinal Hospital is the nearest hospital with a 24-hour emergency room. The Umm Suqeim Clinic is also close and there are many specialists along Beach Road.

Schools: Emirates International School is the biggest secondary school. There are many other schools in Jumeirah, which is right next door. Nurseries such as Emirates British Nursery and Alphabet Street Nursery are also close by.

Leisure: Souk Madinat Jumeirah and Mall of the Emirates are very close by. There is also a Choithram supermarket on Al Wasl Road and Spinneys is not very far. Public beaches are very close as are hotels like Jumeirah Beach Hotel, with restaurants and Wild Wadi water park. The nearest cinema is in Mercato Mall.

Cons

This area can get noisy and is generally safe, but since it is open, you have to be more careful about keeping doors locked and your valuables locked up.

Approximate rental for 3-bedroom villa is between Dhs165,000 and 205,000.

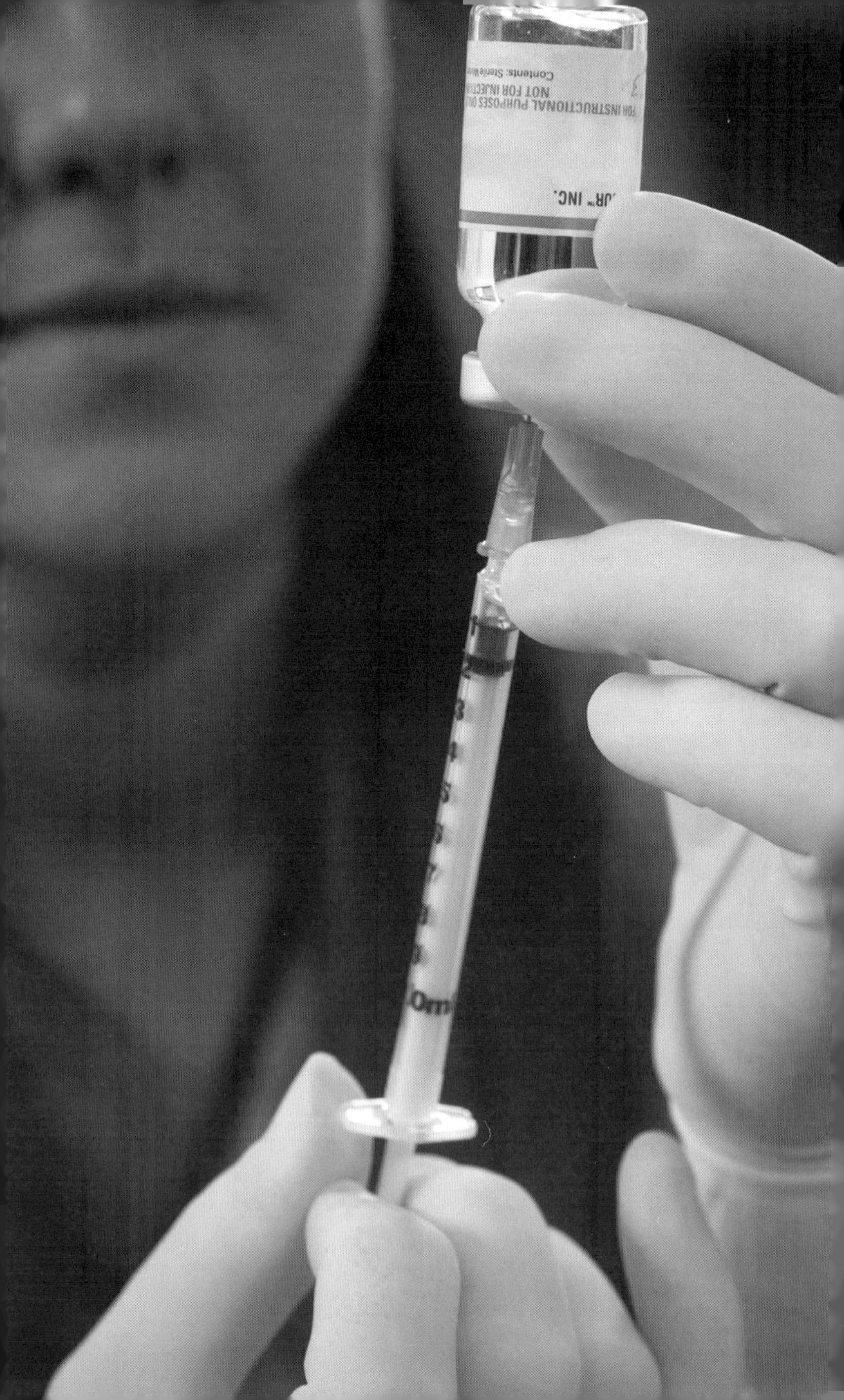
FOR INSTRUCTIONAL PURPOSES
Contents:

Chapter 13

Health care

Even though private healthcare is seen as better – as it is in most countries – the general standard of healthcare in Dubai, both government and private, is high. The government has invested heavily in the health sector and thus all types of advanced medical treatment are available.

HEALTH CARD

You need a health card in order to qualify for subsidised medical care in government hospitals. Your health card will also state the hospital to which you're assigned, although it is not necessary to use that particular hospital.

EMERGENCY TREATMENT

Whether or not you have a health card, emergency treatment is provided free of charge. However, residents in Dubai who do not have a health card may be charged for any follow-up treatments.

HEALTH INSURANCE

Many residents have private medical insurance with companies like Alliance Insurance, AXA Insurance, BUPA, Mednet, National General Insurance and others. Employers often provide their employees with medical insurance as part of the employment package. It is advisable to get health insurance (a law declaring that all employees must have health insurance is also taking effect and is currently in its transition period).

Health insurance companies

Name	Area	Telephone	Website
Abu Dhabi National Insurance Company	Deira	04 2222223	www.adnic.ae
Al Buhaira National Insurance	Deira	04 2319444	www.albuhaira.com
Alliance Insurance	Deira	04 6051111	www.alliance-uae.com
American Life Insurance	DIFC	04 3600555	www.uae.alico.com
Arab Orient Insurance	Bur Dubai	04 2944457	www.insuranceuae.com
AXA Insurance Gulf	Wafi	04 3243434	www.axa-gulf.com
Dubai National Insurance and Reinsurance	Bur Dubai	04 3259700	www.dnirc.com
Gargash Insurance	Bur Dubai	04 3377888	www.gargashinsurance.com
National General Insurance	Deira	04 2222772	www.ngi.ae
Royal and Sun Alliance	Oud Metha	04 3029800	www.rsagroup.ae
SALAMA – Islamic Arab Insurance Co	Oud Metha	04 3374460	www.salama.ae
Wehbe Insurance Services	Wafi City	04 3242345	www.wisuae.com
Zurich International Life	DIFC	04 3634444	www.zurich.com

For more information, visit Dubai Health Authority on www.dha.gov.ae.

MAIN GOVERNMENT HOSPITALS

There are many government hospitals in Dubai, and most are of a high standard. The government health card that all residents should have (see pp 56–7) gives them access to essential subsidised healthcare. The hospitals listed below are all of the highest standard amongst government hospitals. It is also indicated whether or not they have a 24-hour emergency facility. Rashid Hospital is the main hospital for emergencies and has a good A&E department. Dubai Hospital also has emergency facilities and is one of the best hospitals in the Middle East. Al Wasl is a specialist maternity and paediatric hospital and though not a government hospital, does provide subsidised healthcare.

Hospital	Address	Telephone	Website	24 hr emergency
Al Baraha Hospital	Al Baraha, Deira	04 2710000		N
Al Maktoum Hospital	Near Fish Roundabout, Deira	04 2221211	www.dohms.gov.ae	N
Al Wasl Hospital	Oud Metha Road, Bur Dubai	04 3241111	www.dohms.gov.ae	Y
Dubai Hospital	Al Baraha, Deira	04 2714444	www.dohms.gov.ae	Y
Iranian Hospital	Al Wasl Rd, Jumeirah	04 3440250	www.irhosp.ae	Y
Rashid Hospital	Downtown Bur Dubai	04 3374000	www.dohms.gov.ae	Y

MAIN PRIVATE HOSPITALS

The increasing number of private hospitals provide world-class medical facilities. The Welcare Hospital is regarded as the provider of the best quality healthcare in Dubai, followed by The American Hospital. Do make sure you have health insurance in order to receive treatment at any of these hospitals, but double check which hospitals are covered by the insurance.

Hospital	Address	Telephone	Website	24 hr emergency
American Hospital	Oud Metha Rd, Oud Metha	04 3367777	www.ahdubai.com	Y
Belhoul Speciality Hospital	Al Khaleej Rd, Deira	04 2733333	www.belhoul speciality.com	Y
Cedars-Jebel Ali International Hospital	Dugas Rd, Jebel Ali	04 8814000	www.cedars-jaih. com	Y
Emirates Hospital	Jumeirah Beach Rd	04 3446678	www.emirates hospital.ae	Y

Neuro Spinal Hospital	Jumeirah Beach Rd	04 3420000	www.nshdubai.com	Y
Welcare Hospital	Near Aviation Club, Garhoud	04 2827788	www.ehl.ae	Y
Zulekha Hospital	Al Qusais	04 2678866	www.zulekhahospitals.com	Y
Belhoul European Hospital	Dhiyafa Street Satwa	04 3454000	www.belhouleuropean.com	Y

Private health and medical centres

Health and medical centre	Address	Telephone	Website
Al Rafa Poly Clinic	Al Rafa Police Station Rd, Bur Dubai	04 3935115	www.drmoopensgroup.com
Al Rashid Medical Clinic	Al Mulla Bldg, Baniyas St	04 2235121	
Al Wasl Clinic	Near Park n Shop, Al Wasl Rd	04 3955448	www.groupgmc.com
Allied Diagnostic Centre	Al Diyafa St, Satwa	04 3328111	www.allieddiagnostics.net
American Chiropractic Clinic	Villa 491-B Jumeirah 3, Beach Rd	04 3944877	www.thedentalspa.org
Consultant Physicians – Dubai HCC	Bldg 55, Dubai Health Care City	04 3622999	www.drsulaimanalhabib.com
Dubai Medical Village	Jumeirah Rd, Jumeirah	04 3956200	
Emirates Diagnostic Clinic	Union Coop Bldg, Satwa	04 3315155	www.ehl.ae/Emirates Diagnostic
French Medical Centre	Village Shopping Centre, Beach Rd	04 3495020	www.groupgmc.net
General Medical Centre	Magrudy's Shopping, Beach Rd	04 3495959	www.groupgmc.net
German Medical Center – Dubai Healthcare City	Block-B 302 Dubai Health Care City	04 3622929	www.germanmedicalcenterdhcc.com
International Aesthetic Medical Centre	Villa 438-B, Al Wasl Rd, Jumeirah 1	04 3498000	www.iamc.ae

International Medical Centre	Jumeirah Rd, opp Mercato Centre	04 3441142	www.international medicalcentre.com
Jehad International Medical Clinic	Flat 706 Holiday Inn Crowne Plaza, Sheikh Zayed Rd	04 3311773	www.jimc.ae
Joslin Diabetes Centre at Dubai Health Authority	Al Wasl Hospital Campus	04 2194141	www.joslindubai.com
Jumeira Prime Medical Centre	Jumeirah Beach Rd, near Jumeirah Plaza	04 3494545	www.pmcdubai.com
Manchester Clinic	Jumeirah Beach Rd, Jumeirah	04 3440300	www.manchester-clinic.com
Medical International Specialists Centre	Al Wasl Rd, Jumeirah	04 3499100	www.plasticsurgery.ae

OPTICIANS

The opticians in malls are reputable and can carry out good eye tests and give suggestions for glasses, contact lenses, etc. Most of them have large selections of frames and a range of contact lenses available. If you have eye problems or want any other specialist treatment, there are some clinics:

Eye clinic	Address	Telephone	Website
American Hospital	Oud Metha Rd, near Lamcy Plaza	04 3367777	www.ahdubai.com
Atlanta Vision Clinic	Jumeirah Beach Rd, opp Jumeirah Beach Hotel	04 3486233	www.atlantavision2020.com
Gulf Eye Centre	Office Suite 615 Fairmont Hotel, Sheikh Zayed Rd	04 3291977	www.gulfeyecenter.com
Moorfields Eye Hospital	Block E, 3rd flr Al Razi Bldg, Dubai Healthcare City	04 4297888	www.moorfields.ae
Welcare Hospital	Behind Millennium Airport Hotel, Al Garhoud	04 2827788	www.ehl.ae

DENTISTS

As with everything else, dentistry is of a very high standard in Dubai. The government also provides subsidised dental care to residents, for which you need a health card. Dental care is not usually covered by private health insurance. Check www.dubaidentistsnetwork.com for a more detailed list of dentists.

Dental clinic	Address	Telephone	Website
American Dental Clinic	Villa 54 next to Dubai Zoo, Jumeirah Beach Rd	04 3440668	www.americandental clinic.com
Blue Dental Clinic	579 Jumeirah Beach Rd	04 3944233	www.bluedental clinic.com
British Dental Clinic	Al Wasl Rd, Jumeirah 1	04 3421318	www.britishdental clinic.com
Drs.Nicolas and ASP	A/P 30 Unit 302/303 Dubai Healthcare City	04 3624788	www.nicolasandasp. com
Dubai Sky Clinic	Level 21 Burjuman Business Tower, Bur Dubai	04 3558808	www.dubaiskyclinic. com
Dubai Smile Dental Center	Emirates Islamic Bldg, Al Diyafah Rd	04 3986662	www.dubaismile.com
Emirates Hospital	Jumeirah Beach Rd, opp Jumeirah Beach Park	04 3496666	www.emirates hospital.ae
International Dental Clinic	Al Hawai Tower, Sheikh Zayed Rd	04 3433360	www.identalc.com
Jumeirah Beach Dental Clinic	Along Jumeirah Beach Rd, opp Beach Centre	04 3499433	
Swedish Dental Clinic	NASA Travel Bldg, Al Maktoum St, Deira	04 2231297	www.swedishdental clinic.net
The Dental Spa	Jumeirah Beach Rd near Umm Al Sheif St	04 3952005	www.thedentalspa. org
Towerclinic	Ibn Sina Bldg D-104 Dubai Healthcare City	04 3300220	www.towerclinic. com

PHARMACIES

There are many pharmacies in Dubai and you will easily be able to find one that is close to you. They sell many drugs over the counter, often not available without prescription in other countries. Each Emirate has at least one pharmacy open 24 hours a day. The local newspapers will list these or you can call Dubai Municipality on 04 2232323 to find out.

ALTERNATIVE MEDICINE

With the blend of cultures in Dubai, you will find practices from all corners of the world. A lot of the spas do have reflexology as part of their menu of treatments, but there are also specialist clinics for acupuncture, homeopathy, reflexology and physiotherapy. And of course there is a plethora of spas that offer hundreds of different treatments from luxury massages to Ayurvedic treatments (see pp 189–195).

Clinic	Speciality	Address	Telephone	Website
Bliss Relaxology	Reflexology, Thai and other massage	Emirates Building, Garhoud	04 2869444	
Dubai Bone and Joint Center	Physiotherapy	Al Razi Bldg, Dubai Healthcare City	04 3302000	www.dbaj.ae
Dubai Community Health Centre	Homeopathy, psychotherapy	Jumeirah Beach Rd, after Jumeirah Beach Park	04 3953939	www.dubaicommunityhealthcentre.org
Dubai Herbal and Treatment Centre	Acupuncture, homeopathy, Chinese treatments	Zabeel 1, opp Al Wasl Hospital	04 3351200	www.dubaihtc.com
Dubai Physiotherapy Clinic	Acupuncture, physiotherapy	Al Wasl Rd, Jumeirah	04 3496333	www.dubaiphysio.com
Feet First	Reflexology, massage, facials	Town Centre, Jumeirah	04 3494334	www.feet1st.com

General Medical Centre	Physiotherapy	Magrudy's Shopping Complex, Beach Rd	04 3495959	www.groupgmc.net
Holistic Healing Medical Centre	Acupuncture, Ayurveda, colon therapy	Villa 783, Jumeirah Beach Rd	04 3487172	www.healthholistic.com
House of Chi and House of Healing	Acupuncture, reflexology, cupping massage	6th Flr Al Musalla Towers, Bur Dubai	04 3974446	www.hofchi.com
OrthoSports Medical Centre	Physiotherapy, ortho specialist	Jumeirah Beach Rd, near Jumeirah Mosque	04 3450601	www.orthosp.com
The Healing Zone	Reflexology, Reiki, Bowen therapy	Umm Suqueim	04 3940604	www.thehealingzone.net

GIVING BIRTH

Maternity leave

Although mums-to-be should be allowed 45 days of leave on full pay directly before or after birth, many employers in Dubai are not willing to give any further leave, even if unpaid. New fathers aren't allowed any paternity leave.

Maternity hospitals

If choosing a government hospital as it is cheaper than private (though government hospitals still charge for maternity services), Al Wasl has an excellent reputation for maternity and paediatrics. However, many government hospitals do not allow men into the labour room until the point of final delivery. Of the private maternity hospitals, the best are American Hospital, where you will receive very luxurious service, and Welcare Hospital. There are also some relatively new hospitals such as Med Care in Jumeirah, which have great facilities.

It's always good to get advice from people you know and from women who have been through childbirth in Dubai. Visit all the hospitals and clinics and make an informed decision.

To be able to deliver in a government hospital in Dubai, you will need a valid health card and your original marriage certificate and passports (it is a criminal offence to be unmarried and pregnant in Dubai).

Maternity hospital	Address	Telephone	Website	24-hr emergency
Al Wasl Hospital	Oud Metha Rd, Bur Dubai	04 3241111	www.dohms.gov.ae	Y
American Hospital	Oud Metha Rd, Oud Metha	04 3367777	www.ahdubai.com	Y
Belhoul European Hospital	Dune Centre, Diyafah Rd, Satwa	04 3454000	www.belhouleuropean.com	N
Dubai London Clinic	Al Wasl Rd, Jumeirah	04 3446191	www.dubailondonclinic.com	N
Dubai Hospital	Al Baraha, Deira	04 2714444	www.dohms.gov.ae	Y
Med Care Hospital	Adjacent to Safa Park, Jumeirah	04 4079100	www.medcarehospital.com	Y
Welcare Hospital	Near Aviation Club, Garhoud	04 2827788	www.ehl.ae	Y

Obtaining a birth certificate

It is always advisable to check the rules with your embassy before you give birth so that you can confirm the citizenship of your baby and apply for a passport. Every expat baby born in the UAE needs to be registered with the parents' embassy.

The hospital where you have given birth will issue a 'notification of birth certificate' in Arabic. You will need this in English as well as Arabic, each of which costs Dhs50. Translation will cost Dhs15. Al Baraha Hospital will be able to provide an English birth certificate.

You will need:

- Original and a copy of parents' passports with residence permits
- Copy of marriage certificate

- Discharge summary from hospital of mother and child.

You will then need to get this attested at the Ministry of Health Counter at Al Baraha Hospital for Dhs20 and then at the Ministry of Foreign Affairs for Dhs150.

There is also a private company called Medi Express (04 2727772) at Al Baraha Hospital which can handle all translation, attestations and processes for around Dhs130.

The maximum period to register your child's birth is 30 days. Therefore, you don't need to rush to get everything done. You can wait till you decide on a name and then get the certificate.

You then also need to get a passport for your newborn and apply for a residency permit within 120 days.

PART 3

Enjoying life in Dubai

Chapter 14

Touring

There is no shortage of places to explore at weekends and during holiday time in and around Dubai. Why not make the most of the opportunity to learn about the culture and visit the sights? After all, plenty of visitors come to Dubai just for holidays.

It's quite easy to see why Dubai is known as an architectural haven when you just drive down Sheikh Zayed Road or Jumeirah and glance at all the famous buildings like the Burj-Al-Arab, Emirates Towers, and of course the famous tallest tower, Burj Khalifa. But there are many different and exciting ways of seeing Dubai.

BUS TOURS

Big Bus Tour

04 3407709, www.bigbustours.com
Dhs175, children Dhs100, Dhs450 (inc 2 adults and 2 children)

To get an overview of the whole city in just a couple of hours, take the Big Bus Tour. Just choose one of the two routes – City Tour or Beach Tour – sit back and enjoy the views. The ticket also includes an optional *dhow* cruise, an Arabian Treasures Walking Tour, entrance into Dubai Museum and Sheikh Saeed Al Maktoum's house, along with some shopping vouchers. Depending on the time you have, you can do as much or as little as you want by hopping on and off at the 23 stops throughout the city. Tickets are valid for 24 hours.

Wonder Bus Tours

04 3595656, www.wonderbusdubai.net
Dhs150, children Dhs75

This bus can drive on road and water – so as you sit on the same comfortable seat, you'll be transported through the architectural gems and the historic buildings on both shores of the creek and from land to water.

CITY TOURS

Arabian Adventures

04 3439966, www.arabian-adventures.com
Dhs135, children Dhs70 for a half day city tour

Choose from the city tour, Arabian culture tour, future of Dubai tour and more. They organise excursions and dinner cruises as well as activities such as diving, fishing and golf.

Net Tours Group

04 2666655, www.nettoursdubai.com
Dhs110, children Dhs75

They organise half day modern and cultural tours of Dubai as well as desert safaris and tours of other emirates.

CRUISING IN A *DHOW*

A great way to see Dubai's landmarks and glittering lights or to unwind with your partner over a romantic dinner is to take a traditional wooden *dhow* and sail along the Dubai creek in the moonlight. There's a buffet dinner, traditional Arabic coffee and usually some kind of entertainment. The cruise lasts for around 2 hours and starts at approximately 8:30pm.

Al Boom Tourist Village

04 324300

Al Mansour Dhow
04 2057033

Bateaux Dubai
04 3994994

Creek Cruises
04 3939860

Creekside Leisure
04 3368406

SEEING DUBAI FROM THE SKIES

With beautiful turquoise waters, high-rise buildings, various hues of the desert and other incredible landmarks, there's nothing better than seeing all this from high above. It's a totally different view from up here and there are so many different ways of seeing everything.

Did you know?

The Arabic word *burj* means 'Tower'. The Burj Khalifa's design is based on the geometric shape of the *hymenocallis*, a desert flower and has incorporated patterns in Islamic architecture.

Once completed, it is set to become the tallest man-made structure in the world.

Helicopter tours

Blue Banana, 044368100, www.bluebanana.ae
Dhs1250 for 30 mins, max of 6 people

Indulge in this easy ride which lets you have a bird's eye view of Dubai. Enjoy your helicopter travelling backwards, sideways and hanging motionless in mid-air. The cabin can seat up to six people and is suitable for all ages.

Hot air ballooning

Balloon Adventures, 04 2854949, www.ballooning.ae
Dhs950 for one hour, max of 20 people (Blue Banana also offer hot air ballooning)

View the red shades of giant dunes and the striking landscape of Dubai early in the morning.

Seaplane safaris

Seawings, 04 8832999, www.seawings.ae
From Dhs895 for 30 mins, max of 9 people

This is a journey along Dubai's dramatic and ever changing coastal skyline. After taking off smoothly on the water you get, at 1500 feet, a bird's eye view of Dubai's famous landmarks. You can also combine golf and deep sea fishing, and if you're feeling sporty, then sailing is available, too.

Skydiving

Umm Al Quwain Aeroclub, 06 7681447, www.uaqaeroclub.com
Dhs1000 plus Dhs400 for a video (Blue Banana also offer skydiving)

This is one of the most exhilarating, adrenalin-pumping activities. You can see the ocean and rich desert colours from 9000 feet up and then jump out strapped to a qualified instructor.

IN THE DESERT

Leave the busy city life and head out to the legendary Arabian Desert. There's a lot you can do out there, and its proximity means that you can go for a morning or evening tour or even stay there overnight.

Surfing the dunes

A visit to the desert is incomplete without a desert safari tour, a roller-coaster ride across the dunes, swerving from angle to angle in powerful 4x4s. If you like camels, then ride atop this 'ship of the desert', watching the rippling sands catch the golden glow of the sun. This is an adventure not to be missed. Tours can also include a traditional Bedouin-style dinner, often accompanied by some great belly dancing and the aromatic *shisha* pipe if you fancy smoking some delicious flavours.

Arabian Adventures, 04 3034888, www.arabian-adventures.com

Desert Rangers, 04 3402408, www.desertrangers.com

Net Tours, 04 2666655, www.netgroupdubai.com

Knight Tours, 04 2686555, www.knighttours.co.ae

Gulf Ventures, 04 4045880, www.gulfventures.ae

Sand-skiing

Lama Tours, 04 3344230, www.lama-tours.ae
Dhs220 per person for sand-skiing and dune bashing (minimum of four people)

For the adventurous, try this unusual yet easy to learn sport. Get onto a ski board ride over the harmless sand dunes, which will cushion you if you fall. Desert Safaris can usually include this.

Quad biking

Blue Banana, 04 4368100, www.bluebanana.ae
Dhs375 per person for 1 hour, minimum booking of 2 people

Open air in the desert, sand spraying all around, easy to ride, go as fast or as slow as you want – it's all fun and great for a group of friends or with the family.

Camping

Absolute Adventure, 04 3459900, www.adventure.ae, organises corporate camping trips with team-building activities

Sunshine and fantastic locations make camping a popular and perfect weekend activity in Dubai. The best time to go camping is from October to April as sleeping outside in the extreme summer heat isn't exactly easy. You can choose the desert or the *wadis* and mountains. There are plenty of amazing camp sites available. But make sure you go equipped with tents, insect repellent, a first aid kit, map and compass, toilet roll, suncream, water and some on-the-go food, rubbish bags and a fully charged mobile phone.

Drumming

www.dubaidrums.com
Dhs175 for barbeque dinner and drumming, Dhs75 for children aged 5–14

Experience full moon drumming in the desert and feel your stress disappear. It's great for all ages, so take along your family or a group of friends. It's organised by Dubai Drums. Yep, sounds random but that's why it's so cool. It's worth going along for just letting yourself go. Dubai Drums also specialise in team-building events. Don't forget to print out the map before you leave – getting lost in the desert is not recommended.

Now you know

If your car gets stuck in the sand, which is very possible (it happened to me), then kick lots of sand onto the bottom of your wheel on one side, use a few people's force to rock the car back and forth from that side and do exactly the same with the other side. This way, sand will get under your car wheels, lift your car a bit and then, when you start driving again, it should be fine ... hopefully!

HISTORICAL AND CULTURAL ATTRACTIONS

In search of some history? While Dubai is known for its high-rise towers, unbelievable luxury and excessive glamour, there is also a slice of tradition you can explore, which will give you that feeling of old, authentic and perhaps just real.

Visit one of the oldest areas in Bur Dubai called Bastakiya, where you'll find the old windtowers as you walk through the narrow lanes. Dubai Museum will teach you a lot about what the city was like years ago. You can also enjoy a historical journey of Sheikh Saeed's House and understand more about the Islamic religion at the Jumeirah Mosque. And, with all these places and, with the many *souks* and *abras*, you can truly experience the rich Arabic culture.

Al Ahmadiya School and Heritage House
Al Khor St, Deira, 04 2260286
Sun–Thu 7:30am–7:30pm, Fri 2pm–7:30pm

This was the first school in Dubai, established in 1912 and allows you to understand the history of education in Dubai. The Heritage House next door is a traditional Emirati House from 1890.

Bastakiya quarter
Bur Dubai

This is one of the most picturesque sites in Dubai and gives a real feeling of the traditional, old Dubai. It was built in the late 19th century by Persian merchants and still has narrow alleys, courtyard houses and windtowers. Years ago, there was a mass of windtowers on either side of the Creek, a way of cooling houses.

Dubai Museum
Al Fahidi Fort, Bur Dubai, 04 3531862
Sat–Thurs 8:30am–8:30pm, Fri 2:30pm–8:30pm, Dhs3

Housed within the beautiful Al Fahidi Fort, which was built around 1799 to defend the city against invasion, the museum has pottery, stone and metallic items, as well as engravings and skeletons from 4000 years back discovered during digs. It depicts life before the discovery of oil and is a fascinating insight into the history and culture of Dubai.

Don't miss

Dubai Museum has recreated scenes from the past including from Dubai Creek, where the *dhows* first set sail, and how locals used to find pearls.

Sheikh Saeed Al Maktoum House

Shindagha area, Dubai Creek, 04 3937139
Sat–Thurs 8am–8:30pm, Fri 3:30pm–9:30pm

The official residence of Sheikh Saeed Al Maktoum, Ruler of Dubai (1912–1958) and grandfather of the present Ruler, Sheikh Maktoum Bin Rashid Al Maktoum, this house overlooks the mouth of the Creek at Shindagha and is a listed national monument housing a collection of historic photographs, coins, stamps and documents. The magnificent building reopened as a museum in 1986 and offers breathtaking views of the creek.

Grand Mosque

Bur Dubai

Considered one of the largest mosques in the UAE, the Grand Mosque is an important landmark and place of worship, able to house 1200 people at once. It has Dubai's tallest minaret (tower from which the call to prayer is broadcast), countless beautiful domes and handmade stained glass. Even though non-Muslims are not allowed inside the mosque, it's worth visiting just to see its incredible exterior and take photos.

Jumeirah Grand Mosque

Jumeirah Beach Road, 04 3536666

This is a beautiful white stone structure with towering twin minarets. The Islamic style architecture of Jumeirah Mosque is captivating and even more so if you visit at night. It is also one of the very few mosques in Dubai which you can visit as a non-Muslim. There are organised tours of the mosque every Saturday, Sunday, Tuesday and Thursday at 10am.

Dubai Creek and *souks*

(also see pp 200–3 for *souks*)

Located in the historical part of Dubai, the Creek is a natural inlet that cuts right through the centre of the city, with Deira on one side and Bur Dubai on the other. At the Creek, you can experience the fascinating old *souks* offering gold, textiles, spices and fish and stroll around the wharf. These *souks* are on either side of the creek and it's worth taking an *abra* (small water taxi) from one side to other. It's a very, very picturesque ride, from which you'll be able to see the old trading port and *dhows*. You can also take an hour-long trip from the mouth of the Creek to the Maktoum Bridge, passing many historic and modern landmarks along the way.

Dubai Heritage and Diving Village

Shindagha area, Bur Dubai, 04 3937151
Sat–Thurs 8:30am–10:30pm, Fri 3:30pm–11pm

Also known as Hatta Village, the Dubai Heritage and Diving Village near the Creek offers an insight into Dubai's traditional culture and lifestyle. You'll find demonstrations of pearl diving and fishing. It is constructed around an old settlement and has houses which have been recreated in the Hatta style. A large fort and tower, built in the 1880s to protect the city from external attacks, overlooks the village.

Sheikh Mohammed Centre for Cultural Understanding (SMCCU)

Bastakiya, Bur Dubai, 04 3536666, www.cultures.ae

In an effort to help others understand the customs of the UAE, SMCCU organises tours, courses, cultural breakfasts and coffee mornings.

PARKS AND BEACHES

If you want to spend a day away from the busy city life, you'll be able to find a beautifully-landscaped green park near you. And parks in Dubai aren't just child-orientated, unless you go on a 'women and children only' day ... They have a wide array of activities available from taking an *abra* ride and paddling in the lake to playing on video games and enjoying bumper cars. And some parks like Jumeirah Beach Park, Creekside Park, Al Mamzar Park and Safa Park also have access to the beach. Many of the beach hotels offer access to the beach and pool area with varying entry charges (see pp 173–4).

Al Mamzar Beach Park

Deira, north of Al Hamriya Port, 04 2966201
Sat–Wed 8am–11pm, Thurs–Fri 8am–11:30pm, Wed for ladies only, Dhs5 per person, Dhs30 per car, Chalets Dhs150–200

This comprises a large park full of trees, an ampitheatre, children's playground and full beach facilities with lifeguards. You can also hire a chalet for your family.

Creekside Park

Bur Dubai, between Al Maktoum and Al Gharoud Bridge, entry behind Dubai Court, 04 3667633
Daily 8am–11pm, Wed for ladies and children only, Dhs5 per person

This is one of Dubai's most popular and largest parks with botanical gardens, fishing piers, jogging tracks, barbecue sites with equipment, children's play areas, restaurants and a large amphitheatre. And if that's not enough, there's also an 18-hole mini golf course. You can sit on cable cars and enjoy the views, hire bikes and go for a ride or choose to experience an *abra* ride.

Jumeirah Beach Park

Jumeirah Beach Road, 043492555
Fri–Tues 8am–11pm, Wed–Thurs 8am–11:30pm, Mon – for ladies and children only. Dhs5 per person, Dhs20 per car

With full beach facilities and lifeguard service, this is great for picnics. There's a children's playground, barbecue areas and even a helipad.

Jumeirah Open Beach Park

Jumeirah Beach on a 1km long area, 04 3443379
24 hours daily

With a beach front, this is great for picnics, swimming and sunbathing. There are picnic tables, a barbecue area, small play areas for children and volleyball area.

Mushrif Park

On Al Awir Road, Al Rashidiya, 04 2883624
Fri–Tues 8am–11pm, Wed–Thurs 8am–11:30pm, Dhs3 per person, Dhs10 per car

About a half-hour drive from Dubai, Mushrif Park has a miniature train, merry-go-round, offers camel rides and includes 'World Village' which has miniature architectural samples from every continent – Dutch windmills, English Tudor cottages and Thai stilt dwellings. There are also separate swimming pools for men and women.

Safa Park

Bur Dubai, Al Hamriya, 04 3492111
Fri–Tues 8am–11pm, Wed–Thurs 8am–11:30pm, Dhs3 per person

This is a mini-city with small-scale roads, traffic lights and signs for children, a video game parlour for teenagers, bumper cars and a big wheel. You can also hire a paddle boat on the lake, play tennis, cricket, volleyball, basketball ... and they even have football pitches. It is very popular with joggers and walkers.

HOTELS

Dubai, as you'll have heard and seen, is home to some of the swankiest, plushest, bling-bling hotels in the world. At the top end of this list you have Burj al-Arab in Dubai and Emirates Palace Hotel in Abu Dhabi. Others such as Al Qasr, Park Hyatt, Emirates Towers, Jumeirah Beach, Fairmont, Intercontinental and so many others rank just as highly with stylish designs, fantastic eateries, luxurious spas, swimming pools and the works. Some of the hotels have outstanding architecture and are worth paying a visit just for this. Most waterfront hotels have lush beaches and watersports facilities.

The latest and most hyped-up addition, The Atlantis, with a huge aquarium, great water park and some of the poshest restaurants, built on the peak of the Palm Jumeirah, has only added to the glamour of Dubai. So, all in all, you're never short of luxury in Dubai, whether you want to spa at the weekend (see pp 189–95), indulge in the most decadent of Friday brunches (see pp 277–81), or just head out somewhere not too far for a long weekend (see pp 144–52).

Hotel prices are constantly fluctuating. It's therefore advisable to check with the hotel when you travel. You may, of course, get better deals from travel agencies in your home country, especially if it is a package.

There are also some slightly cheaper hotels which also have great facilities such as the Premier Inn (04 8850999), where an overnight stay costs Dhs350, and the Ibis in Al Barsha (04 5156868), which has similar rates.

City hotels

Al Murooj Rotana
Sheikh Zayed Road opp Dubai Mall
04 3211111
www.rotana.com/property-10.htm

Angsana
Sheikh Zayed Road
04 3230000
www.angsana.com

Burjuman – Arjaan Rotana
Burjuman Centre, Trade Centre Road
04 3524444
www.rotana.com/property-11.htm

Crowne Plaza Dubai Festival City
Dubai Festival City, Deira
04 7012222
www.crowneplaza.com/dfc

Fairmont
Sheikh Zayed Road
04 3325555
www.fairmont.com/dubai

Grand Hyatt
Oud Metha, Bur Dubai
04 3171234
www.dubai.grand.hyatt.com

Hilton Dubai Creek Hotel
Baniyas Road, Deira, close to City Centre Shopping Mall
04 2271111
www.hilton.com

Hyatt Regency Dubai
Al Khaleej Road, Corniche, Deira
04 2091234
www.dubai.regency.hyatt.com

InterContinental Dubai Festival City
Festival City, Deira
04 7011111
www.ichotelsgroup.com/dubai

Jumeirah Emirates Towers
Sheikh Zayed Road
04 3300000
www.jumeirah.com

JW Marriott Hotel
Abu Baker Al Siddique Road, Deira,
04 2624444
www.jwmarriottdubai.com

Kempinski Hotel Mall of the Emirates
Sheikh Zayed Road
04 3410000
www.kempinski-dubai.com

Le Meridien Dubai
Deira, Airport Road
04 2170000
www.lemeridien.com/dubai

Moevenpick Hotel Bur Dubai
Oud Metha, Bur Dubai
04 3366000
www.moevenpick-hotels.com

Park Hyatt Dubai
Baniyas Road, Deira
04 602 1234/209 6661
www.dubai.park.hyatt.com

Raffles
Sheikh Rashid Road, Wafi
04 3248888
www.raffles.com

Rimal Rotana Suites
Murraqabat Street, Deira
04 2688000
www.rotana.com/property-19.htm

Shangri-La
Sheikh Zayed Road
04 3438888
www.shangri-la.com

Sheraton Dubai Creek Hotel and Towers
Baniyas Street, Creek Road, Deira
04 2281111
www.starwoodhotels.com/sheraton

The Address Hotels
There are several Address Hotels in the city; see www.theaddress.com for full contact details.

Towers Rotana
Sheikh Zayed Road
04 3438000
www.rotana.com/property-20.htm

Beach Hotels

Al Qasr – Madinat Jumeirah
Jumeirah Beach Road, Jumeirah
04 3668888
www.jumeirah.com

Atlantis The Palm Jumeirah
The Palm Jumeirah
04 4261000
www.atlantisthepalm.com

Burj Al Arab
Sheikh Zayed Road
04 3017777
www.burj-al-arab.com

Dar Al Masyaf
Jumeirah Beach Road, Jumeirah
04 3668888
www.jumeirah.com

Dubai Marine Beach Resort and Spa
Jumeirah Beach Road, Jumeirah
04 3461111
www.dxbmarine.com

Grosvenor House Dubai
Dubai Marina
04 3998888
www.grosvenorhouse-dubai.com

Habtoor Grand Resort and Spa
Al Sufouh Road, Jumeirah
04 3995000
www.grandjumeirah.habtoorhotels.com

Hilton Dubai Jumeirah Beach Resort
Jumeirah Beach Residence Walk
04 3991111
www1.hilton.com

Jebel Ali Golf Resort and Spa
Jebel Ali (Jebel Ali Free Zone)
04 8836000
www.jebelali-international.com

Jumeirah Beach Hotel
Jumeirah Beach Road, Jumeirah
04 3480000
www.jumeirahbeachhotel.com

Le Meridien Mina Seyahi Beach Resort and Marina
Al Sufouh Road, Jumeirah
04 3993333
www.starwoodhotels.com/lemeridien

Le Royal Meridien Beach Resort and Spa
Al Sufouh Road, Jumeirah
04 3995555
www.starwoodhotels.com/lemeridien

Mina A' Salam
Jumeirah Beach Road, Jumeirah
04 3668888
www.jumeirah.com

One and Only Royal Mirage
Jumeirah
04 3999999
www.oneandonlyresorts.com

Sheraton Jumeirah Beach Resort and Towers
Al Sufouh Road, Jumeirah
04 3995533
www.starwoodhotels.com/sheraton

The Ritz-Carlton
Jumeirah Beach Road, Jumeirah
04 3994000
www.ritzcarlton.com

Desert Hotels

Al Maha Desert Resort and Spa
Al Ain Road
04 3034222
www.al-maha.com

Desert Palm Hotel
Al Awir Road
04 3238888
www.desertpalm.ae

Hatta Fort Hotel
Hatta Village
04 8523211
www.hattaforthotel.com

Jumeirah Bab Al Shams
Endurance Village
04 8096100
www.jumeirah.com

WEEKEND BREAKS

Surely every weekend can't be spent shopping in the malls, going to fancy restaurants and bars and sitting for four-hour brunches. It's always great to escape from the hustle and bustle of demanding city life.

And while Dubai has some fantastic beach hotels, if you're living here, chances are you won't want to escape to a resort so close to home or so close to all the razzmatazz of this city.

Well, lucky for Dubaians, there are fantastic areas to explore and gorgeous resorts to escape to not very far away. And even if you fancy going further afield, destinations like Oman, India, Sri Lanka, Bahrain, Jordan, even Africa are only a few hours away.

In this section, I've only given a selection of resorts and places to escape to. Abu Dhabi, Fujairah and Ajman, three of the seven Emirates, are very close by and can make for a great weekend break. If you want to head a few hours away to Oman or Bahrain, then there's some more information on these countries other than just luxurious resorts.

Resorts close to Dubai

Al Maha Desert Resort and Spa

04 3034222, www.al-maha.com

Just 45 minutes from Dubai and you're in for a very special weekend, tucked away in a nature reserve. There are only 42 rooms built in the style of Bedouin tents, a fantastic spa and good food.

Jumeirah Bab Al Shams Desert Resort and Spa

04 8096100, www.jumeirahbabalshams.com

Just 45 minutes from Dubai, this is an elegant desert resort set in a traditional Arabic fort. It features 113 rooms built in a rustic traditional style and offers an authentic experience of Arabic culture.

One to watch

Ibn Battuta Gate Hotel

Already being dubbed the gateway to Abu Dhabi due to its iconic entrance arch which is larger than Paris's Arc de Triomphe, this hotel is scheduled to open towards the end of 2009.

Bani Yas Island

02 8015400, www.desertislands.anantara.com

Just off the coast of Abu Dhabi is the lush Sir Bani Yas Island, developed by Sheikh Zayed Bin Sultan Al Nahyan as a private Royal Nature Reserve. It recently opened to international tourism as the Anantara Desert Islands Resort and Spa as part of the Desert Islands project. With a focus on nature, you'll find indigenous Arabian wildlife such as the endangered oryx from the Arabian National Park, which roam by the waters. You can go by car or take a flight.

Emirates Palace, Abu Dhabi
02 6909000, www.emiratespalace.com

Just an hour away in Abu Dhabi, this is both magnificent and majestic – very palace-like. It is located on 1.3km of a private beach and is surrounded by 85 hectares of landscaped gardens.

The rooms are pretty lavish, but it does take almost 15 minutes to walk from one end of the Palace to the other.

Hilton, Fujairah
09 2222411, www.hilton.com

Just a 90-minute drive from Dubai, Fujairah lies on the east coast of the UAE. This Hilton is located by the Hajar mountains and on the shores of the Arabian Gulf. It is a charming and relaxing resort, where you can sit by the beach, or play tennis, basketball or watersports. There is a variety of dining options from exotic Mediterranean-style to seafood, and don't forget to enjoy a *shisha* at the beachfront Sailor's restaurant at dusk.

Le Meridien Al Aqah, Fujairah
09 244 9000, www.lemeridien-alaqah.com

Under two hours' drive from Dubai, Fujairah has some great beach resorts. At Le Meridien, all the 218 rooms have incredible sea views and with the backdrop of the majestic mountains, this resort is quite an escape. There are also eight dining options, a professional diving centre, penguin club for kids and, of course, a luxurious spa, not to mention the in-house cinema.

Kempinski, Ajman
06 7145555, www.ajmankempinski.com

Less than a 30-minute drive from Dubai, Ajman is the smallest of the seven United Arab Emirates and quite an idyllic place. Relax on the enormous white sandy beach and swim in the crystal clear blue waters of the Arabian Sea. There's also an Ayurveda spa here, so go get detoxed and discover the healing powers of this ancient science.

Banyan Tree Al Wadi, Ras Al Khaimah
www.banyantree.com

This will be Ras Al Khaimah's first luxury resort of its kind, set to open at the end of 2009. It will have private pools, a hydrotherapy spa, private beach club and kids' club as well as a nature reserve.

Hatta

Drive time: Just over 1 hour
Bus: every hour of the day from Deira bus station.

The ancient, fortressed village of Hatta lies along the foothills of the dramatic Hajar Mountains. It has fantastic mountain scenery as well as the magnificent Hatta rock pools. You'll find plunging waterfalls and unspoilt environment. Its close proximity to Dubai makes it a very popular getaway, even if it's a day trip. It is also home to the Hatta Fort Hotel (www.hattaforthotel.com), an isolated mountain resort overlooking the Hajar mountains.

The mountains are best explored by 4x4 vehicles, though during the winter months, water may be found in the *wadis*. Visit Wadi Hatta, filled with greenery and wildlife and Juma Mosque, which stands amidst palm groves.

Oman

Fly time: 1 hour
Drive time: 4 hours
Warning – in case you're renting a car, your insurance won't cover accidents in Oman.

Oman has plenty to offer, from pristine beaches to history and adventure, and it's all very accessible. And a weekend away in Oman will give you a totally different taste of the Middle East. If you're in for luxury, the beach and just a relaxing escape, then stay at one of the world-class resorts that Oman boasts.

The Chedi
+968 24524400, www.ghmhotels.com

The Chedi is undoubtedly romantic in every way. The pool, elegant and with that vanishing edge, has a spectacular view of the Gulf of Oman. It has 167 rooms and private villas, but is spread out so well that it doesn't feel crowded. What is spectacular about the Chedi is its appearance in the evening with the water courtyards in perfect lighting.

Shangri-La
+968 24776269, www.shangri-la.com

Shangri-La's Barr Al Jissah Resort and Spa comprises three luxurious hotels, so it's almost like a mini-village. Its location along the bay of Al Jissah and with the dramatic backdrop of rugged mountains makes it an exclusive destination resort. Each of the three hotels has a different allure. Al Waha (The Oasis) is the perfect family getaway, with a kids' club, several swimming pools and a fantastic lazy river, which will keep kids occupied. Children also eat for free. The second hotel, Al Bandar (The Town), is more geared to couples and for business trips. The final Al Husn (The Castle) is the flagship and most exclusive, with six-star indulgence.

Al Bustan Palace
+968 24799666, www.al-bustan.intercontinental.com

Set in the midst of a mountain range and the Gulf of Oman, Al Bustan Palace overlooks a beautifully clear beach and has just reopened after a two year, multi-million dollar, lavish refurbishment. It is far more grand inside than it is outside. There are numerous dining options, with the all-day restaurant Al Khiran Terrace, serving Asian, Italian and French, the French Al Marjan and China Mood, featuring the best in Szechwan, Cantonese and Shangai cuisine.

Six Senses Hideaway Zighy Bay
+968 26735555, www.sixsenses.com/Six-Senses-Hideaway-Zighy-Bay

The setting of the indigenous, village-style accommodations and private marina is dramatic, with mountains on one side and a 1.6-kilometre sandy beach at Zighy Bay, on the other.

What else?
Oman isn't just about luxury. You can go for walks or long hikes in the scenic Al Hajar mountain range. And if walks aren't your thing, then a picnic in between the mountains in the dry *wadis* will serve well. If you are the adventurous type, then further away is the Al Hoota Cave, which has an underground lake and can be explored by anyone, regardless of whether or not you have caving experience (www.alhootacave.com).

Oman is also a diver's haven, providing plenty of opportunity for diving. Dive with Oman Dive Centre, (+968 24824240, www.omandivecenter.com), one of the top diving centres in the world. It's worth trying out night dives while you're here. The phosphorescence in the water, released by plankton, makes the water beautifully visible after dark.

If you want an insight into the culture and heritage of Oman, head into Muscat Old Town, visit one of the best and oldest *souks*, Muttrah Souk, where you'll find traditional craft, old silver, spices, embroidery, incense, the traditional *khanjar* swords and so much more. Take a tour of the modern, large and lavish Grand Mosque. Learn about the history of Oman at Muscat Gate Museum and visit the beautiful Alam Palace, home of Sultan Qaboos.

And apart from Muscat, there is also Musandam and Salalah, both of which have resorts and fantastic beaches, but are much further away.

Bahrain

Fly time: Just over half an hour
Drive time: over 5 hours

Bahrain is very close to Dubai; you can very quickly be in a country rich in history where you can stay in one of the luxurious resorts or indulge in a bit of sightseeing.

Banyan Tree Desert Spa and Resort, Al Areen, Bahrain
+973 17845000, www.banyantree.com/en/alareen/index.html

A luxurious hideaway, the Banyan Tree has lush pool villas with azure swimming pools, jet-pools and private gardens, one of the world's most extensive spas and hydrotherapy complexes, a complete body wellness centre and the award winning Banyan Tree Gallery.

Ritz Carlton, Bahrain Hotel and Spa
+973 17580000, www.ritzcarlton.com/en/Properties/Bahrain

This beautiful resort is located in a 20-acre urban resort complex on the seafront of Manama. Stay in one of the seafront villas, with a butler, swimming pool and private beach access.

What else?
If you want to delve into a bit of culture, head to the *souk* in Manama, then to Bahrain's National Museum, home to a vast collection of Bahraini artwork. One of the most historic buildings in Bahrain houses the Museum of Pearl Diving, a pursuit that has been Bahrain's heritage for over 100 years. There's also the Riffa Fort and Arad Fort, where you'll learn more about the history of this country.

You can spot an Arabian gazelle, oryx or a desert hedgehog at The Al Areen Wildlife Park in the village of Zallaq, which provides a natural habitat for several kinds of plants and more than 500 species of animals and birds.

And finally, Bahrain is fantastic for water sports enthusiasts. You can do anything from game fishing, scuba diving and snorkelling to water-skiing, windsurfing and parasailing.

Qatar

Fly time: 1 hour

Qatar is becoming increasingly popular with tourists. With large energy reserves and recent development, it has become a regional economic powerhouse. The capital, Doha, has a fantastic mixture of rich, traditional Arabic and modern architecture.

Ritz-Carlton Doha

+974 4848000, www.ritzcarlton.com/doha

Gazing over the waters of the Arabian Gulf, this is an idyllic setting for both business and leisure. There are a total of 374 rooms and suites with fantastic views, nine restaurants with local and international cuisine and bars, a world class spa and indoor and outdoor swimming pools.

Four Seasons Hotel Doha

+974 4948888, www.fourseasons.com/doha

With its own private beach and a marina, this hotel is opulent and exclusive, a traveller's haven. It is a beautiful property and has 232 luxurious and tastefully decorated rooms. There are several restaurants and a fantastic spa with 11 chic treatment rooms and a kids club.

Sharq Village and Spa

+974 4256666, www.ritzcarlton.com/en/Properties/SharqVillage

This is a breathtaking waterfront property with 174 rooms and traditional architecture. You can meander through the lane of the surrounding Sharq Village, sit by the stunning pools or in the outdoor *majlis*. There are plentiful, exceptionally-fine dining options and a Six Senses Spa built in the style of a Qatari bazaar, featuring 23 treatment rooms, relaxation rooms, heated marble wet beds, two Hammam rooms and dry flotation beds.

W Hotel Hotel and Residences
+974 4535353. www.whoteldoha.com

This recently opened W Hotel is swanky, plush and stylish and houses a Bliss spa. It is located in West Bay and isn't far from the City Centre Shopping Mall. Among the restaurants, W Hotel also houses the prestigious La Maison du Caviar.

What else?
For a spot of culture, The Grand Mosque and the Abu Bakir al-Siddiq Mosque are particularly interesting. The National Museum in Doha offers a glimpse into the country's past. Stroll through the narrow alleys of Souq Waqif, the oldest *souq* in Doha where you'll find handicrafts, mounds of spices, coffees and enticing perfumes.

Drive along the picturesque cornice and visit Al Shaqab Stud owned by the Emir, on the outskirts of Doha, where you'll find pure-bred show and race horses and a riding school. Not far from Doha, you can see hundreds of camels at the Camel Track. And for watersports, you have everything from sailing and waterskiing to scuba diving.

Other short breaks with flights times

Qatar, Doha, 1 hr
Saudi Arabia, Riyadh, 1 hr 50
Iran, Tehran, 2 hr 05
India, Delhi, 3 hr
Cyprus, 3 hr 40
Jordan, Amman, 3 hr 15
Syria, Damascus, 3 hr 30
Lebanon, Beirut, 3 hr 40
Greece, 4 hr 55
Maldives, 4 hr 15
Sri Lanka, Colombo, 4 hr 10
Egypt, Cairo, 4 hr 20
Seychelles, 4 hr 30
Turkey, Istanbul, 4 hr 45

Safari tour

Camel tour

Emirates palace (Abu Dhabi)

Dubai Marina

Sheikh Zayad Road

Mina A'Salam and Burj

Barasti bar and restaurant

Falcon City of Wonders

Atlantis, The Palm

Buddha Bar

Mall of the Emirates

Montgomery golf club

Burj Al Arab seafood restaurant

Evening light, Dubai

Chapter 15

Activities and sports

There is just so much going on in Dubai, it's hard to think of something you can't do, learn or practise here. Facilities are great and there are a number of international sporting tournaments which take place in Dubai, attracting the best players in various sports including golf, tennis, rugby, cricket, horse racing, sailing and others.

Taking part in activities that interest you will help you make new friends. You can also meet others through www.meetup.com/dubai-new-in-town, www.rendezvousdubai.com, www.expatexchange.com and www.socialcirclesdubai.com. You can also join 'Friends of Dubai' on Facebook.

ARCHERY

Hatta Fort Club House

Hatta Fort Hotel, 04 8523211

Games of 30 mins. If you have a group of five or more, they can arrange for a class.

Jebel Ali Shooting Club

Jebel Ali Golf Resort and Spa, 04 8836555

Offers regular classes three times a week.

BOOTCAMP AND KICKBOXING

Fitness 02

050 9556129, www.fitness02.com

Fitness 02 offers kickboxing classes in Safa Park, Booty Bootcamp classes for women on Kite Beach, challenging Renegade Boot Camps and fitness programmes for kids.

Physical Advantage

04 3116570, www.physicaladvantage.ae

With three bootcamp sessions a week, this intense and motivational programme is run in various locations.

BIRD WATCHING

The varied landscape and different habitats from mountains and mangrove swamps to tidal wetlands and desert scrub attracts a wide variety of birds. Dubai is also on a migration route for birds travelling from Central Asia to Africa and vice versa. There are over 390 bird species, of which many are unusual or rare. Ras Al Khor Wildlife Sanctuary, at the end of Dubai Creek, is a wetland reserve which attracts many migratory birds and is also home to over 500 greater flamingoes. Other locations for bird watching are the Emirates Golf Club (where you will need special permission), Safa Park and Mushrif Park. And if you're prepared to venture further out, then take a short boat ride from Hamdan Port in Abu Dhabi to Al Futaisi Island (02 6666601). The natural reserve here is home to a hugely diverse selection of birds.

CAVING

If you're experienced or going with someone who knows what they're doing, you'll get to see some of best caves with spectacular stalagmites and stalactites. Al Ain, Jebel Hafeet and near the Oman border are the areas you should head to. Since there are currently no companies organising cave tours and no mountain rescue services, you do need to have an experienced person with you.

CLIMBING

Ras Al Khamah, Dibba, Hatta and Al Ain/Buraimi offers some great climbing. In Wadi Bih or the indoor climbing wall at Pharaohs' Club, you'll find other climbers at the weekends. Dubai's World Trade Centre also boasts the highest climbing wall in the UAE, just over 15 metres high.

www.globalclimbing.com – this website will give you more information on climbing in various areas.

Pharaohs' Club

04 3240000

Based in Wafi City, Pharaohs' Club runs classes in climbing.

Bluebanana

04 436 8100, www.bluebanana.com

Take three hour outdoor lessons in Dibba, perfect for beginners.

COOKING

L'Atelier des Chefs

Le Meridien, 04 7022604, adc@lmdubai.com, www.atelierdeschefsdubai.com

For the first time outside of Europe, L'Atelier des Chefs is offering daily cooking class at Le Meridien. There are one hour express daily classes as well as evening classes.

CYCLING

Dubai Roadsters

www.dubairoadsters.com

Dubai Roadsters are a group of cyclists who enjoy leisure and recreational cycling in Dubai. They have weekly club rides, training rides, tours through the desert and mountains and some races. They also organise annual cycle tours overseas.

DANCE

Salsa

For all different Salsa classes check www.dubaisalsa.com.

Diego Galvis & Julie Andrea Ramirez

Malecon, Dubai Marine Beach Resort &Spa, 050 8429252

James and Alex

Crowne Plaza Hotel; Shoreline Clubhouse 2, Palm Jumeirah, www.jamesandalex.com

Ritmo De Havana

DUCTAC, Mall of Emirates, Del Piero – delpiero2000me@yahoo.com, www.ritmo-de-havana.com

Roger and Guillermo Baez

Shangri-la Hotel; Aviation Club, Garhoud; Knowledge Village Block no 17, 050 4248832 , salsamaster24x7@yahoo.com

Salsa Dubai

Wafi, Phil – salsadxb@emirates.net.ae

Gurukul Dubai

DUCTAC, Mall of the Emirates and Mirdif
Somna – 050 5087180, somna@gurukuldubai.com, www.gurukuldubai.com

Gurukul offers dance programmes in Kathak, Yoga Dance and personalised training for all ages. Pali Chandra, the force behind Gurukul, trained rigorously in Kathak for over 15 years and is an internationally-recognised performing artist.

Nora Dance Group

DUCTAC, Mall of the Emirates and Palm Jumeirah
Nora – 050 8750111, www.noradancegroup.com

Learn belly dancing, Bollywood moves, hip hop, yoga or judo.

Street Jazz and Tap

King's School, Umm Suqueim. Jacqueline Sweed – 050 2275255

This dance school, sponsored by Emirates Entertainment, teaches all types of dance including ballroom, modern jazz and street dancing.

The Ballet Centre

Behind Jumeirah Plaza, 04 3449776

FENCING

Dubai Fencing Club

Mihail – 0507944190, www.dubaifencingclub.com

Experienced fencing coaches provides individual and group training sessions for adults and children. Masks, gloves and weapons are provided.

International Fencing Club of Dubai

Seraj Al Ali – 0506267440, www.fencingdxb.com

They cater to all levels of experience from beginners through to advanced national and international standards. It is the first fencing club in Dubai meeting international standards, equipped with three metallic pistes and all-electric signalisation.

FISHING

Al Wasl Cruising and Sport Fishing

Deira, 04 2681468, www.cruiseindubai.com

Club Joumana

Jebel Ali Golf Resort and Spa, 04 8048023, www.jebelali-international.com

Dubai Creek Golf and Yacht Club

Deira Creek, 04 2054646, www.dubaigolf.com

Nautica 1992

Habtoor Grand Hotel
Suzy Dillon – 0504262415, www.nautica1992.ae

Ocean Active

04 8821070, Email nick@oceanactive.com, www.oceanactive.com

FOOTBALL

Football has become a very popular sport over the years and is promoted in Dubai schools, colleges, locally and nationally. Here are some clubs and groups you can join:

Barclays International Football Academy

04 3371698, www.intlfootballacademy.com

DHL Dubai Amateur Football League

Dean O' Grady – 050 3965135, www.dafleague.com

Dubai Football Academy

04 2824540, www.esportsdubai.com

Dubai Women's Football Association

Lisa Buscheck – 050 7027841, dubaiwf@hotmail.com, www.dubaiwfa.com

FLYING

Emirates Flying School

Terminal 2, Dubai International Airport, 04 2995155

Jazirah Aviation

Ras Al Khaimah, 07 2446416

Umm Al Quwain Aeroclub

Umm Al Quwain, 06 7681447

GOLF

With fantastic weather and great facilities, Dubai is becoming a premier golfing destination. The Dubai Desert Classic tournament attracts big names including

Tiger Woods, Ernie Els and Colin Montgomerie. Dubai Golf (04 3475201, www.dubaigolf.com), a government organisation, operates a central reservation system for those wishing to book a round of golf in any of the major courses. Here are some golf courses where you can play:

Al Badia Golf Resort

04 2325778, www.albadiagolfresort.com

Arabian Ranches Golf Club

04 3663000, www.arabianranchesgolfdubai.com

Dubai Country Club

www.dubaicountryclub.ae

Dubai Creek Golf and Yacht Club

04 2956000

Emirates Golf Club

04 3802222

Montgomerie Golf Club

04 3905600, www.themontgomerie.com

The Resort Course

04 8836000, www.jebelali-international.com

HOCKEY

Dubai Hockey Club

info@dubaihockeyclub.com, www.dubaihockeyclub.com

For old and young of varying abilities. They have matches several evenings a week.

Dubai Mighty Camels Ice Hockey Club

www.dubaimightycamels.com

They play from September to May, with an annual tournament in April.

HORSE RIDING

Horse racing is part of the Arabic tradition, celebrated at Dubai World Cup (www.dubaiworldcup.com, see p 26), the richest horse race in the world held annually in March. There are a number of places you can go horse riding and take classes:

Club Joumana

Jebel Ali Golf Resort and Spa, 04 8836000

Emirates Equestrian Centre

050 5537986, www.emiratesequestriancentre.com

Emirates Riding Centre

Nad Al Sheba, 04 3361394

Jebel Ali Equestrian Club

04 8845101, www.jaec-me.com

ICE SKATING

Al Nasr Leisureland

04 3371234, www.alnasrleisureland.ae

This complex houses an ice rink, a bowling alley, a pool, tennis courts, a gym, arcade games and food court. Dhs25 for two hours.

Dubai Ice Rink

Dubai Mall, 04 4373111, www.dubaiicerink.com

This Olympic-size ice rink is Dubai's latest and boasts world-class facilities for those who want to learn skating or even if you just want to have fun with friends. Dhs50 for two hours.

Galleria Ice Rink

The Galleria Mall at Hyatt Regency, Deira, 04 2096551, www.thegalleria.hyatt.com

A unique feature for those at Galleria Residence, the ice rink offers professional coaching and fun entertainment for all. The rink is a little smaller than an Olympic-size rink. Dhs25 for three hours.

KITE FLYING

Dubai Kite Club

www.dubaikiteclub.com

MARTIAL ARTS

There are a number of courses you can take in martial arts – everything from Karate, Judo and Aikido to Muay Thai, Kudo and Taekwondo.

Dubai Karate Centre

04 3447797, www.dubaikarate.com

Golden Falcon Karate Centre

04 3360243, www.goldenfalconkarate.com

Golden Fist Karate Club

04 3551029

World Black Belt Centre

04 3434397, www.blackbeltscenter.com

MOTOR RACING AND GO-KARTING

Dubai Autodrome

04 3678700, www.dubaiautodrome.com

The Dubai Autodrome and Business Park in Dubailand is the first fully integrated motorsports facility. It includes a 5.39 kilometre circuit offering six different configurations, a race and driving school and an approved karting track.

Dubai also has two smaller outdoor go-kart tracks: Formula One at Nad Al Sheba and the Dubai Kart Club beside the Jebel Ali Hotel.

NETBALL

Dubai Netball League

www.dxbnetball.com

With weekly matches and training schedules, players and coaches are kept on their toes. They organise social events and hold trials for international tournaments. Any players over the age of 14 are welcome. They play at the UAE Tennis Association in Mirdiff. There is also a men's team.

ORCHESTRA

Get together with other singers and musicians to put on various shows, concerts and musicals:

Dubai Singers and Orchestra

04 3491896

Dubai Chamber Orchestra

www.dubaiorchestra.org

UAE Philharmonic Orchestra

www.uaephilharmonic.com

PAINTBALLING

Pursuit Games Paintball

Behind Grand Hyatt, 0506514583, www.paintballdubai.com

Outdoor paintballing.

Dubai Autodrome (Kartdrome)

04 4361422

Described as indoor paintballing without the paint and without the mess, this is a laser-tag game at the Laserdrome Dubai.

RUGBY

Dubai Dragons

James Wellings – 0507096898, www.dragonsrugbydubai.com

Dubai Exiles Club

www.dubaiexiles.com

Dubai Hurricanes

Chris Gregory – 0506266107, www.dubaihurricanes.com

RUNNING

The weather in Dubai is great for running for at least half the year. There is, of course, the Dubai Marathon (www.dubaimarathon.org, see p 24) in January each year. There are also several groups that meet up to run regularly.

Dubai Creek Striders

04 3211999, www.dubaicreekstriders.com

Dubai Road Runners

www.dubai-road-runners.com

SKATING

You'll find the city's best skate ramp in Festival City. It's right behind Toys R Us and is a highly professional course with ramps for beginners and experts.

SKIING

Ski Dubai

04 4094000, www.skidxb.com

Skiing in a desert sounds odd, but in Dubai anything's possible. Get into your ski boots and head to Mall of the Emirates, which has the only indoor ski resort in the region. With five runs and plenty of snow, this can be a fun outing, especially when you want to get away from the heat outside.

SNOOKER

Dubai Snooker Club

04 3375338, www.dubaisnooker.com

Based in Al Karama, this club is open to the public and has many snooker and pool tables. They also organise tournaments.

SPORT LEAGUES

Duplays

www.duplays.com

Looking for ways to socialise and stay fit? Duplays organise both mixed- and single-gender recreational and competitive sport leagues for people in their 20s, 30s and 40s. They organise everything from basketball and beach volleyball to netball, rugby and ultimate frisbee. They also do five-a-side football and racquet sports.

STREET-RUNNING

www.uaeparkour.moonfruit.com

The Parkour and Freerunning scene in Dubai is small, but growing. There's a club that meets in Dubai and Abu Dhabi to throw themselves off walls.

TENNIS

Tennis is one of the most popular sporting options. Courts are available in all the major hotels and many other places throughout Dubai. The Dubai Tennis Stadium at Aviation Club is also home to the Dubai Tennis Championships, attracting many of the leading international tennis stars. A few places offer coaching.

The Aviation Club

04 2824122, www.cftennis.com

Dubai Tennis Academy

04 3444674, www.dubaitennisacademy.com

Emirates Tennis Academy Emirates Golf Club

04 3802222

THAI BOXING

Colosseum

Muay Thai Health and Fitness Club, Zabeel Road, Karama, 04 3372755
www.colosseumuae.com

They also teach Muay Thai, Jeet Kune Do, karate for kids and swimming.

Dubai Fight Academy

Bel Remaitha Club, Rashidiya, 04 2899844, www2.fightacademy.ae

Classes are only for men.

TRIATHLON

Dubai Triathlon Club

julie@dubaitriclub.net, www.dubaitriclub.net

YOGA

Yoga has become increasingly popular in Dubai as it has elsewhere, so many of the fitness centres here teach yoga as part of their weekly schedule. There are also some centres which concentrate on just yoga, listed below. And if you like the sound of doing yoga in fresh air with the sun shining, then there are classes in Safa Park. Or even in the moonlight at Madinat Jumeirah.

Al Karama Ayurvedic and Yoga Centre
Karama Centre, 04 3378921, www.alkaramahealthcare.com

Artistic Yoga
various locations, 04 3981351, www.artisticyoga.com

Club Stretch (Bikram yoga and Pilates)
Near Capitol Hotel, Bur Dubai, 04 3452131, www.clubstretch.ae

Exhale (Pilates, yoga, toning, Hulaerobics, African dance)
Murjan 1, The Walk at JBR, 04 4243777, www.exhaledubai.com

Gems of Yoga
White Crown Building, Trade Centre 1, 04 3315161,
www.gemsofyogadubai.com

Zen Yoga
Various locations, 04 3670435 (Dubai Media City), www.yoga.ae

Yogilates (fusion of yoga and Pilates)
Safa Park Gate 2, 04 3626385, www.coredirection.com

Talise Spa
Madinat Jumeirah, 04 3666818

Evening and moonlight yoga.

SPECTATOR SPORTS

There are sport events throughout the year, attracting some of the best international players in the different fields. You will find more information on these events in the Festivals section (see pp 23–9).

Dubai Tennis Open

04 2824122, www.dubaitennischampionships.com

Usually in February.

Dubai Racing Club (horse race)

04 3270077, www.dubairacingclub.com

Usually in March.

Dubai Desert Classic at the Emirates Hills Golf Club (Golf Tournament)

04 3802112 www.dubaidesertclassic.com

Usually in February.

Dubai Rugby Sevens

04 3210008, www.dubairugby7s.com

Usually last week of November up to early December.

Masters Football Cup

04 3671991, www.mastersfootballdubai.com

Usually in October.

Camel Racing

04 3388170

Watch the unique sport of Camel Racing which is an important part of the culture here. You can watch a camel race at the new race track on Al Ain Road during the winter months (see p 21).

WATERSPORTS

Whether you're a keen diver or want to try it out for the first time, this is the perfect place to dive into the deep turquoise oceans. You'll find some exotic fish, perhaps spotted eagle rays, small sharks, barracuda, sea snakes and stingrays. Choose one of the challenging dives for ship wrecks, marine life or coral reefs.

There are plenty of diving schools in Dubai and across the UAE. Most diving centres offer PADI certification courses. And in case you aren't absolutely sure whether you want to take the full course, most offer a trial experience, from which you can decide whether or not you want to get your diving licence.

www.divingindubai.com – this website will tell you more about diving and give recommendations for dive schools.

Diving schools

7 Seas Divers
09 2387400, www.7seasdivers.com

Al Boom Diving
04 3422993, www.alboomdiving.com

Emirates Diving Association
04 3939390, www.emiratesdiving.com

Other watersports

Water skiing
Zip across the waves of the Arabian sea and feel the thrill as the water sprays all over you.

Parasailing
Take in the awesome views of the ocean from above as you parasail.

Wakeboarding

Step on a wakeboard and be pulled through the waves by a speed boat.

Kite surfing

The wind will pull your kite from one direction to another as you freely kite surf through the high winds in Dubai.

Windsurfing

Feel the rush in the water and let the wind carry you in this thrilling sport.

Speed boating

Race against the wind in some of the fastest boats you'll ever find.

Sailing

You can choose one of the sailing boats, dinghies or traditional *dhows* and indulge in one of the most popular pastimes in Dubai.

www.surfersofdubai.com will give you all the information for surfing in Dubai as well as the other Emirates and Oman, and where you can buy boards.

Watersport locations

Club Mina, Le Meridien Mina Seyahi

04 3181420

Club Mina offers a range of watersports for hotel guests, members and non-members. This includes windsurfing, kayaking, waterskiing, wakeboarding, knee boarding, boat cruise, banana and donut boat rides.

Club Joumana, Jebel Ali Golf Resort and Spa

04 8048023

Club Joumana offers windsurfing, waterskiing, sailing, fishing and kayaking as well as banana and donut boat rides.

Umm Al Quwain Marine Club
06 7666644, www.uaqmarineclub.com

They offer fantastic wakeboarding, skiing and kayaking and can organise fishing trips and trips to the mangrove island.

Bluesail Dubai
04 8880234, www.bluesailyachts.com

Bluesail offers sail training for all levels. All instructors are RYA Yachtmaster Ocean qualified.

Fun Sports
050 4657311

Fun Sports offer sail training, speedboating and other sports.

Waterparks (see p 221–2)
Wild Wadi Waterpark
04 4384444, www.jumeirah.com

Wonderland Splashland
04 3241222, www.wonderlanduae.com

HEALTH AND BEACH CLUBS

Health clubs				
	Telephone	**Location**	**Yearly/Dhs**	**Daily/Dhs**
Active Plus Health	04 3360001	Opp American Hospital	4,500	-
Al Nasr Fitness	04 3371234	Al Nasr Leisureland	1,400	-
Assawan Health Club	04 3017777	Burj Al Arab	35,000	500
Aviation Club	04 2424122	Garhoud	8,750	250
Bodylines Leisure and Fitness	04 3122556	Towers Rotana, SZ Rd	3,500	150
Colosseum	04 3372755	Montana Bldg, Zabeel Rd	2,400	50
Dubai Ladies Club	04 3499922	Jumeirah Beach Rd	12,000	175
Elixir Spa	04 3995000	Al Habtoor Grand Resort	21,000	225 *
Fitness First	04 3510044	Various locations	5,500	-
Fitness Planet	04 2699773	Mamzar	3,390	40
Nautilus Fitness Centre	04 3314055	Crowne Plaza, SZ Rd	4,800	70
Pharaohs' Club	04 3240000	Wafi	6,600	-
Quay Healthclub	04 3668888	Madinat Jumeirah	16,000	-
Shape Express	04 3516141	Beach Rd, Bur Dubai	3,900	75
Shapes Wellness	04 3672137	Knowledge Village	2,500	35
The Big Apple	04 3198661	Emirates Towers, SZ Rd	4,470	55
U Concept	04 3449060	Village Mall, Jumeirah	7,200	350

Beach clubs				
	Telephone	**Location**	**Yearly/Dhs**	**Daily/Dhs**
Club Joumana	04 8836000	Jebel Ali Golf Resort and Spa	8,500	300
Club Mina	04 3993333	Le Meridien Mina Seyahi	25,000	250
Dubai Marine Beach Resort	04 3461111	Jumeirah 1, opp Jumeirah Mosque	14,000	300
Jumeirah Health and Fitness Club	04 3995533	Jumeirah Sheraton	14,500	180 *
Palace of the Royal Mirage	04 3999999	One and Only Royal Mirage		300 *
The Pavilion Marina and Sports Club	04 4068800	Jumeirah Beach Hotel	49,500	500 *
The Ritz-Carlton Health Club and Spa	04 3186184	Ritz-Carlton Dubai	40,000	1,000 *

*pool and beach access only

Chapter 16

Art, drama and theatre

Dubai's art scene is very much alive and expanding, with a variety of galleries and exhibitions displaying traditional and contemporary art, both local and international. There's something to do and see for all of Dubai's art aficionados.

I have only concentrated on a select few galleries in this section, but browse through *Time Out Dubai* magazine for details on weekly exhibitions and other galleries. And if you aren't much of a gallery-goer but love art, then visit www.emorat.deviantart.com, where you'll find over 500 pieces of art waiting to be bought. If you're a budding artist, there are places to work from including the fantastic Tashkeel.

ART CLASSES AND CREATIVE SPACES

Dubai International Art Centre (DIAC)

Street 75b, between Town Centre and Mercato Mall, Villa 27, 04 3444398, www.artdubai.com

This is Dubai's oldest and largest art organisation. With over 90 courses such as writing, fashion design, painting, Arabic calligraphy, sewing, pottery and photography, there's something here for everyone. It functions as an important resource as a gallery, library and learning centre.

Dubai Community Theatre and Arts Centre (DUCTAC)
Level 2, Mall of the Emirates, 04 3414777, www.ductac.org

DUCTAC offers various classes from drawing, painting, sculpting and photography to theatre and drama and Indian, salsa, tap and other forms of dance. There is also an art gallery and theatre for performances.

Jam Jar
Near Gold and Diamond Park, Al Quoz, 04 3417303, www.thejamjardubai.com
Sat–Thurs 10am–10pm

Exhibits include contemporary art from emerging local talent and international artists. This is an urban DIY painting studio and art gallery, offering a unique art experience with unlimited acrylic paint on canvas.

Riot Art
04 4224166, www.riot-art.com

Here, you can print all your paintings and photographs onto various types of canvas.

Shelter
04 4345655, www.shelter.ae

Shelter is not necessarily for artists, but for anyone in the creative fields. It is a community workspace that allows individuals from various creative disciplines to engage in an environment that nurtures entrepreneurial small businesses.

Tashkeel
Nad Al Sheba, 04 3363313, www.tashkeel.org
Sat–Thurs 8am–10pm

An independent resource for artists and designers in the UAE, facilitating art practice, cross-cultural dialogue and creative exchange. Once you have paid membership (weekly or yearly), you have access to studios equipped with creative software, large format digital printing, jewellery workstations, painting studios, photographic dark rooms and a printmaking studio. There is also a journals and reference library, members' room and exhibition gallery. Tashkeel also organises workshops.

DRAMA

Dubai Drama Group

DUCTAC, Mall of the Emirates
Abhishek Reddy – 050 5094211, www.dubaidramagroup.com

This is a non-profit, amateur theatrical group initially formed to bring people together with a common interest in theatre. Its purpose is to encourage the performance of dramatic and musical works related to theatre.

Drama Dubai

DUCTAC, Mall of Emirates Tiffany – 050 9861761
www.dramaworkshopsdubai.com

Drama Dubai offers versatile drama-based courses for individuals of all ages and abilities. Each individual is encouraged to push the boundaries of their creativity and imagination to explore where their talents can lead them.

Helen O'Grady Drama Academy

Trade Centre, Al Hayya Club and various locations, 04 2351952
www.helenogrady.net

This drama academy offers drama for children from the age of 5 to 17. Each class is filled with a wide variety of high energy exercises and theatre games designed by a team of professionals at the UK headquarters.

GALLERIES

Art Attack Gallery

Dubai Zoo, Jumeirah Beach Road, 04 3444398, www.artattackgallery.net
Sat–Thurs 10am–7pm

Showcases important work from the Gulf, Europe, Africa, India, America and Canada. You will find a large selection of art on canvas as well as water colours. Art Attack also strives to introduce vibrant new local artists.

Artsawa

Exit 43 opp Al Shirawi Equipment, Al Quoz, 04 3408660, www.artsawa.com
Sat–Thurs 9:30am–7pm

Showcasing contemporary art from the Middle East, North Africa and neighbouring countries.

Artspace

Bldg 3, Dubai International Financial Centre, 04 3230820
www.artspace-dubai.com
Sat–Thurs 10am–8pm

Dedicated to the promotion of Contemporary Middle Eastern Art and Artists from paintings to sculpture.

Courtyard Gallery and Café

Al Rasaas Rd, off Sheikh Zayed Road, 04 3479090
www.courtyardgallerydubai.com
Sat–Thurs 10am–6pm

This gallery has modern art exhibits and provides a rich and inspiring mix of contemporary and traditional art design. Have a meal or coffee in this inspiring atmosphere.

Cuadro Museum and Fine Art Gallery

Gate Village Bldg 10, Dubai International Financial Centre, 04 4250400
www.cuadroart.com
Daily 10am–8pm, Sat 12–6pm

A large space in DIFC, Cuadro showcases international, contemporary art of both established and emerging artists.

Interview with Mira and Tala Achkar

Sisters who have grown up in Dubai, moved to Canada to study and are now back here.

How has Dubai changed for you?

When I was younger and living in Dubai, it was a smaller society – I would know everyone that I bumped into. In the past seven years, with the expansion, there has been an increase in everything and there's so many new people. It's expanding at a monstrous rate.

What about culture?

I think artistically and culturally, it's becoming more developed. The independent artists' side of it is really expanding. There are amazingly talented people here, so it's great that the UAE is supporting this. Although it's a shallow, materialistic place, it does have this depth – it's not just an empty shellcase. Dubai sure does have a future and if I lived elsewhere, then I would definitely move to Dubai out of choice.

Four Seasons Ramesh Gallery

Al Zomorrodah Building, Za'abeel Road, 04 3349090
www.fourseasonsgallery.com
Daily 9am–9pm

One of the largest galleries in Dubai, featuring and selling work by local and international artists. The gallery also has a collection of decorative furniture and accessories.

Green Art Gallery

Behind Dubai Zoo, Jumeirah, 04 3449888, www.gagallery.com
Sat–Thurs 10am–9pm

Plays a vital role in introducing modern Arab art from across the Middle East and North Africa to the city and beyond and in nurturing the establishment of the city's earliest collector base.

Majlis Gallery

Al Fahidi Roundabout, Bur Dubai, 04 3536233, www.themajlisgallery.com
Sat–Thurs 9:30am–8pm

Based in a traditional windtower house, this gallery promotes the work of artists of international standing and is a meeting place for creative minds. You will find fine art, handmade glass, crafts, frames and pottery.

Port of Call Gallery

Al Attar Business Tower, Sheikh Zayed Road, 04 3326006
www.portofcallgallery.com
Sat–Thurs 10am–1:30pm, 4:30–7:30pm

This gallery focuses on oriental arts from Far Eastern countries including China, Japan and Myanmar. There are valuable pieces of furniture, ceramics, textiles and more.

The Third Line

Between Marlin Furniture and Spinneys, Al Quoz 3, 04 3411367,
www.thethirdline.com
Sat–Thurs 11am–8pm

Located in a former warehouse in Al Quoz, The Third Line brings to the forefront talented young Gulf artists. It has high-level exhibitions as well as films by Arab directors, book presentations and talks with artists.

Interview with Katrina

Katrina is Artist Liaison and Institution Manager, Third Line Gallery.

What made you move to Dubai?

I moved to Dubai to live near my fiancé's family and explore the region. We were both looking for a change from where we living at the time (New York and Philadelphia) and have definitely found that in the UAE. We've made some very dear friends and, although I have not learned as much Arabic as I had hoped, I have certainly had an interesting time and learned a great deal while living here.

Were you working elsewhere previously?

The Third Line was actually my first job in Dubai. Working in the arts completely transformed my experience of living here, as Dubai has a very vibrant arts community that attracts the most interesting people – from the UAE, across the Gulf and wider region, as well as internationally.

What are your thoughts on culture in Dubai?

Although the culture history of the UAE and the Gulf in general is often underestimated there is a very rich cultural history here ... and it is fascinating to see how the UAE is transforming itself into a regional hub for contemporary arts. As the international contemporary art world begins to focus on the Middle East, the UAE and Dubai in particular is playing a large role in shaping the development of the scene.

The arts and culture sector in Dubai is undergoing a tremendous growth and I believe having a real impact regionally. That is why The Third Line set up and why I am so excited to work here, because we focus on supporting Middle Eastern emerging artists, providing a thoughtful and professional platform for their work, and educating regional and local collectors about art from the region. Dubai's cultural scene has a very key role to play in supporting art from the Middle East beyond the borders of the UAE.

What is Dubai like for artists?

Dubai offers a very vibrant mix of cultures, high energy, and a growing number of arts-related organisations. There are groups like Pecha Kucha, Tashkeel, Shelter and DUCTAC that are providing more resources for artists and other creative types. Along with a burgeoning gallery scene, the governmental arm focused on the arts, Dubai Culture, is enacting policies that help art institutions and individual artists operate here and there is a lot of support nationally from the Emirates Foundation and the Sharjah Art Foundation. The Sharjah Biennale and art fairs like Art Dubai, the Bastakiya Art Fair, Abu Dhabi Fringe Festival, as well as the countless film festivals are bringing another level of attention to the arts here, regionally and internationally. Dubai is the sort of place where, if you have a dream and passion, you can create it – you can play part in shaping the growth of the arts scene here, which is just an amazing opportunity.

XVA Gallery
Behind Majlis Gallery, Bastakiya, Bur Dubai, 04 3535383, www.xvagallery.com
Sat–Thurs 9am–9pm

Housed in an old traditional building, XVA has local and regional art and sometimes European and American exhibitors. They display installation art, portraits, paintings and photography.

Sharjah
This is another place you'll be able to find some fantastic art, a definite must-visit for the art enthusiasts. Known as 'The Cultural Capital of Arabia', an honour awarded by UNESCO in 1998, Sharjah has a rich tapestry of monuments and relics organised in almost 25 museums. This is quite an attraction for those with an interest in cultural tourism. Among the museums is Sharjah Art Museum (06 5688222), which has a good permanent collection of art that originally belonged to the Ruler of Sharjah, and the Very Special Arts Centre, a workshop and gallery for disabled artists.

Interview with Jill Hoyle

Manager of Tashkeel, a creative hub for artists and designers in Dubai. Lived in the United Arab Emirates for almost 12 years.

What made you move to Dubai?

Like many people, I moved to Dubai when my husband accepted a post in Dubai. However, this has proved to be a very positive move for us both and I have been fortunate to have been able to advance my own career in new and unexpected ways whilst we have been living here.

Were you working elsewhere in Dubai previously?

Yes, I taught at The American University in Dubai, at Latifa College and Zayed University.

What are your thoughts on culture in Dubai?

When we first arrived in Dubai there was very little in the way of the arts happening in Dubai at all, but over the last five or so years there has been a huge growth in activities in these areas. I think that it will be extremely interesting to see how things develop over the next few years as artists, musicians and other creative people working in the region gain confidence and find their own creative voice.

Do you think Dubai is a great place for budding artists and other creative people?

Absolutely. There is a great interest in these areas and, gradually, these are being accepted as worthy activities and occupations. There is an exciting generation of young Emarati artists just beginning to exhibit their work, who are acting as positive role models for others. The universities are now beginning to develop specialist programmes in visual arts, in addition to the design courses that have been taught for some time, which is helping to bring credibility to the arts too. But it's important that the arts are allowed to develop here at their own pace and that the structure and character of the arts scene emerges from within the society, rather than being imposed from outside.

How has the arts scene changed and grown over the past years?

There are so many more galleries and events happening now. At one time there were perhaps three openings a month – now there are sometimes three a night and it is impossible to keep up with everything. Art Dubai has also played a major role in educating the public about the art scene and in introducing international galleries to Dubai.

THEATRE

Dubai Community Theatre and Arts Centre

04 3414777, www.ductac.org

Conveniently located inside the Mall of the Emirates, performances here are centred on dancing and storytelling. It also has a whole host of classes (see pp 182–3).

Madinat Theatre

04 3666546, www.madinattheatre.com

This modern 442-seat theatre inside the famous Madinat Souk is the first of its kind in the Middle East. It has a busy event calendar throughout the year.

FESTIVALS

KITAB – Abu Dhabi International Book Fair

02 6212975, www.adbookfair.com

An annual, very large and well-developed event with author talks and many booksellers from all over the world.

Emirates Airline International Festival of Literature (EAIFL)

04 3420060, www.eaifl.com

The first festival of literature of its kind was held in Dubai in February 2009 and aims to become an annual event. This festival saw some of the best authors come together to speak on their books and lives and on a variety of different topics and issues.

Sharjah Book Fair

06 5673139, www.swbf.gov.ae

This is a little less developed than Abu Dhabi Book Fair, but a great way for Arabic readers to get books.

Art Dubai

www.artdubai.ae

This is the first contemporary art fair in Dubai, which began in 2007 and takes place at the Madinat Jumeirah during March each year. In 2009, it hosted nearly 70 international galleries.

Dubai International Film Festival

www.dubaifilmfest.com

A non-profit cultural event featuring short films and documentaries from around the world, highlighting Dubai's multicultural nature. This festival takes place in December each year and focuses on cinema from the Arab countries and India.

BOOK CLUBS

Dubai Page Turners

www.meetup.com/dubaipageturners

A female book club, for those aged between 20 and 40, which meets monthly.

Kutub

The Third Line Gallery, Al Quoz, 04 3411367, www.thethirdline.com, www.readkutub.wordpress.com, kutub@thethirdline.com

Reads a broad range of diverse, Middle Eastern writers and holds cross-cultural discussions about books that are available in both English and Arabic. Kutub meets monthly mostly at Third Line Gallery.

Sharjah Book Group

Sharjah Ladies Club, Sharjah
Fiona Jack – fgbwj@hotmail.com

This book club meets on the last Sunday of the month at the restaurant in Sharjah Ladies Club. They pick a wide variety of books from women's topics to classics and try to include authors from various countries.

LANGUAGES

Alliance Française

Oud Metha, Bur Dubai, 04 3358712, www.afdubai.com

French and Arabic

Arabic Language Centre

Dubai International Convention and Exhibition Centre, 04 3086036 www.dwtc.com/ArabicLanguageCentre

Arabic

Berlitz Language Centre

Jumeirah Beach Rd, 04 3440034, www.berlitz.ae

Arabic, English, French, Spanish, Italian, Mandarin, Japanese, Russian, German

Dar El Lim School of Languages

Sheikh Zayed Rd, Emirates Hills, 04 3310221

Arabic, German, French, Spanish, Italian, Portuguese, Farsi, English

Dubai International Art Centre

Off Jumeirah Rd near Town Centre, 04 3444398, www.artdubai.com

Arabic and Spanish

Eton International Languages

Blk 3, F01 Dubai Knowledge Village, 8003866, www.eton.ac

Spanish, German, Italian, Chinese, Japanese, English, Turkish, Urdu, Hindi

Goethe Institut
04 3590529, www.goethe.de/gulfregion

German

Sheikh Mohammed Centre for Cultural Understanding
Bastakiya, near Dubai Creek, 04 3536666, www.cultures.ae

Arabic

Chapter 17

Beauty and spa

Dubai urbanites work hard, but who can complain when there is so much sunshine and a whole array of heavenly spas? Such a plush and opulent destination calls for luxury and indulgence. And sometimes, all you'll want to do is escape to a place of calmness for that much needed mini-break.

This is another of the favourite pastimes of people here: relaxation, switching off and turning on that relaxing holiday mode for a day. Spas here are experiences, not mere treatments. Dubai has become quite a spa-centric destination and with the plethora of nationalities that have settled here, the spas are also just as varied, being influenced by disciplines from around the world.

It's also a great gift to buy someone ... and with the number of spas and amazing variety of treatments in Dubai, you could become a spa-holic. But prices do vary a great deal, so just check and compare.

SPAS

1847, Grosvenor House or Emirates Towers

04 3301847
Dhs290 – 60 mins: well-being relaxing massage

Relaxation and spa indulgence isn't only for women. 1847 is a fantastic head-to-toe grooming lounge for men, where they can get a manicure or pedicure, a shave, a full body massage and their shoes shined. It's stylish and soothing and exclusive.

Akaru, Aviation Club

04 2828578
Dhs315 – 60 mins: equilibrium massage

This large private spa has 14 treatment rooms, a sauna and *hammam*, and offers facials, massages and body wraps using Payot and Thalgo products. Try microdermabrasion for the skin, or the Pure Oxygen Capsule where your body is immersed in oxygen. The Aviation Club also has a hair salon and a nail spa.

Alasalla Spa, Dubai Ladies Club

04 3449445
Dhs280 – 60 mins: relaxing massage

This holistic spa will allow you to unwind after a workout in their fitness centre. The spa has traditional Arabic treatments including the *rasul* and royal *hammam*.

Amara Spa, Park Hyatt

04 6021234
Dhs420 – 60 mins: Swedish or aromatherapy

This secluded spa is a true haven of beauty and tranquillity. It's also one of the only spas where you can indulge in a couple's treatment. There are optional packages such as the Diamond, Emerald, Ruby and Sapphire 'Ceremonies'. Arabian teas and dried fruit and nuts taken while you sit in your own private outdoor area, add that pampering touch.

Angsana Spa

04 3684356
Dhs350 – 60 mins: aroma, Thai, Hawaiian massage

With branches in Arabian Ranches, Montgomerie and Emirates Hills, Dubai Marina, and in the Angsana Hotel on Sheikh Zayed Road. Angsana is an oasis of calm with rich dark wood, incense and dim lighting. It combines Asian and European techniques and offers fusion baths such as 'Coco Coffee' and 'Orange Milk' along with the usual massages, body polishes and facials.

Aroma Spa, Dubai Marine Beach Resort

04 3468081

Dhs385 – 60 mins: combination of relaxing and aroma body massage

This is a very private and low-key spa – not quite as lavish as some of the other spas in Dubai. Nonetheless, it has a fantastic range of Guinot and Payot treatments including a detoxifying algae wrap and the Ionithermie slimming treatment.

Assawan Spa and Health Club, Burj Al Arab

04 3017338

Dhs675 – 60 mins: full body, well-being massage

A lavishly and tastefully decorated spa on the 18th floor of this iconic hotel provides spectacular views. Revive yourself in some of the finest massages including Thai, Indian, Swedish, Shiatsu and Balinese. There are separate ladies and gents sauna, steam room, jacuzzi and a choice of mixed or ladies-only infinity swimming pool.

Cleopatra Spa, Wafi City

04 3247700

Dhs350 – 60 mins: full body massage

Located in the Pyramids, Wafi City, this spa has an Egyptian theme and has luxurious and opulent surroundings. The spa menu is extensive with treatments including Ayurvedic massages, a stone massage with hot 'batu' stones from Indonesia and separate male and female spas.

Lime Spa, Desert Palm just after Dragon Mart

04 3238888

Dhs420 – 60 mins: full body, Thai massage

There are organic facials, massages, scrubs and cocoons. Try the 'Intuitive Organic

Facial' which uses botanical sea plant extracts or the 'Lime Intuitive' massage which combines Swedish, Aromatherapy and Balinese methods. And look onto the lush polo fields while you have your treatment done.

Mandara Spa, The Monarch Hotel
04 5018270
Dhs470 – 65 mins: deep tissue massage

A blissful calm oasis away from the hectic life of Sheikh Zayed Road, this hotel is just minutes from DIFC and Dubai World Trade Centre. Try the Mandara massage with two therapists, combining five different kinds of massages including Japanese Shiatsu. Relax in the jacuzzi afterwards.

Natural Healing Holistic Wellness Spa, Jumeirah Beach Road
04 3483896
Dhs230 – 60 mins: Oriental massage

Located opposite Burj Al Arab, this spa is a nice change to the usual opulence of hotel spas. The spa has a calm yet cosy atmosphere using warm earth tones and is based on the ancient science of *feng shui*. Treatments range from acupuncture and reflexology to Oriental body healing with footwork and stress buster massage.

Oriental Hammam, One&Only Royal Mirage
04 3999999
Dhs330 – 50 mins: deep tissue massage

Go for the Oriental Hammam, where the treatment begins with thorough exfoliation and cleansing of each area of the body, after which you lie on a heated marble slab while the therapist massages you. The Oriental Hammam operates separate hours for men and women.

Ritz-Carlton Spa
04 3186184
Dhs450 – 50 mins: Swedish, Balinese, aromatherapy massage

There is a variety of Oriental and Far Eastern therapeutic techniques. As well as the Balinese massages, facials and Scentao hot stone therapy, you can also go for hydrotherapy treatment. Then have your hair done and nails painted at the hair and beauty salon. They also offer a unique 24-carat gold massage ...

SensAsia

04 3498850
Dhs310 – 60 mins: Balinese, Islander massage

This is an award-winning boutique, women-only day spa where each treatment room is named and decorated after a destination in Bali, Thailand or Japan. With dim lighting, water features and Buddhist statues, you get a real sense of escape. And what could be more natural than products like honey, coconut and green tea, which are used in the treatments?

Sisters Beauty Lounge, Dubai Mall

04 3398500
Dhs300 – 60 mins: full body massage

After a day of shopping in the world's biggest mall (just in case you didn't know), pop into this spa for a 'Sweet Rose Facial', which uses fresh roses, cranberries and pomegranates, or indulge in an intensive hair treatment, wash and blow dry in time for dinner.

Softouch Spa, Kempinski

04 4095909
Dhs350 – 55 mins: Swedish massage

Touching Mall of the Emirates, this is the perfect place to escape and experience the ancient healing powers of Ayurveda. The therapists will use exotic ingredients, tailor-made for your unique body type. And if you fancy a more normal massage, there's a range of those from deep tissue and Balinese to Oriental and hot stone therapy.

Spa Dunya, The Walk at JBR

04 4393669
Dhs390 – 60 mins; Thai, lymphatic massage

This spa uses the effects of colour on the body and has an organic cosmetic product range using the principles of chromotherapy and aromatherapy. You can choose from a harmonising colour massage, lymphatic drainage, colour reflexology, infrared sauna and colour energy baths. The spa also has a salon where you can get colouring, highlights, waxing and more.

Spa Intercontinental, Festival City

04 7011111

Dhs380 – 60 mins: Swedish, deep tissue, Balinese massage

Enjoy a ginger and lemon tea and then go for the Jasmine Rosewood Body Pack or one of the facial therapies using Natura Bisse products. Then lounge by the large outdoor swimming pool overlooking the Creek.

Talise Wellness Spa, Al Qasr, Madinat Jumeirah

04 3666818

Dhs465 – 50 mins: Thai, Balinese, hot stone massage

This is one of the most beautiful spas in Dubai and getting there by a small *abra* will give you pre-treatment relaxation. By combining the best and oldest of global healing traditions with the latest international techniques, the expert therapists are able to nurture the body through five key methods to wellness. Talise use Sodashi products, a natural skin care range.

Tilia and Finn, Boutique 1, The Walk at JBR

04 4380636

Dhs260 – 60 mins: aromatherapy massage

Recently opened, this is Boutique 1's in-store spa which has a selection of natural therapies using plant-based, organic products. You can get massages, facials and hair styling – so after an afternoon of shopping in Boutique 1, be pampered away.

The Spa, The Palace Hotel

04 4287805

Dhs475 – 50 mins: signature deep tissue massage

With great bath houses, *hammams*, monsoon showers and steam and hydro baths, this is true Arabian luxury. Try a Carita facial or one of the Hammam rituals.

The Spa at Shangri-La

04 4052441
Dhs400 – 60 mins: full body massage

This is quite a minimalist spa, with a menu of mostly Asian treatments from Thai and Balinese massages to Javanese Lulur, an Indonesian cleansing treatment and a caviar facial. The club also has a huge rooftop swimming pool, separate spas for men and women, with a plunge pool, sauna and steam.

Westin Heavenly Spa, Westin Mina Seyahi

04 3994141
Dhs420 – 55 mins: full body massage

Indulge in the 'Arabian Massage Ritual' or if you fancy a massage, then go for 'The Butterfly Effect', using techniques from Thai, deep tissue and sports massage or the 'Heaven on Earth', a four handed massage. The atmosphere is warm and cosy, with soothing hues of woods and whites.

Willow Stream Spa, the Fairmont Hotel

04 3325555
Dhs320 – 60 mins: relaxation massage

The white pillars and mosaics give this spa a Romanesque feel – a refreshing change to the more common Asian dim interiors. The separate male and female sections feature a jacuzzi, steam rooms, ice shower, and relaxing footbaths. After your treatment, sit by the outdoor swimming pool and order a smoothie.

Spa at home

Fancy a massage in the comforts of your home? **Chez Toi** (04 3397117, www.cheztoibeauty.com) does this and more. Massages, pedicures, waxing, facials ... the works. 1 hour Swedish massage is Dhs180.

BEAUTY, HAIR AND NAILS

Beauty salons are just as popular as spas in Dubai, if not more so. There is such a variety of beauty and hair salons and so many of them that it might be a task to choose which one you want to go to. Word of mouth is usually the way to go, or just find a salon that's most convenient and closest to you. Most hotels and some malls have salons, and you'll find that a lot of them also do henna designs as this is very common for Arabic ladies. There are a number of nail bars in malls where you can get pedicures and manicures, along with half-hour back massages.

Beauty salons		
Beautiful Times Salon	Khalid Bin Walid Road (Bank Street), Bur Dubai	04 3529966
Cleopatra Beauty Salon	Opp Lal's Al Maya Supermarket, Satwa	04 3444423
Cut Above	Jumeirah Beach Road, next to Magrudy's	04 344 6444
Essential	Al Wasl Rd, Umm Suqueim	04 3955909
Patsi Collins	RAK Bank Building, Garhoud	04 2869923
Pebbles	Al Attar Tower, Sheikh Zayed Road	04 3437220
Sasha Beauty Salon	Wafi City	04 3242070
Sisters Beauty Lounge	Village Mall, Jumeirah Beach Road and Dubai Mall	04 3420787
Tilia and Finn	Boutique 1, The Walk at JBR	04 4257888

Dermatologists		
Cosmesurge	Jumeirah Beach Road, near Emirates Hospital	04 3445915
Dermalogica Institute	Dubai Mall	04 3398250
Eternal Medspa	Jumeirah Beach Road, Villa 5	04 3440008
Kaya Skin Clinic	Various locations including Town Centre Mall, Sultan Business Centre, Dubai Marina, Uptown Mirdiff	04 3498982

Hair salons		
Cut Above	The Jumeirah Centre, Jumeirah Beach Road	04 3446444
Dessange	Kempinski, Mall of the Emirates	04 3417733
Frank Provost	Dubai Marina, Mall of the Emirates, World Trade Centre	04 3629865
Roots	Jumeirah Beach Road and Sheikh Zayed Road	04 3444040
The Hair Shop	Trade Centre Apartments	04 3326616
Toni and Guy	Emirates Towers and Grand Hyatt	04 3303345
Trendz	Raffles Amrita Spa	04 3149870

Nail bars		
N. Bar	Various locations including Ibn Battuta, Palm Strip, Emirates Towers Boulevard	04 3669828
The Nail Spa	Aviation Club, Mercato Mall and Ibn Battuta	04 2821617
NStyle Nail Lounge	DIFC, Madinat Souk and Mall of the Emirates	04 4250347

Chapter 17

Shopping

Shopping and Dubai – the two words are synonymous. Dubai is often described as a shopper's paradise. Okay, so there are also the beaches and the food ... but shopping is so much of a pastime that there are new glittering world-class malls sprouting up all over the place, not to mention Dubai Mall, the world's largest mall.

And when most shops are open till 10pm or even later, you're really not stuck for what to do in the evenings, if shopping turns out to be your thing. You also have plenty of refreshment, entertainment and dining options at most of the malls from multiplex cinemas and arcades to food courts and fantastic restaurants. And don't forget the traditional *souks*, a flavour of old Arabia ...

As the year begins, the city jumps into the famous Dubai Shopping Festival, a month-long fiesta of parties and money-splashing fun. It's become a huge tourist attraction, bringing in an awesome Dhs3 billion in 2007.

The celebrations during this festival make it what it is. There are fireworks, laser shows and various events including the recent and new Dubai Food Festival. And malls also have performers and processions. So it really is a feast for all your senses. In 2009 House of Talents provided a platform for local women to exhibit their skills. To find out more about DSF, visit www.mydsf.com. It certainly is a fun and festive time in Dubai.

But shopping isn't just about the malls. You can also head to one of the fantastic *souks,* quite a striking contrast to the modern malls. They give you a glimpse into the past, into what Dubai was all about before we had even heard of it. The amount of gold sprawled across the windows is mesmerising, the aroma of spices as you walk through Spice Souk is enticing and the masses of fabrics and materials you'll find at Meena Bazaar can be tiring. What makes the *souks* even more interesting is the opportunity to haggle and bargain.

A note of caution

These *souks* are outdoor and involve a fair amount of walking. So if it's summer time, don't head out in the peak afternoon heat.

And since I think *souks* are cooler than malls, I'm starting this section with the *souks.*

THE OLD TRADITIONAL *SOUKS*

These timeless *souks* really are the heart of Arabia. A long time ago, when Dubai was a coastal village, merchants and traders would come from India and Iran and sell their merchandise in the tiny shops by the creek – Deira and Bur Dubai. These shops turned into *souks* selling spices, dates, tobacco, charcoal, textiles and other goods. Now, years later, you will discover the rustic charm of these old shops as you stroll through the *souks* and take in a slice of history. The *souks* are usually open from 10am to 1pm and from 4pm to 10pm.

Gold *Souk*

Located in Deira, this is Dubai's most famous *souk,* and the reason why Dubai is known as the city of gold. It is quite a dazzling sight. There are lanes filled with small shops selling gold, silver, stones, pearls and everything that falls under the name of jewellery. And if nothing suits your tastes, get something altered by one of the craftsmen. The Gold *Souk* is always busy but don't visit between 1pm and 4pm as many shops will be closed.

Tips

- You'll need to use cash and bargaining can be fun.
- While you're shopping around, stop for a *shawarma* and fresh juice at one of the small food outlets.

Spice *Souk*

The scents of cinnamon, cloves and other luscious, strong spices will lure as you walk through Deira's Gold *Souk*. Located right next to the Gold *Souk*, there are piles of vibrant colours of spices and a mixture of strong aromas. Shopkeepers will happily advise you on spices and their uses. You can also buy various dried fruits and nuts here, as well as different kinds of incense burners. When buying saffron, at a fraction of Western prices, be careful to make sure it's authentic.

Textile *Souk*

This is in Bur Dubai, on the opposite side of the creek. Textiles are imported from all over the world and you'll just about find every colour and fabric here. Make sure you bargain.

Dubai Perfume *Souk*

This is near Gold *Souk* and if you can't find it, the plethora of aromas and fragrances floating around will allure you. You'll be able to get traditional, Arabic spicy *ittars*, designer perfumes and a variety of incense powders, crystals and woods. The shopkeepers can also concoct a unique perfume that fits your personality.

Meena Bazaar

This 30-year-old bazaar is on the Bur Dubai side, near Bastakiya and Dubai Museum. Parking is a nightmare, so get there by taxi. Here, you'll find a maze of shops selling handlooms, silks, cottons, brocades, gold and other jewellery. It has, over the years, become a 'Little India' and some shopkeepers even quote prices in rupees.

Souk Al Bastakiya

This *souk* is held on Saturdays from 10am till sunset in Bastakiya, where you'll see the old wind towers of Dubai. There are vendors selling clothes, crafts and representing local culture through henna stands, Arabic coffee and authentic ethnic cuisine. It's quite a festive day with live music. The Al Bastakiya Art Fair is also held here during March.

NEWLY-RECREATED *SOUKS*

There are also some new creations of *souks*, which give a more plush and lavish, not to mention air-conditioned experience of walking through an Arabic market place.

Madinat Jumeirah

Close to the Burj Al Arab, Madinat Jumeirah is always buzzing and gives you a real feel of Arabia. Meander through the lanes of unique shops and galleries, interspersed with cafés and fantastic waterfront bars and restaurants. And in between all this is a beautiful little river in which hotel guests (Al Qasr hotel is touching Madinat) can travel to and fro by boat. One of the best theatres in town is also based here, as is the Trilogy nightclub.

Souk Khan Murjan

On the lower level or underground of the Wafi Mall, this is a less busy *souk* boasting an Islamic theme, inspired by a 14th century Baghdad *souk*. You could easily miss it if you don't know it's there. There are two entrances from inside Wafi and, once you enter, you'll find craftsmen from across the region and more than 150 stalls offering arts and crafts.

Souk Al Bahar

Right next to the Dubai Mall in Downtown Dubai, *Souk* Al Bahar has Arabesque architecture and views of Burj Khalifa. The boutiques here sell handicrafts, accessories and art. You'll also find some great restaurants and quaint cafés.

Dubai Mall Gold *Souk*

This is on the bottom floor of the Dubai Mall and though it doesn't quite provide the same authentic and real experience as Deira Gold *Souk*, it's still interesting to just browse around the stalls and shops. The upside is that you can get absolutely all your shopping done under one roof, even if your legs might hurt by the end of the day.

OTHER MARKETS

Arte *Souk*

Times Square Mall, info@arte.ae, www.arte.ae

This is a fantastic arts and crafts market that takes place on the second Friday of every month. You'll find all sorts of jewellery, paintings, cards, clothes and more from all around the world, but made locally.

Covent Garden Market Dubai

www.marinamarket.ae, 050 2445795, www.coventgardenmarket.ae
Thurs 5pm–midnight, Fri and Sat 10am–8pm

The market, which used to be held at Marina Walk, has now moved to the Walk at Jumeirah Beach Residence and been rebranded Covent Garden Market Dubai. With over 75 stalls selling homeware, clothes, flip flops, trinkets, arts and crafts and so many other things, this provides the perfect day out. And don't think shopping's all there is – musicians, singers, jugglers, mime artists, caricaturists and portrait painters ... well that really is Covent Garden with the added beach factor.

Dubai Flea Market

www.dubai-fleamarket.com
Melanie Beese – 050 2969680, melanie.beese@dubai-fleamarket.com,

Interested in buying second hand goods and hand crafts, or do you fancy selling them? Check the website for the next flea market and head to Al Safa Park. It's scenic and interactive.

Karama Market

Karama Market is an outdoor market selling everything from clothes, shoes and belts to souvenirs and other knick-knacks. You can really bargain and get some pretty cheap stuff.

AREAS TO SHOP

Karama

Out to get some good bargains? Head to Karama, filled with energy and character its two central streets are brimming with lots of small shops with goods spilling out onto the streets. You'll find clothes, fashion accessories, leather handbags and watches, as well as souvenir shops selling everything from rosewood boxes and *shisha* pipes to Arabic coffee pots and Omani silver jewellery. If you enter Karama Shopping Complex, you'll find vendors shouting at you, enticing you with fantastic Prada and Versace imitations, designer watches and handbags. You will find anything you want, but make sure you haggle. In the evening, head to Time Café (04 3522277), where you can watch sports, play pool, darts and even mini-golf. And if you're after spicy food, then Pakistani restaurant Karachi Darbar (04 3347272) will do the trick.

Deira

This is old Dubai, not lined with tall buildings, but with timeless *souks* and alleyways. The main attractions are, of course, the Gold *Souk* and Spice *Souk* (see pp 200–1), but don't forget to take a ride in an *abra*. There are also the fish and vegetable *souks* along the cornice, certainly worth a visit.

Satwa

This neon-lit area is known for its fabric shops and tailors. Get a suit or dress made up for unbelievably low prices. You can also get your car windows tinted here and buy funky accessories for your car. Diyafah Street is home to the famous All Mallah (04 3984723), where you'll get a succulent *shawarma*. And if you fancy a spicy curry, then head to the famous Ravi's (04 3315353). Take a stroll through this lively main street at night.

Bur Dubai

This old bustling area is where you'll find the real bargains for electronic goods. Al Fahidi Street is the main street you should head to, while Khalid Bin Al Waleed Street, also known as Computer Street, is where you'll find computers and laptops. Always ask for a service warranty and make sure you bargain. You'll also find clothes and jewellery for sale and this is where the famous Meena Bazaar is located (see p 201). Be warned – you'll end up doing a lot of walking.

The Walk at Jumeirah Beach Residence

This long stretch of beachfront shopping hosts nearly 170 retailers with many more opening up. European fashion store Zadig et Voltaire, Saks Fifth Avenue and London's Aiyanna are some of the top brands that have opened up. There are also plenty of great choices for restaurants and cafés. It's got a great atmosphere for an evening out. You'll find people jogging, taking long walks and dining on the tables spilling out on the street.

MALLS

Burjuman

Trade Centre Road, Bur Dubai, 04 3527755, www.burjuman.com
Sat–Thurs 10am–10pm, Fri 2pm–10pm

This slick and stylish mall has more than 180 prestigious stores including Saks Fifth Avenue and designers such as Donna Karan, Valentino, Escada and Louis Vuitton. If that's too pricey, the mall also has the high-street fashion stores. There's a selection of restaurants, a food court and cafés, as well as a play area for children. And in case you want to live or even work a few seconds away from the mall, you can! Burjuman residences are literally touching the mall and they are nothing short of luxurious. The office tower is also right next door.

Deira City Centre

Garhoud, 04 2951010, www.deiracitycentre.com
Sat–Thurs 10am–10pm, Fri 2pm–10pm

With over 340 shops, Deira City Centre houses the popular Carrefour, an 11-screen Cinestar Cinemas, an office tower, Magic Planet (leisure complex), and the Sofitel City Centre Hotel and Residence.

Dragon Mart

International City, Emirates Road, 04 3687205, www.dragonmart.ae
Sat–Thurs 10am–10pm, Fri 2pm–10:30pm

The outlets here sell a vast and varied selection of Chinese products made in China. It is said to have the largest concentration of Chinese traders outside of China.

Dubai Festival City

Al Rebat Street, adjacent to Garhoud Bridge, 04 2136135,
www.dubaifestivalcity
Thurs–Sat 10am–midnight, Sun–Wed 10am–10pm

This is quite the retail resort with over 500 shops, over 100 restaurants, cafés and bistro and a 12-screen Grand Festival Cinema. You can choose to eat at one of the *al fresco* dining venues along the water, and jump into an *abra* if your legs are aching. Large stores include Marks and Spencer, IKEA and Toys R Us. With the sparkling Intercontinental Hotel connected to the mall, what better place to stay? There's also a Fitness First inside the mall.

Dubai Mall

Sheikh Zayed Road, 1st Interchange, Downtown Dubai, 04 3627500,
www.dubaimall.com
Sun–Wed 10am–10pm, Thurs–Sat 10am–midnight

Wow

- Dubai Mall is the biggest mall in the world.
- It houses the famous Dubai Aquarium, with 33,000 animals.
- There's a massive ice rink and SEGA Republic.

The largest mall in the world. And let's not even dwell on the shops – there won't be many things you can't find here, especially with international stores like Bloomingdales and Galeries Lafayette. There's a large cinema and an unbelievable range of dining options. For all things sweet, there's Candylicious, the world's largest candy shop, lots of frozen yoghurt places dotted around and the famous New York Magnolia cupcakes inside Bloomingdales (see p 268 for cupcakes). You can leave your kids at Kidzania (www.kidzania.com) while you shop. And if the walking has taken a toll on your legs, why not have an al fresco dining experience with views of the Burj Khalifa, tallest tower in the world and the Dubai fountains, which are on every evening across the Burj lake. If you want to spa, head next door to The Address hotel.

Dubai Marina Mall

Dubai Marina, 04 4361000, www.dubaimarinamall.com
Sun–Sat 10am–10pm

Opened recently, this mall has 155 stores on four levels, boutiques, a kids' entertainment area, a fantastic range of cafés and dining options as well as a cinema. The breathtaking Marina views, as you shop, is what makes this mall special. There's also a Waitrose.

Dubai Outlet Mall

Al Ain Road (Route 66) at Dubailand, 04 4234666, www.dubaioutletmall.com
Sun–Wed 10am–10pm, Thurs–Sat 10am–midnight

A must if you're looking for great bargains. This is the only 'outlet' concept mall in the region and has over 800 of the world's top fashion brands. It includes high-end names such as Prada, Christian Dior and Gucci. It is home to the first ever Chuck E Cheese's family entertainment venue in the UAE, which includes great food, games, rides and a bowling alley.

Bargain-hunter

If you like furniture from *The One* but find the prices a little high, *The One* in Outlet Mall has a section called Seconds, where you can pick up things a lot cheaper – they might be chipped a little, but they will be good value.

Ibn Battuta Mall

Between Interchange 5 and 6, Sheikh Zayed Road, 04 3621901
www.ibnbattutamall.com
Sun–Wed 10am–midnight, Thurs–Sat 10am–1am

This themed mall is named after the legendary Islamic traveller Ibn Battuta who journeyed around the world as a young man in quest of knowledge. The mall traces the route through six richly-decorated, themed courts – Tunisia, China, Egypt, India, Persia and Andalusia, each one visited by the great adventurer. It's fairly spacious and large, so be sure to wear comfy shoes. And if you do get tired, then there is an in-mall shuttle service that takes you from one end to the other. And in the evening, you can catch a movie at the 21-screen IMAX cinema. The mall also houses a Fitness First gym.

Did you know?

- Ibn Battuta was born in 1304 in Morocco and travelled 73,000 miles over a period of nearly 30 years.
- What he achieved in one lifetime makes him a shining Islamic icon.

Lamcy Plaza

Oud Mehta Street, Near American Hospital, 04 3359999, www.lamcyplaza.com
Sat–Tues 9am–10pm, Wed–Fri 9am–10:30pm

A slightly less glamorous and smaller mall. However, don't be fooled by size. Lamcy still has 150 retail outlets, along with a supermarket, a cinema and a big food court. Other stores include Paris Gallery, Bhs, Damas, Giordano and Guess.

Mall of the Emirates

Interchange 4, Sheikh Zayed Road, 04 4099000, www.malloftheemirates.com
Sun–Wed 10am–10pm, Thurs–Sat 10am–midnight

Filled with designer brands, furniture stores, electronics and so much more, Mall of the Emirates is one of the most popular malls in Dubai. Harvey Nichols and Debenhams have huge stores inside. And the fantastic Kempinski Hotel is connected to the mall. You'll never run of activities if you're spending the day here – the famous Ski Dubai is on site.

Mercato Mall

Jumeirah Beach Road, Jumeirah, 04 3444161, www.mercatoshoppingmall.com
Sat–Thurs 10am–10pm, Fri 2pm–10pm

Named after the Italian word for 'market', this mall has been designed in a distinctive Renaissance architectural style, capturing Italian, French and Spanish flavours. It also houses a 12-screen Century Cinema. There is a Spinneys, Home Centre, Virgin Megastore, and an Early Learning Centre, as well as a range of fantastic clothes shops.

Mirdif City Centre

Off Emirates Road, Mirdif, www.mirdiffcitycentre.info
Newest mall, opened in April 2010

A large mall with a plethora of shops and food outlets, cafes, restaurants, a Carrefour hypermarket, cinema complex, an outside cinema, children's entertainment area, and indoor skydiving centre.

The Boulevard Emirates Towers

Sheikh Zayed Road, linked to Emirates Towers Hotel, 043198999
www.jumeirahemiratestowers.com
Sat–Thurs 10am–10pm, Fridays 4pm–10pm

This fairly small shopping boulevard links the Emirates Hotel and office tower. It's more high-end and smart with designer-label boutiques such as Gucci, Giorgio Armani, Jimmy Choo and Bvlgari.

The Village

Jumeirah Beach Road, Jumeirah, 04 3447713, www.thevillagedubai.com
Sat–Thurs 10am–10pm, Fri 4pm–10pm

Browse through the glitzy boutiques of select clothing and fancy home furnishings. End your day by going for a yoga class at Zen Yoga and indulge in delicious cup cakes from the Sugar Daddy Bakery.

Wafi City

Oud Metha Road, 04 3244555, www.wafi.com
Sat–Wed 10am–10pm, Thurs–Fri 10–midnight

The Egyptian-themed Wafi is a large and very elegant shopping complex, with pyramid-shaped atrium roofs. Wafi is focused more on luxury brands and expensive boutiques and has over 200 stores, restaurants, an entertainment centre called Encounter Zone, a roller-blading rink and a traditional *souk* called Khan Murjan. Among the shops are Marks and Spencer, Tanagra, Tiffany and Co, Mont Blanc, and Versace. Where better to stay than the opulent Raffles Hotel, situated next door?

SUPERMARKETS AND HYPERMARKETS

Al Maya Supermarket

www.almayagroup.com

A good range of brands, affordable prices and conveniently located in the centre of each area.

Al Mamzar 04 2624949, Al Murooj 04 3215552, Al Rigga 04 2236976, Satwa 04 3420626, Jumeirah Beach Residence (Al Sadaf) 04 4389676, Jumeirah Beach Residence (Bahar) 04 4370166, Lamcy Plaza 04 3351397, Reef Mall 04 2229898

Carrefour

www.carrefouruae.com

This French chain now has four branches in Dubai. There is a large range of foods, as well as sections for electronics, household goods, luggage, clothes, garden furniture, DVDs and stationery. Pricing is very competitive.

Al Shindagha 04 3939395, Al Mamzar, Century Mall 04 2035699, Deira City Centre 04 2951600, Mall of the Emirates 04 4094899

Choithram

www.choithram.com

One of the largest supermarket chains, where you will find a good selection of British, American and Asian products. However, it is also quite expensive.

Al Fahidi St 04 3523651, Al Wasl Rd opp. Safa Park 04 3943852, Dubai Tower Al Nasr Sq 04 2232488, Garhoud 04 2825494, Green Community 04 8852299, Greens 04 3663160, Holiday Centre 04 3311377, Hyatt Galleria 04 2710605, Jebel Ali 04 8845585, Jumeirah Beach Rd 04 3442424, Karama 04 3371021, Lakes 04 3801010, Springs 04 3602262, opp. Ramada Hotel 04 3526946, Umm Suqeim 04 3481864

Géant Hypermarket

www.geant-dubai.com

This hypermarket is in Ibn Battuta Mall and has a very large selection of foods. They stock clothes, electronics, household goods and outdoor goods.

Ibn Battuta Mall, between Interchange 5 and 6 on Sheikh Zayed Road, 04 3685858

Hyperpanda

This is a huge hypermarket, has a large healthcare centre and an electronics department.

Dubai Festival City, Al Garhoud, 04 2325997

Lifco

www.lifco.com

There are only two branches in Dubai, but Lifco has a large range of items.

Garhoud 04 2868685, Zabeel 04 3327899

Lulu

www.luluhypermarket.com

With outlets in Al Barsha, Karama and Qusais, Lulu has low prices and sells a large range of foods as well as clothing, luggage, electronics and home appliances.

Hypermarket: Al Barsha 04 3418888, Al Qusais 04 2988880, Karama 04 3346333
Centre: Al Muteena opp. Sheraton 04 2626141, Karama 04 3353354
Supermarket: Karama 04 3367070

Park n Shop

This isn't a chain, but has a fantastic bakery and butchery. The bakery sells famous jam doughnuts and birthday cakes as well as a good range of wheat-free breads.

Al Wasl Road, Al Wasl 04 3945671

Spinneys

www.spinneys-dubai.com

With numerous branches across the city, Spinneys is very convenient. You'll find a range of South African, Australian, British and American items. They also have a selection of Waitrose products from the UK. Vegetarian options are good.

Al Ghurair Centre 04 2222886, Bin Sougat Centre 04 2862442, Dubai Marina 04 3674810, Jumeirah 04 3674810, Mazaya Centre 04 3212225, Mercato 04 3496900, Mirdiff 04 2880335, Ramada 04 3555251, Trade Centre Rd 04 3511777, Umm Suqeim 04 3941657

Union Co-op

www.ucs.ae

This chain has some of the best fruit and vegetables.

Mankhool 04 3980944, Al Tawar 04 2643100, Al Wasl 04 3212263, Aweer 04 3331816, Hamriya 04 2629191, Jumeirah 04 3945999, Rashidiya 04 2862434, Satwa 04 3312891

HIDDEN GEMS

Hidden behind the facade of super-glitzy malls, designer-stores galore and top high street fashion brands are some very talented local designers, whose clothes have that unique edge and are gaining popularity.

Burlesque

This is a stunning new concept store, a surreal feast for the eyes. It's difficult to describe – a grown-up grotto peppered with ironic references at every twist and turn. It's sensuous, wild and sophisticated. Think *Alice in Wonderland*. Think precocious. Think art. From funky jewellery and tattooed tables to iconic furniture pieces and sexy handbags, Burlesque is a paradise of fashion-forward accessories. It's like nothing else and it's a must. Burlesque is a paradise of fashion-forward accessories, and is located on Al Wasl Road beside the Al-Ghazal centre.

Esra

A very high-end designer in Dubai who sells amazing bridal gowns and cocktail party dresses to the affluent. They sell it through their high-end studios but don't have any retail outlets.

Glamour Collection

Designed by Heba, this collection brings colorful patterns and designs to women's everyday wear. The soft fabrics she uses to design elegant flowing tops, perfect for beach, evening and casual wear are from Egypt, Syria, India and Pakistan. Her designs are displayed at Sunny Days boutique, Jumeirah Centre on Al Wasl Road. Contact Heba on 050 7593 956.

Hatzys and Bitzis

Sisters Gulnaz, Nazgul and Nilufer Nejmi made quite an impression with their hats at the Dubai World Cup this year. They have now launched their 'Hatzys and Bitzis' hat collection, under the brand Fashion Monsters, which also concentrates on make-up, fashion design and photography. They make their hats from scratch in different styles from elegant to crazy. To place an order, contact 050 5457895.

Mapochette

If you don't want to max out your credit card at times like these, rent a stylish designer bag from www.mapochette.com. They'll deliver it to you in no time.

Meher and Riddhima

This home grown brand by friends Meher and Riddhima, selling both Western and ethnic clothes, is a top seller in Dubai and India and set to go international. Buy their signature clothes at Sauce (www.shopatsauce.com) in Village Mall (04 3447270), Dubai Mall and XVA Gallery, Bastakiya.

Reem's Closet

Find some awesome designer bags and clothes in Reem's Closet in Mazaya Centre (04 3439553). And they really are affordable.

Royal Rickshaw

This designer (www.royalrickshaw.com) sells funky, stylish and fashionable dresses, versatile and trendy kaftans, and tops. Their collection is available from Tiger Lily (04 3248088), Wafi Mall and Boutique 1 (04 3304555), Emirates Towers Boulevard.

SugarVintage

Childhood friends Leila and Hedaya have created a range inspired by their travels. Sauce (Dubai Mall and other locations) stocks SugarVintage clothes.

BOOKSTORES

Kinokuniya

Dubai Mall, 04 4340111

Inside the Dubai Mall, this giant bookstore is 68,000 square feet which stocks more than half a million books and a thousand magazines in various languages.

Booksplus

Lamcy Plaza/Spinney's Umm Suqeim, 04 3366362

Books Gallery

Village Mall, Jumeirah, 04 3445770, www.jashanmal.ae

Borders

Various locations, 04 2943344

Magrudy's

Various locations, 04 3444009, www.magrudy.com

Magrudy's sell cards, toys, stationery, and art materials as well as books. You can buy school uniforms and shoes at their Jumeirah and Ibn Battuta branches. Magrudy's also run book clubs for adults and children.

Spinney's Bookshop

Near Burjuman Centre, 04 3511777

The Bookworm Bookshop

Park n Shop, Al Wasl Road, 04 3945770

This bookshop is great for children's books and features an enchanting Bedouin tent with cushions, where children can lounge and read. They also hold story-telling sessions and craft activity sessions.

White Star Bookshop

Beach Centre, Jumeirah, 04 3446628

SECOND HAND BOOKSHOPS

House of Prose

Jumeirah Plaza (04 3449021), Ibn Battuta Mall (04 3685526)

This is the place to go for paperback fiction. A second-hand book store where you can find good deals.

Book World Trading

Satwa (04 3491914), Karama (04 3969697)

Satwa's foremost bookshop with 75,000 books. It's a mixed shop of old and new titles where you can return the books you bought and get half the price back.

Chapter 19

Looking after your kids

Fitness, energy and creativity through fun activities are vital to a child's growth and learning. Dubai boasts a wide range of activities for kids. Sunshine most, if not all year round is the biggest bonus.

If you're moving to this city with youngsters, this section will give you a taster of the sporty, creative and educational things your children can do. And there's sure to be something going on in each area of Dubai. In fact, there's so much happening out there, you'll need to be quite selective. And that's exactly what I've had to do here ... just pick some of the many things going on for children.

INTERNET RESOURCES

DubaiKidz

www.dubaikidz.biz

An online directory of everything your kids can do in Dubai, from finding a nursery or school to suggestions for interesting after-school activities and planning birthday parties.

DubaiParent

www.dubaiparent.com

Everything you need to know as a parent in Dubai from nurseries and schools to shopping and parties.

SHOP ONLINE

BabySouk

www.babysouk.com

This website is the idea of two mothers with twins, whose aim is to provide customers in Dubai and the UAE with the best of well-designed, innovative, educational and fun children's products. They also have a next-day delivery service.

DubaiBabies

www.dubaibabies.com

DubaiBabies sources innovative baby products and gifts, bringing choice to Dubai mums and making them available here. Shopping for baby products is made more convenient as DubaiBabies deliver, but they also have a kiosk in Mercato Mall for anyone who doesn't fancy internet shopping.

Just Kidding

www.justkidding-me.com

A one-stop-shop for everything from colourful strollers to super-safe car seats, fashionable furniture with choices of interior design accessories and some hip clothing labels for babies, young children and mothers-to-be.

NEW MUMS AND BABIES

Alpha Tots

Jumeirah, Near Safa Park, 050 6985165

Holly Grattan organises a range of activities such as 'Little Scholars', 'Funky Monkey' and 'Dragonfly Yoga'. Classes range from baby and child swimming and arts and crafts to first aid courses and self-defence classes for mums.

Boogie Babies

Various locations including Mall of Emirates, 050 884 1966
www.boogiebabies.org

They run lively, fun and musical sessions for babies, toddlers and mums, dancing and funky fun for children aged 3–6 and BoogieBabies aerobic exercise for ages 4 and up. Classes are held at a variety of locations including Arabian Ranches Golf Club, Mall of the Emirates, Hayya Club at Emirates Hills and Dubai Ladies Club on Jumeirah Beach Road.

Deira Mums and Tots

Fun City Play area, Reef Mall, Deira, Nargis – 050 6781168 or
deiramums@gmail.com, www.deiramums.blogspot.com

Mums-to-be, mums with babies, infants and toddlers get together to relax in the company of other mums while their children gain social and physical skills in some free play. They also have a singing class and an art and craft class.

Mommy and Me Yoga

Town Centre, Emirates Hills, 04 3670435

Stay in shape and spend time with baby. Classes assist in the development of the child's motor skills.

TopTots

Al Wasl Road, Jumeirah
Lauren Fenton – 050 3542120, toptots10@hotmail.com

An early learning enrichment programme to encourage all round development in toddlers between 3 months and 4 years. Also gives an opportunity for mums to meet other mums.

Baby signing language workshops

Liz Jackson – 050 7592844

This course is for babies 6 months and up before they speak. Moms are taught how to communicate with their kids through signs. This helps to enrich the child's vocabulary and ability to speak.

Baby massage

There are some courses in Dubai teaching parents how to massage their babies to help with colic, constipation, teething, sleeping and other things:

Liz Jackson (050 759 2844) Kinder Music Instructor/Baby Massage
Paula Miller (050 650 1189) Lactation Consultant/Infant Massage

CREATIVITY

Dubai International Art Centre

Villa 27, Street 75b, between Town Centre and Mercato Mall, 04 3444398
www.artdubai.com

This is Dubai's oldest and largest art organisation. With over 90 courses such as writing, fashion design, painting, Arabic calligraphy, sewing, pottery and photography, there's something here for everyone.

Dubai Community Theatre and Arts Centre, DUCTAC

Mall of the Emirates, 04 3414777, www.ductac.org

DUCTAC offers various classes from drawing and painting, theatre and drama to Indian, salsa, tap and other forms of dance for children (as well as adults) from the age of 6 years. There is also an art gallery and theatre for performances.

Jam Jar

Behind Dubai Garden Centre on Sheikh Zayed Road, 04 3417303
www.thejamjardubai.com
Open Sat–Thurs 10am–10pm

This is an urban DIY painting studio and art gallery, offering a unique art experience with unlimited acrylic paint on canvas, regardless of age, experience or profession.

Bead Palace

Opposite Mercato Mall, Jumeirah Beach Road, 04 3497858/59
beadpalace@regencyglobal.ae
Sat–Thurs 10am–7pm, Fri 2pm–6pm

This is a unique do-it-yourself concept in jewellery making and design. There are classes available and there's a variety of crafts to choose from like beading, pottery, cooking, T-shirt painting, glass painting, card designing or woodcraft. For children aged 5–15, there is a bead and craft camp every Saturday, which also includes a cooking programme.

Café Ceramique

Various locations including Town Centre JBR (04 3447331) and Mall of the Emirates (04 3410144), www.café-ceramique.com

Inspire some creativity as the kids get a taste of art, paint and fun while yummy mummies indulge in coffee and a bite. Of course, with lots of little clay pieces around, mums might also be tempted to have a paint.

FUN DAYS OUT

Amusement and Water Parks

Aquaventure

The Atlantis, Palm Jumeirah, 04 4260000
www.atlantisthepalm.com/aquaventure
Daily 10.00am to sunset
Admission – Dhs285 per adult, Dhs220 for ages 3–7 and free for ages 0–2

At the Atlantis Hotel, set at the peak of the amazing Palm Island Jumeirah, this extravagant water park has something incredible for all ages. While you brave the famous Ziggurat or 'Leap of Faith' which features a near vertical slide almost 100 feet high and which then continues through a shark-filled lagoon, or whether you are whisked away by the exciting river ride of over 2 kilometres that includes tidal pools, waterfalls and rapids, your kids can plunge into Splashers, a water playground with tipping water buckets, slides, climbing frames and rope bridges. You can also send them to the supervised marine adventure where they can learn about sea life or to the Lost Chambers Atlantis-themed aquarium with 65,000 marine creatures, not to mention the chance to swim with dolphins (but book this early). Aquaventure also has a 700-metre beach – so if you fancy having a lazy day in the sun, then it's all there.

Dreamland Aqua Park

Umm Al Quwain, 06 7681888, www.dreamlanduae.com
Daily 10.00am–7.00pm
Admission Dhs100 per adult, Dhs70 children under 1.4 metres tall, children 3 years old and below 1.1 metre are free of charge

You might have to drive 45 minutes to get to Umm Al Quwain, but Dreamland Aquapark is a great place for some water-splashing fun if you have kids. The Aqua Play area has water bouncers for babies, see-saws, a splashers area and water bikes. There are also bumper boats and a wave pool for the older swimmers, along with some adrenaline-pumping slides like the Twister and Twisting Dragons. You can try the family raft ride, or fall asleep as you drift along in the lazy river. And if the adults want to sit back and have a drink, they can head to the pool bar.

Wild Wadi

Jumierah Beach Hotel, 04 3484444, www.wildwadi.com
Daily 11am–7pm; in October, opens at 8am
Admission – Dhs195 per adult, Dhs165 for children less than 1.1 metres tall

Located between the Burj Al Arab and the Jumeirah Beach Hotel, Wild Wadi is an Arabian-themed water park, featuring 30 water rides and several restaurants. The rides have names like Wadi Wash, Jumeirah Sceirah and Rushdown Ravine. There are also several Master Blaster rides, in which riders sit in inflatable rings which are propelled uphill by high-power water jets.

Wonderland

Next to Garhoud Bridge, opposite Grand Hyatt, 04 3241222
www.wonderlanduae.com
Please contact Wonderland to find out updated prices and timings as they change often.

This theme park in Garhoud is divided in to three distinct areas: Splashland features a wide range of water attractions, then there's The Main Street and finally the Theme Park which includes a roller coaster. There's an electronic games parlour, bumper cars, paddle boats, tennis courts, volleyball, football and basketball areas, as well as numerous barbecue sites.

Wildlife

Dubai Zoo
Jumeirah Beach Road, 04 3496444
Admission: Dhs2

This zoo has grown over the years and is now home to over 1200 animals including lions, tigers, monkeys, giraffes, bears, deer, herons, parakeets, mongooses and other dangerous and exotic animals. Some of these are also rescue animals, confiscated at customs and saved from maltreatment at shows and circuses. Space, however, is very tight and though there have been plans to move the zoo to a larger premises, nothing has happened as yet. The zookeepers do their very best to take care of the animals in such conditions, but it is sad to see that nothing has been done about this.

Sharjah Natural History Museum
06 5311999

The Arabian Wildlife Centre, inside the Museum, has plenty of animals and endangered species including the famous Arabian leopard. A fantastic interactive day out for children.

Amusement Centres

Children's City
Creekside Park, www.childrencity.ae, 04 3340808
Dhs10 for children, Dhs40 for a family of 4

This educational city for children aged 2–15 has interactive exhibits focusing on nature and space travel, as well as culture and history. It's a place where children can explore, play, discover, and learn about the world in which we live.

Encounter Zone
Wafi City Mall, Oud Metha, 04 3247747
Dhs35 for first 2 hours, Dhs25 for every 2 thereafter

A large playground with Lunarland, a play area for under 8s, and Galactica, with a skate park, 3D cinema, video games and Crystal Maze for teens.

Kidzania

Dubai Mall, www.kidzania.com

Due to open towards the end of 2009, this will be a mini-city with offices, homes, schools, theatre and the works. Children can play various roles from being doctors and teachers to mechanics and artists.

Magic Planet

Deira City Centre, 04 2954333, www.deiracitycentre.com
Entrance is free, but you need to load a card or buy Dhs50 pass for unlimited play.

A great place to leave your kids while you shop away. You know they'll be entertained with a merry-go-round, a train, bumper cars and video games. There is also an activity play gym and a small soft-play area for the younger ones.

Toby's Adventureland

Burjuman Centre, 04 3552868, www.tobysdubai.com
Dhs19 for under 4 years (90 mins), Dhs25 for 4–7 yrs, Dhs30 8+ yrs

This large indoor play area is for kids 10 years and younger. There is a ball pit and soft play area for younger kids, slides and punch bags for the older ones and children's programmes showing on the large plasma television.

Other things to do

Bowling

Al Nasr Leisureland, Behind American Hospital, Oud Metha, 04 3371234

City Bowling, City Centre, Deira, 04 2959139

Dubai International Bowling Centre, next to Century Mall, 04 2969222

Dubai Bowling Centre, Al Quoz, 04 3391010

Magic Planet, Mall of the Emirates, 04 3414444

Dolphinarium
Creek Park Gate No 1, 04 3369773, www.dubaidolphinarium.ae

Do you love dolphins? Watch the dolphin show, which runs daily except Sunday and has various timings. You can also swim with the dolphins. Dhs100 for adults and Dhs50 for children.

Ice Skating
Al Nasr Leisureland, behind American Hospital, Oud Metha, 04 3371234

Dubai Ice Rink, Dubai Mall, 04 4373111

Galleria Ice Rink, Hyatt Regency, Deira, 04 2096550

Libraries

Library		
	Location	**Telephone**
Al Ras Library	Near Dubai Creek	04 2262788
Al Safa Library	Al Wasl Rd, Jumeirah	04 3947279
Al Twar Library	Al Twar	04 2630013
Hatta Library	Main St, Hatta	04 8521022
Hor Al Anz Library	Hor Al Anz	04 2661788
Rashidiya Library	29B St, Rashidiya	04 2858065
The Old Library, DUCTAC	Mall of the Emirates	04 3414777
Umm Suqeim Library	Jumeirah Beach Rd	04 3482512

Mad Science
Al Khaleej Building, Zabeel Road, Karama, 04 3366528, www.madscience.org/uae

Mad Science sparks imaginative learning and provides after-school, preschool and vacation programmes, as well as workshops and birthday parties. The science classes are both entertaining and educational and parties can have lasers and indoor fireworks.

Ski Dubai
Mall of the Emirates, www.skidxb.com, 04 4094000
Daily 9am-midnight
A one-day ski slope pass costs Dhs300 and Dhs240 for children

With an area of 22,500 snow-covered square metres, this huge indoor ski park in Mall of the Emirates can be quite an outing. They also run skiing classes.

Sharjah

There's a lot to do in Sharjah, especially if you have kids, and since it's only a 30-minute drive from Dubai, it can make a great day out.

The Science Museum and Discovery Centre
Before Sharjah Television, 06 5586577

An interactive museum where kids can learn about the world.

Adventureland
Sahara Centre, Al Nahda Interchange, 06 5316363
www.adventureland-sharjah.com

On the first floor of the Sahara Centre, this is a real indoor funfair with a number of good rides for all ages, as well as video games, a climbing wall and bowling.

Sharjah Aquarium
Al Khan near the Lagoon, 06 5285288, www.sharjahaquarium.ae

Kids will be amazed by the 250 species of sea life from the smallest clownfish to reef sharks. You can choose either to walk by the sea outside or walk under the sea inside the aquarium.

Al Qasba
06 5560777, www.alqasba.ae

Set on the waterfront, Al Qasba is full of culture, art, food and entertainment. There is a theatre gallery, a musical fountain and a kids' zone with edutainment activities created for children of various age groups. And don't forget to ride on the 'Eye of the Emirates', the giant wheel with breathtaking views of Sharjah and neighbouring Dubai.

SPORT

Bradenton Preparatory Academy

Dubai Sports City, 04 4251111, www.dubaisportscity.ae

This world class academy, which has trained the likes of Andre Agassi in Florida, plans to open its Dubai campus September 2009.

Dorrell Tennis School

www.tennisdubai.com
Maurice – 050 6598500

Tennis lessons and programmes are held at Dubai World Trade Centre Club or Shangri-La Hotel for various age groups. They also have sports clinics for corporate clients as well as international tennis tours and tournaments.

Dubai Swim

Uptown Primary School, 15th St Mirdif, info@dubaiswim.com,
www.dubaiswim.com

Provides swimming teaching and coaching for all ages from infants to children and adults.

DuGym

Various locations
050 5536283, suzanne@dugym.com, www.dugym.com

Gymnastics and trampoline coaching for children of all ages. The club operates at 15 different locations including Jumeirah English Speaking School and The Ballet Centre. DuGym also has an Academy of Gymnastic for its higher level students.

Kids Foot

Uptown Mirdif/Etisalat Academy, 04 2543070, www.semmarsport.com

Enrol your children on a Football Training Programme which promotes courage and a positive attitude to enable them reach their highest potential. The programmes are managed by Semmar Sport Services whose aim is to increase sport awareness, particularly for children aged 2–14. They run junior club sports programmes to summer fitness camps and special need children programmes.

E-sports Dubai

The Aviation Club, Tennis Stadium
04 2824540, www.esportsdubai.com

With a focus on enjoyment through learning, E-sports have sports training academies for children and adults of all levels. Sports include tennis, football, swimming, cricket, rugby, climbing and holiday camps.

E-Sports Climbing Academy

Sadi Saad – 050 9757316
Dhs45 for a one-hour session

The Kids' climbing club meets at GEMS World Academy in Al Barsha, which has 22 different climbing routes and is open to 5–18-year-olds. It takes place every Saturday at 10am–12:30pm. Classes are also held at Wellington International School.

Horse Riding

050 5537986/ 050 5587656, www.emiratesequestriancentre.com

During a session, children have a ride session and a games session or they go on a hack, along with a stable management lesson. At the end of the season, the children take the BHS progressive Riding Test which is awarded to those who successfully ride and answer questions about horse knowledge. They will receive a certificate and a badge.

My Gym
520 Jumeira Beach Road, 04 3943962, www.mygymuae.com

Award-winning programmes for children from 6 weeks to 13 years in fitness, games, sport, music and more.

Soccer Kids Dubai
Various locations including Emirates Hills
Ben – 050 3560960, James – 050 4764877, www.soccerkidsdubai.com

This is the largest soccer coaching academy in the UAE, teaching over 900 children aged 4–17 in ten different locations. They also offer holiday camps and footie parties. Training takes place throughout the week at different venues.

DANCE

Ballet Centre
Road 16C, behind Jumeirah Centre, 04 3449776, www.balletcentre.com

Ballet Centre has a range of classes for different age groups from drama, piano and Irish dancing to Taekwondo, street jazz and gymnastics for tots.

Turning Pointe Dance Studios
Russian Cluster, International City, 800 32623, www.turningpoint.ae

Initially training in classical ballet, Turning Pointe Dance Studios, formerly known as The Dance Centre, has now expanded to include funky dance, modern, jazz and tap. They teach students aged 3–18 years and have locations all around Dubai.

Dubai Community Theatre and Arts Centre (DUCTAC)
Mall of the Emirates, 04 3414777

Offers many styles of dance including salsa and Irish dancing.

Crystal Dance and Music
Opposite Dubai Municipality, Karama, 04 3969898

Classical Indian dance including Bharatnatyam and Bollywood dance classes. They also teach instruments including organ, guitar, piano, drums, violin, flute, *tabla* and *mridangam*.

MUSIC

Centre for Musical Arts
Gold and Diamond Park, Al Quoz, 04 3418872, www.cmadubai.com

Lessons in piano, guitar, violin, singing and more for all levels.

Dubai Music School
Karama, 04 3964834

Lessons in singing, piano, guitar, violin, drums, brass and more for all levels.

Jumeirah Music Centre
Jumeirah Centre, Jumeirah Beach Road, 04 3492662, www.jumeirahmusic.com

Lessons in singing, piano, guitar, flute, violin and drums.

Popular Music Institute
Wafi City Mall, Oud Metha, 04 3242626

Lessons in guitar, drums, violin and piano.

Shruthi Music and Dance Training Centre
Karama, Sana Fashion Bldg, 04 3377398

Aside from piano, guitar, drums, etc., they also offer classes in *tabla*, Indian vocal music and Indian dance.

The Music Institute

Murjan 1 Plaza, Jumeirah Beach Residence, 04 4243818
www.themusic-uae.com

Lessons in singing as well as playing instruments such as guitar, violin, drums and piano.

BIRTHDAY PARTIES

Bead Palace

Opposite Mercato Mall, Jumeirah Beach Road, 04 3497858/59
beadpalace@regencyglobal.ae

You'll have a karaoke machine, juice, cookies, popcorn as well as staff to instruct the children on how to make jewellery. You can get catered food including both a birthday cake and hot foods.

Bowling Party

Magic Planet Zone
Dubai City Centre or Mall of the Emirates, 04 3424747

Dubai International Bowling Centre
Next to Century Mall, 04 2969222

With pool tables and arcade games.

Dubai Bowling Centre
Al Quoz, 04 3391010

With pool tables, air hockey.

Bowling City
Festival City, 04 2328600

With karaoke cabins, network and touch-screen games.

Café Ceramique

Various locations including Town Centre JBR (04 3447331) and Mall of the Emirates (04 3410144), www.café-ceramique.com

Inspire some creativity as the kids get a taste of art, paint and fun while yummy mummies indulge in coffee and a bite. Of course, with lots of little clay pieces around, mums might also be tempted to have a paint.

Flying Elephants

Al Quoz, 04 3479170, www.flyingelephantuae.com

Experienced party organisers will make sure the kids are entertained all day.

Mad Science

Al Khaleej Building, Zabeel Road, Karama, 04 3366528, www.madscience.org/uae

Mad Science birthday parties are both entertaining and educational and can include lasers and indoor fireworks.

Me and Riley

Emma – emmariedel@yahoo.com, 050 2867896

They organise stylish birthday parties in fantastic different settings such as 'the beach', 'animal safari', 'skull and cross chic' and 'mini Arab fashionista'.

Spa parties for kids

This may be something of a shock (I was certainly horrified), but there is now a spa craze for kids in Dubai. Manicures, pedicures, massages ... for kids? Colour Nail (04 3418848) at Times Square Centre offers spa parties, and for parties at home, call Brush and Co (04 4308465), based at France Cluster, International City.

Spot On Kidz

Sheikh Zayed Road, 04 3216536, www.spotonkidz.com

Entertains kids and organises special events tailor-made for all occasions.

NURSERIES

It is best to choose nurseries depending on where you live. This section lists some of the best nurseries in Dubai. The regular nursery week is Sunday to Thursday, though you can usually enrol your kids for as many days a week as is convenient for you. The average nursery fees are Dhs22–30,000 a year.

Art Kids

Al Manara, Mankhool, 04 3989335
Sun–Thurs, Age: 4 months–4 years
Classes: 9am–1pm
Daycare: 7:30am–7pm

Babyland Nursery

Opposite Choitram, Jumeirah, 04 3486874, www.babylandnursery.com
Sun–Thurs, Age: 1 year–4½ years
Classes: 8am–12:30pm
Daycare: 8:30am–4pm

Bright Morning

Jumeirah 3, 04 3946118
Sun–Thurs, Age: up to 4½ years
Classes: 8am–12noon
Daycare: 12noon–7pm

British Orchard

Jumeirah Beach Rd, 04 3953570,www.britishorchardnursery.com
Sun–Thurs, Age: 15 months–5 years
Toddlers 8am–11am, Nursery: 8:30am–12noon,
Foundation: 8:30am–12:30pm

Children's Garden

Green Community, 04 8853484, www.childrensgarden.ae
Sun–Thurs (flexible attendance), Age: 2 years–5 years
Classes: 8:30am–2pm
Daycare: 2:15pm–5pm

Emerald City Nursery

21st St, Jumeirah 2, 04 3490848, www.emeraldcitynursery.com
Sun–Thurs (flexible attendance), Age: 4 months–4 years
Classes: 7:30am–3pm
Daycare: 3pm–6pm

Emirates British Nursery

Opp Dubai Police Academy, Umm Suqeim, 04 3489996, www.ebninfo.ae
Sun–Thurs, Age: 11 months–4½ years
Classes: 8am–12:30pm
Daycare: 12:30pm–3pm

Jumeirah International Nursery

Al Wasl, 04 3499065, www.jinschools.com
Sun–Thurs (flexible attendance for under 3s), Age: 1½ years–5 years
Nursery: 8am–3pm

Kangaroo Kids

Burj Khalifa, 04 4205250, www.kangarookids.ae
Sun–Thurs, Age: 6 months–4 years
Toddler: 8am–12:30pm, Nursery: 8am–2:30pm, Foundation: 8am–5pm

Kid's Cottage Nursery

Jumeirah Beach Rd, 04 3942145, www.kids-cottage.com
Sun–Thurs, Age: 1 year–4 years
Classes: 8am–12:30pm, 12:30pm–2pm

Kid's Island Nursery

Al Hamra Jumeirah 3, 04 3942578, www.kidsislandnursery.com
Sun–Thurs, Age: 13 months–3 years, (for 3–4 yrs – Cocoon Nursery, www.cocoonnursery.com)
Classes: 8am–12:30pm, 12:45pm–2:30pm

Knightsbridge Nursery

Near Wild Wadi, Jumeirah, 04 3481666, www.theivychild.com
Sun–Thurs (flexible attendance), Age: 6 months–4¾ years
Classes: 7:30am–2pm, 7:30am–6pm

Ladybird Nursery

Al Wasl Rd, Jumeirah, 04 3441011, www.ladybirdnursery.ae
Sun–Thurs, Age: 1 year–6 years
Classes: 8am–12:30pm

Seashells Nursery

Al Barsha, 04 3413404, www.seashellsnursery.com
Sun–Thurs, Age: 18 months–4 years
Classes: 8am–12:30pm, 12:30pm–2pm

Small World Nursery

Jumeirah 2, 04 3490770, www.smallworldnurserydubai.com
Sun–Thurs (flexible attendance), Age: 1 year–4 years
Classes: 8am–12:30pm

Super Kids Nursery

Mirdiff, 04 2881949
Sun–Thurs, Age: 11 months–4 years
Classes: 8:30am–1pm
Daycare: until 5pm

Yellow Brick Road Nursery

Al Garhoud, 04 2828290, www.yellowbrickroad.ws
Sun–Thurs, Age: 4 months–5 years
Classes: 7:30am–3pm, 3pm–6pm

SCHOOLS

Which school you send your child to is one of the most important decisions to make. There are many schools you can choose from in Dubai, but where do you start and how do you find the right one? One thing's for sure – with the waiting lists some schools have, you will have to start early and start doing the groundwork even before you get to Dubai. You should note that if you move to Dubai after 1st May, you will not be able to enrol your child into school for that particular school year and will instead need to wait till September.

1 The first and most important thing to understand is that you will need to send your child to a private school, and school fees vary a lot, so it's worth comparing.

2 School first, then house. Distances can be a nightmare in Dubai, so first find the school you want to send your child to, then look for accommodation. The last thing you want is to find that your drive to school is almost two hours.

3 Now you need to decide which curriculum you want your child to study. For most expats, it is determined by the educational system of their home country. So, if you're from the UK and are planning to return to England in a few years, then the safest bet is to choose a school offering the English National Curriculum. There are three main curricula – American, British and International Baccalaureate (IB).

American – There aren't any set exams, though American universities usually require students to pass SAT exams. The American style of education allows children to study a wide variety of subjects, so they don't need to specialise early on. Even once they begin university, they will have two years of courses before deciding what to specialise in. However, standards vary from school to school. The obvious follow-on to having studied in an American school is an American university, but universities elsewhere in the world do recognise the American education system.

British – GCSE exams are taken in Year 11, A-level exams in Years 12 and 13. This is an all-round and well-respected curriculum. However, it requires the student to specialise in 3–5 subjects for A-levels, which means they narrow down quite early on, though it also means a shorter number of years in university (3–4 on average) as compared with the American system. British universities are the natural follow-on, but other international universities recognise and respect the British curriculum.

IB – IB exams are given at the end of a two-year programme in Year 13. The IB system draws on various international educational systems and is gaining more recognition and popularity all over the world. IB also regulates the schools that offer this curriculum. Universities worldwide recognise the IB. If you're unsure about which part of the world you're going to next, it's best to choose the IB system as your child will most easily be able to adjust from this system to another due to its international element.

4 While it's great to speak to other parents about their experiences of schools in Dubai, it is equally important for you to visit different schools to see what they are offering. At the end of the day, you need to develop a relationship with the school and the teachers – so the comfort level is critical.

5 If you have a child with special needs, you will need to search even harder since facilities for such children are very limited. Many schools will not accept dyslexic children.

6 What you need for enrolling your child in a school:

- Application form
- Copies of student's and parents' passports (information page and residence visa)
- Passport photographs (usually eight)
- Copies of student's birth certificate
- School records for past two years
- Immunisation records and medical history
- Transfer certificate from student's previous school.

7 School term dates are similar to the UK:

Autumn: mid September to mid December

Spring: early January to early April

Summer: mid April to early July.

8 Useful Resources: the Dubai Schools Inspection Bureau has given a detailed assessment of educational standards and performance of every school in Dubai. Visit The Knowledge and Human Development Authority website for these assessments (www.khda.gov.ae/En/DSIB/InspectionBureau.aspx). Education Oasis (www.education-dubai.com) will also help you understand more about the system here.

American curriculum

Al Mawakeb School

Near Dubai International Airport, Al Garhoud, 04 2851415
info@almawakeb.sch.ae, www.almawakeb.sch.ae
Kindergarten – Grade 12

Al Mizhar American Academy for Girls

Near Spinney's Mirdif, 04 2887250, admissions@aag.ae, www.taaleem.ae
Kindergarten – Grade12

American School of Dubai

Near Dubai Zoo, Jumeirah, 04 3440824, asdadmin@eim.ae, www.asdubai.org
Kindergarten – Grade 12

Al Ittihad Private School

Near Safa Park, Jumeirah (04 3945111) and Near Mamzar Park (04 2966314)
aipsma@ittihadschool.ae, www.ittihadschools.com
Kindergarten – Grade 12

Dubai National School

Near Mall of Emirates, Barsha, (04 3474555) and Al Twar (04 2988555)
barsha@dns.sch.ae, twar@dns.sch.ae, www.dns.sch.ae
Kindergarten – Grade 12

British curriculum

Al Safa Private School

Near Park n Shop, Jumeirah, 04 3947879, school@safaschooldubai.com
www.safaschooldubai.com
Foundation – Year 6

Al Salam Private School
Behind NMC Hospital, Al Ghusais, 04 2679594, info@alsalamschool.sch.ae
www.alsalamschool.sch.ae
Foundation – Year 11

Cambridge International School
Near Dubai Festival City, Garhoud, 04 2824646, cambridge@cis-dxb.ae
www.gemcis-garhoud.com
Foundation – Year 12

Dubai Carmel School
Near Bait Al-Khair Charity, Al Nahda 2, 04 2675424
info@dubaicarmelschool.com, www.dubaicarmelschool.com
Foundation – Year 12

Dubai College
Al Sufouh, 04 3999111, admissions@dubaicollege.org, www.dubaicollege.org
Year 7 – Year 13

Dubai English Speaking College
Academic City, 04 360 4866, admin@descdxb.com, www.descdxb.com
Year 7 – Year 13

Dubai English Speaking School
Near St. Mary's Church, Oud Metha, 04 3371457, admissions@dessdxb.com
www.dessdxb.com
Foundation – Year 6

GEMS Jumeirah Primary School
Near Park n Shop, Jumeirah, 04 3943500, office@jpsdubai.sch.ae
www.jumeirahprimaryschool.com
Foundation – Year 6

GEMS Wellington Primary School
Behind Shangri-La Hotel, 04 3433266, registrar@gemswps.ae
www.gemswps.com
Foundation – Year 6

Horizon (English) School
Near Safa Park, Jumeirah, 04 3422891, hsdubai@emirates.net.ae
www.horizonschooldubai.com
Foundation – Year 6

Jebel Ali Primary School
Near Ibn Battuta Mall, 04 8846485, jaschool@emirates.net.ae
www.jebelalischool.com
Year 1 – Year 6

Jumeirah College
Behind Park n Shop, Jumeirah, 04 3955524, office@jcdubai.sch.ae
www.gemsjc.com
Year 7 – Year 13

Kings School Dubai
Near Madinat Jumeirah, 04 3483939, info@kingsdubai.com
www.kingsdubai.com
Foundation – Year 6

Raffles International School
Near Jumeirah Beach Hotel, Umm Suqeim, 04 4271200
enquiries@rafflesis.com, www.rafflesis.com/english
Foundation – Year 12

St. Mary's Catholic High School
Near Rashid Hospital, Oud Metha, 04 3370252, maryscol@emirates.net.ae
www.stmarysdubai.com
Year 1 – Year 12

Star International School
Near Uptown Mall, Mirdif, 04 2884644, registrar.mirdif@starintl.ae
www.starschoolmirdiff.com
Foundation – Year 6

The English College
Opp Toyota Showroom, Sheikh Zayed Road, 04 3943465
admissions@englishcollege.ac.ae, www.englishcollege.ac.ae
Foundation – Year 13

IB curriculum

Emirates International School
Opp Garden Centre, Jumeirah, 04 3489804, mail@eischools.ae
www.eischools.ae
Kindergarten – Grade 13

Emirates International School
The Meadows, 04 3629009, meadows@eischools.ae, www.eischools.ae
Kindergarten – Grade 13

Dubai American Academy
Behind Mall of Emirates, 04 3479222, dacademy@emirates.net.ae
www.gemsaa-dubai.com
Kindergarten – Grade 12

Dubai International Academy
Near Jebel Ali Race Course, Emirates Hills, 04 3684111
admissions@diadubai.com, www.diadubai.com
Kindergarten – Grade 12

GEMS Wellington International School
Sheikh Zayed Road, 04 3486575, registrar@wisdubai.sch.ae
www.wellingtoninternationalschool.com
Kindergarten – Grade 12

Greenfield Community School
Behind Courtyard by Marriott, Green Community, 04 8856600
info@gcschool.ae, www.gcschool.ae
Kindergarten – Grade 12

Jumeirah English Speaking School
Arabian Ranches, 04 3619019, jess@jess.sch.ae www.jess.sch.ae
Kindergarten – Grade 13

Jumeirah English Speaking School
Near Safa Park, Jumeirah, 04 3945515, jess@jess.sch.ae, www.jess.sch.ae
Kindergarten – Grade 6

Repton School Dubai
Nad Al Sheba 3, 04 4269393, info@reptondubai.org, www.reptondubai.org
Kindergarten – Grade 12

Uptown School
Near Uptown Mall, Mirdif, 04 2886270, fdharsey@uptownprimary.ae
www.uptownprimary.ae
Kindergarten – Grade 5

Chapter 20

Restaurants

Dubai has quickly become one of the leading culinary destinations, on a par with London, Paris and New York. The variety of cuisine available in Dubai clearly represents the array of cultures inhabiting the city. You will be tempted by the local Arabic restaurants, but the choice is endless.

Whichever cuisine you fancy, you will certainly be satisfied and well rewarded. There are various chains, and other stand-alone restaurants, often located in the opulent hotels. This section highlights various restaurants organised by cuisine type.

General food prices in Dubai

The cheapest food around would be a local *shawarma* – around Dhs5–10. An Indian curry in a local restaurant in, say, Deira will also be around Dhs10. If you're just grabbing a sandwich for lunch, it will cost Dhs21 and a jacket potato around Dhs25. If you go to a mid-range restaurant, your main course may cost Dhs30–50 and at a high-end eatery it may cost anything from Dhs80 to over Dhs150. What really bumps up your bill at the restaurant is alcohol, though alcohol is generally only served in restaurants and bars attached to a hotel.

Bookings

If you're eating at a mid- to high-end restaurant especially on Thursday, Friday and Saturday nights, you should definitely book a few days in advance. Some popular restaurants get booked up very quickly, so call early.

For the health-conscious

It's certainly possible to be healthy anywhere you are, if you really want to be, but whether or not a city lends itself to assist you in that mission is a different matter. In Dubai, you may not have the same ranges and varieties as in London, but you certainly have choices and can choose to be healthy. At normal supermarkets, there are the low-fat and skimmed-milk options and you can get some organic food, albeit a small range. There are cafés and lunch spots that can be kind on your belly – Limetree Café (04 3498498), More Café (04 2830224) and Organic Foods and Café (04 4340577) to name a few (see pp 283, 284).

Vegetarian food

- Dubai caters well for vegetarians from a good range of foods in most of the supermarkets and choices in almost all the restaurants except, of course, seafood restaurants and steakhouses.

- In terms of supermarkets, Carrefour is large and well stocked with all the vegetables, the Choitrams and Spinneys supermarket chains also have good stocks and carry frozen vegetarian food such as Linda McCartney, Quorn and Amy's Vegan foods. Spinneys also sell vegetarian food from the Tesco range in the UK. You'll be sure to find some great vege things at Organic Foods and Café which is in both Dubai Mall and Greens (04 4340577, 043617974). Enjoy organic breads, ice creams and lots of other dishes while you do a bit of home shopping.

- For vitamin supplements or other vegetarian foods, Holland and Barrett in Town Centre Mall on Jumeirah Beach Road is pretty good, as are the health shops you'll find in other malls.

- As far as restaurants are concerned, there are some Indian restaurants that cook only vegetarian food, but other than that, most of the restaurants around Dubai have some options on their menus for vegetarians. If they don't, you can request them to prepare something specially for you as they have probably served other vegetarians before. For pure vegetarian restaurants that serve a more European fare, there's the recently-opened Little Italy in Bur Dubai and for fine dining, Magnolia in Al Qasr (04 3666155). Needless to say, avoid the steakhouses!

HOW THIS GUIDE IS ORGANISED

Restaurants listed in this section are organised according to cuisine type and the price guide (in dollars) is given according to the approximate cost of one person's meal (1 starter, 1 main and 1 drink). The following is the guideline for prices:

- Under Dhs100 = $
- Dhs100–200 = $$
- Dhs200–300 = $$$
- Dhs300–500 = $$$$

AMERICAN

Applebee's $
Sheikh Zayed Road, 04 343 7755

Casual dining with large portions of sizzling fajitas, sour cream, salad and guacamole. Finish off with a decadent sticky toffee pudding.

Billy Blues $
Rydges Plaza, 04 3982272

With American décor and a lively atmosphere, you can enjoy large platters of steaks and barbeques.

Chili's $
Various locations, 04 2828484

A casual, lively atmosphere where you'll get fries and nachos and all things greasy but yummy. End with a brownie and ice cream.

Go West $$$

Jumeirah Beach Hotel, 04 4068733

With a fun, lively and colourful atmosphere, Go West offers steaks and Tex-Mex, and big portions of everything.

Gourmet Burger Kitchen $

Various locations, 04 3637401

From London, this burger place has fresh produce, a great choice of toppings and wholesome fries. It's healthy fast food served in a lounge setting.

Planet Hollywood $$

Wafi City, 04 3244100

A loud and fun, movie-themed place to lunch or dine with kids. The menu is as you'd expect in any other Planet Hollywood – large portions and a few vegetarian options.

TGI Friday's $$$

Mall of Emirates, 04 3410030

This international restaurant has a cheerful atmosphere, is great for families and groups and has a wide selection of steaks, ribs, pasta, pizza and fantastic desserts.

ARABIC

Almaz by Momo $$

Mall of the Emirates, 04 4098877

Tucked away in Harvey Nichols, this atmospheric restaurant serves traditional Moroccan and a good fusion of Middle Eastern dishes. Makes for a great lunch away from the hoardes in the mall.

Al Nafoorah $$$

Emirates Towers Hotel, 04 3198088

It might be pricey, but you'll get some exceptionally tasty, authentic Lebanese cuisine, which will always impress. Try the excellent hot and cold mezzeh dishes and enjoy *shisha* on the outdoor terrace.

Al Qasr $$

Dubai Marine Beach Resort and Spa, 04 3461111

A relaxed meal with Lebanese and Middle Eastern delights overlooking the garden, swimming pools and the beach with belly dancers and Arabic music.

Ayam Zaman $$$

Royal Ascot, Bur Dubai, 04 3558500

Designed in the form of a cave and has live Arabian music playing at night. There are belly dancing troupes, violinists as well as singers.

Ever tried a *Shawarma*?

Just as the English have fish and chips, Dubai has *shawarma* – grilled meat (fresh off the rotating skewer) and salad wrapped in Arabic bread, topped with some pickles, tomatoes, onions and fries. It's certainly worth a try and one of the best places to find them is Al Diyafa Street, which has a number of *shawarma* joints.

Picnic Home (opposite Musallah Tower in Bur Dubai), which has been around since 1977, has the best *shawarmas* in Dubai as well as the best roasted chicken. **Al Mallah** (04 3984723) is also very famous for its excellent large *shawarma* topped with lots of garlic sauce and fruit juices as does **Sea Shell Caféteria** (04 3989920, behind Diyafa Street), **Jabal Al Noor** (04 3989800, Diyafah Street) and Ijaza (04 3444874, Jumeirah Beach Road).

You'll generally find the real deal in Deira and Satwa, albeit on the go. Then, of course, there are the well known restaurant chains such as **Zaatar W Zeit**, **Saj Express** and **Automatic**.

Automatic $

Various locations, 04 3214465

For years now, the Automatic has been serving great Arabic food in the region. With a large range of *mezze* and salad, you could make a meal of this alone.

Café Arabesque $$$

Park Hyatt Hotel, 04 6021234

Delicious, Arabian food served in an vibrant, Arabesque atmosphere with elegant décor and stunning views of Dubai Creek. Enjoy the freshly baked breads straight out of the wood-fired oven and the extensive list of *mezze* dishes.

Best Lebanese cuisine

Al Hallab $

Mall of the Emirates, 04 282 3388

Excellent service, fresh hot bread, fine cuisine at affordable prices. They do delicious daily specials. Don't miss out on the fantastic lentil soup, and for mains, try the *siyadiye*, a Lebanese speciality of rice cooked with fish with tahini, lemon, coriander and pine nuts.

Arz Lebanon $

Near Burjuma, opposite Spinneys, 04 3964466

If you like *fattoush*, you'll find the best in Arz Lebanon. The mixed starters dish is particularly good as well as stuffed chicken for main course.

Fakhreldine $$$

Movenpick Hotel, Bur Dubai, 04 3350505

This is a classic Lebanese restaurant with an extensive menu and a fantastic atmosphere with impressive décor and belly dancer.

Flooka $$
Dubai Marine Beach Resort and Spa, 04 3461111

This nice diner has a comprehensive selection of Lebanese *mezze* and fresh fish, which you choose yourself.

Best Lebanese sweets

Al Baba

Main branch opposite Deira City Centre, 04 295 2007

A nice quiet place where you can sit, have tea and select something from the huge choice of different *baklawas*. Make sure you try Al Baba's excellent *knafe*, a famous Lebanese pastry.

Mezza House $$
Downtown Dubai, 04 4205444

This delightful restaurant with fantastic *mezze* is tucked away in Old Town residences. The authentic Arabic atmosphere is complemented by smoking *shisha* pipes.

Shimmers $$$
Mina A' Salam, 04 3368888, (closed from June to August due to the summer heat)

A relaxed romantic escape with *alfresco* dining right on the beach and views of the Burj Al Arab. Don't miss out on the spicy tomato and lemongrass soup.

Shoo Fee Ma Fee $$$
Souk Madinat Jumeirah, 04 3668888

An elegant dinner spot with a terrace where you can *shisha* away. Select from the range of Moroccan and Arabic dishes.

Tagine $$$

The One and Only Royal Mirage, 04 3999999

With a colourful and warm Moroccan atmosphere, Tagine serves up some excellent and authentic cuisine, with crisp salads, garlic zucchini and delicious couscous dishes. Portions are large so don't over-order.

Times of Arabia $$$

Souk Madinat Jumeirah, 04 3686044

Sophisticated and grand with décor inspired by history, Times of Arabia boasts great Arabic *mezzeh* (slightly overpriced) and affordable wines.

ASIAN

Asiana $$$

Raffles Hotel, Wafi, 04 3249888

A sophisticated and atmospheric setting for lunch or dinner, Asiana offers dishes from Indonesia, Japan, Malaysia, Thailand and Vietnam. You can watch the cooks prepare culinary delights in the open kitchen or sit out on the terrace in the evening.

Bamboo Lagoon $$$

JW Marriott, Deira, 04 6077977

The buffet has various stalls with a range of fantastic Oriental dishes. You'll get everything from *sushi* and *teriyaki* to curries, seafood and noodles.

Beachcombers $$

Jumeirah Beach Hotel, 04 4068750

Live-cooking stations and delicious curries, *satay* and stir-fries are great, but what's so special about Beachcombers is its stunning beachfront location with fantastic views of Burj Al Arab. They also have a separate children's menu and a supervised play area.

Eauzone $$

One and Only Royal Mirage, Dubai Marina, 04 3999999

Overlooking the Arabian gulf and tranquil pool, Eauzone's intimate setting is one for romance. Indulge in modern cuisine with an Asian twist. There are good vegetarian and seafood choices. Finish off with a chocolate samosa.

The Noodle House $$

Various locations, Emirates Towers (04 3198758)

A buzzing atmosphere, bench-seating, an open kitchen, self-tick menu and modern design makes Noodle House a favourite. The food is quick and tasty.

Wox $$

Grand Hyatt, Umm Hurair, 04 3172700

You can sit around the noodle bar and enjoy live, sizzling cooking while waiting for your favourite dishes.

CHINESE

China Club $$

Radisson SAS Deira, 04 2057333

Very popular for its delicious *dim sum*, China Club has elegant ambience and tasty Chinese dishes.

China Sea $$

Maktoum Road, Deira, 04 2959816

This large restaurant serves large portions and the most authentic Chinese fare in Dubai. With live cooking, you can pick and choose what you want and it will be stirred and spiced up in no time.

Chopstix $$

Marco Polo Hotel, Deira, 04 2720000

It's not plush, but it is flavoursome. From *kimchi,* the Korean national dish and superb Shanghai prawns to burned-garlic fried rice, you'll get wonderful Chinese food here.

Chinese Treasure $$

Al Nasr Leisureland, Oud Metha, 04 336 2525

A restaurant with authentic décor and tasty Chinese food. It's great value for money. Try the spicy peanut prawns.

Da Shi Dai $

Murjan Building, Jumeirah Beach Residence 04 4264636, Uptown Mirdif, 04 2888314

Freshly prepared *dim sum* at a unique *dim sum* station. The menu is varied and each dish is a snack, served in a modern 'small eats' format. It also caters very well for children.

Lan Kwai Fong $

Opposite Movenpick Hotel, Oud Metha, 04 3353680

You'll get large portions at very good prices. The diners are mostly Chinese, so you know you're getting the real deal. And it's MSG-free.

Shang Palace $$

Shangri-La Hotel, Sheikh Zayed Road, 04 3438888

Top-notch Chinese food at rather high prices. But then it is the Shangri-La. The succulent Beijing Duck is worth a try.

Steam Sum Dim Sum $
Dubai Festival City, 800 78326

An attractive and stylish restaurant with fantastic steamed dumplings and great mocktails.

The Noble House $$$
Raffles Hotel, Wafi, 04 3149731

Brilliant setting, great food. A waiter pouring tea behind his back from a long-spouted pot and the ice cream which has dry ice rising from the bowl will wow you.

Zheng He's $$$
Mina A'Salam, 04 3666159

Next to the water, this is a stylish restaurant; great for some delectable Chinese delicacies – fantastic *dim sum* and other starters with tangy sauces.

EUROPEAN

Al Muntaha $$$$
Burj Al Arab, 04 3017442

High up on the 27th floor with breathtaking views of the sea, the sophisticated Al Muntaha serves Mediterranean cuisine.

Apres $$
Mall of the Emirates, 04 3412575

A stylish cocktail bar and cosy restaurant serving filling food including steaks and pastas. The views of the indoor ski slopes, give a feel of an Alpine ski lodge.

Café Chic $$$

Le Meridien, Garhoud, 04 7022710

This multi award-winning restaurant offers fine, French dining wich pleasant décor and mellow jazz. The food is impressive and you will have small treats, like a soup before your ordered courses.

Da Gama $$

The Aviation Club, Garhoud, 04 2823636

This resembles a Portuguese farmhouse and has an authentic European feel. You'll get a bite of Tex-Mex, Italian and some Portugese. Taste the excellent red house wine and relax in the bar area upstairs.

Glasshouse $$$

Hilton Creek, Deira, 04 2127550

A classy atmosphere with dark wood and glass walls. Modern Mediterranean cuisine, tasty and good, but not so expensive. End with the yummy banoffee cheesecake.

Best fish and chips in town

London Fish and Chips
Ibn Battuta Mall
04 3669939

The Fish and Chip Room
Murjan, Jumeirah Beach Residence
04 4270443

Carter's
Wafi Pyramids
04 3244100

Fish and Co.
Al Ghurair Mall, Deira
04 2270252

Belgian Beer Café
Intercontinental, Festival City
04 7011127

The Irish Village
The Aviation Club
04 2824750

Magnolia $$
Al Qasr, 04 3666155

This is a fine-dining vegetarian restaurant serving delicious salads and soups as well as spinach risotto, potato gnocchi and a millet tofu cake. End with a chocolate tart.

Reflets Par Pierre Gagnaire $$$
Intercontinental Festival City, 04 7011111

French chef Peirre Gagnaire entered the Dubai dining scene with this restaurant in 2009. It has a sleek and almost funky design with purple carpet. You'll find some amazing French classics here.

Rhodes Mezzanine $$$$
Grosvenor House, Dubai Marina, 04 3176862

With white-leather walls, luminous Perspex screens and pink and orange furniture, this restaurant is a fusion of modern furniture and classic British dishes. A masterpiece of celebrity chef Gary Rhodes.

Rivington Grill $$$
Souk Al Bahar, Downtown Dubai, 04 4230903

A recently opened, thoroughly British restaurant in Souk Al Bahar with fish and chips, lamb chops, Welsh rarebit, Yorkshire pudding and anything else that's really British.

Verre $$$$
Hilton Dubai Creek, Deira, 04 2127551

Chef Gordon Ramsay's first restaurant outside the UK, this is an elegant setting with exquisite European and French cuisine. It's pricey but faultless, though not one for the vegetarians.

Vu's $$$$
Jumeirah Emirates Towers, 04 3198771

With innovative European, French and Italian cuisine, superb service and stylish design, this is a top spot for a sophisticated lunch or dinner. It also has great cocktails and bar snacks, not to mention that you're up on the 50th floor.

INDIAN

Aangan $$
Dhow Palace Hotel, Bur Dubai, 04 3599992

Dark rusty wood, candle-lit, live traditional music and tasty food make this one of the top Indian eateries. Try the *tawa kebabs, roomali roti,* thick *dal makhni* and end with one of the delicious *kulfi* ice-creams.

Appa Kadai $
Karama, opp Lulu's, 04 3348030

You'll find the best *appam* here – wafer-thin pancakes which you can fill with egg, *sambhar* or chopped tomato and onion *masalas.*

Antique Bazaar $$
Four Points by Sheraton, Bur Dubai, 04 3977444

A leader of Indian restaurants, Antique Bazaar is intimate with live, soothing music and a range of mouth-watering flavours. Each table tells a different story.

Asha's $$
Wafi Pyramids, 04 3240000

Famous Indian singer Asha Bhosle owns this restaurant. With modern, cosy interiors, an outdoor terrace and tasty north-western Indian dishes, you won't be disappointed.

Ashiana $$
Sheraton Hotel and Towers, 04 2071707

Northern Indian specialities with aromatic and spicy dishes and classical Indian music playing in the background.

Bombay by the Bay $$
Dubai Marina, 04 4297979

This new restaurant offers delicious spicy Indian food in a contemporary yet Mughalite setting. The outdoor terrace is ideal for alfresco dining, offering views of the Marina.

Bombay Chowpatty $
Karama, 04 3964937

One of the best and cheapest for authentic Indian fast food with a huge variety of snacks and juices. Enjoy the ambience inside or relax outside. Try the hot *puris* and the *chai* here is fantastic.

Coconut Grove $
Rydges Plaza, 04 3982222

Up on the ninth floor in Satwa, this is a hidden gem. You'll find astoundingly good South Indian food and other dishes from Kerala, Goa and Sri Lanka.

Daily $
Bur Dubai, near Burjuman, 04 3373123

This is no fine dining, but if you want authentic Pakistani food, this is the place. The *tikkas* are simply fantastic and don't miss out on the *biryani* and *kadais*. But go early – it's packed and the *biryani* runs out quickly.

Gazebo $
Al Mankhool Road, Bur Dubai, 04 3598555

Celebrating cuisines of Lucknow and Hyderabad with rich spicy dishes, devilishly hot curries, all for low prices. Try the *paneer tikka*.

Govinda's $
Karama, 04 3960088

This purely vegetarian restaurant serves sumptuous and traditional Indian food and fresh juices, with a friendly ambience.

Handi $$
Taj Palace Hotel, Deira, 04 2232222

Ornate wooden décor and *tandoori* ovens create a regal Mughalite atmosphere. Taste the rich cuisines of northwestern India.

Romantic dinners

Amaseena, Lebanese
Ritz-Carlton, Dubai Marina, 04 3994000

Pierchic, Seafood
Al Qasr Hotel, Madinat Jumeirah, 04 3668888

Cappana Nuova, Italian
Dubai Marine Beach Resort and Spa, 04 3461111

Pai Thai, Thai
Al Qasr, Madinat Jumeirah, 04 3666740

Segreto, Italian
Souk Madinat Jumeirah, 04 3668888

Shimmers, Arabic
Mina A'Salam, 04 3368888

Majlis Al Bahar
Burj Al Arab, 04 3017600

Or why not make something, or get a take-away and go to a hidden place in Safa Park, where you can have a serene picnic all alone ... or by the beach, if you don't mind the sand.

Indego $$$$

Grosvenor House, Dubai Marina, 04 3176000

The consultant chef here is the Michelin-starred genius Vineet Bhatia. Indego has a suave ambience and definitely worth going on a special day. The lamb shank *rogan josh* is worth a try.

It's Mirchi $$

Ramee Royal Hotel, Karama, 04 3344088

The Bollywood tunes, dancing, Friday karaoke and delicious Indian curries give a real taste of India. There's also a huge buffet.

Nina $$$

Arabian Court, One and Only Royal Mirage, 04 3999999

A charming restaurant offering modern Indian-European fusion cuisine, worth saving for a special occasion.

Ravi's $

Satwa, 04 3315353

Forget the décor, this famous Pakistani diner is about what's on your plate and the cheap prices. Try some of the hot Punjabi dishes and juicy *kebabs* – a spicy delight to the palate.

Rasoi $$

Coral Deira Hotel, 04 2128267

Recently relaunched Mughal restaurant with grand, regal interiors by French fashion designer François Desroches and a live band. Delve into Mughlai delicacies.

Savarna Bhavan $

Karama, 04 3345252

If you're looking for quick South Indian vegetarian food, especially *idlis* and *mendu vada*, you'll be sure to find it here at very cheap prices.

Tanour $
Opposite Century Hotel, Jumeirah, 04 3935990

With subdued lighting, have a private meal with good, reasonably-priced food. Though it's a small restaurant, dishes are quite large, so be warned.

The Bombay Brasserie $
Marco Polo Hotel, Deira, 04 2720000

Concentrating on North Indian delicacies, fish is the speciality here and portions are large. With live entertainment and Mughal court ambience fit for royalty.

The Rupee Room $$
Dubai Marina Walk, 04 3905755

Savour the chunky meat and rich spicy curries, chicken *tikka masala* and onion *bhajis*.

Urban Tadka $
Karama, 04 3961395

Go at night and this place will be buzzing. While the mains are good, Urban Tadka is known more for its snacks and *chaats*.

INTERNATIONAL

Al Dawaar $$$
Hyatt Regency, Deira, 04 2096697

This is Dubai's only rotating restaurant and has a superb international buffet. Don't miss out on their incredible circular dessert buffet.

Boardwalk $$
Creek Golf Club, Al Garhoud, 04 2956000

Enjoy creekside dining with great views. Burgers, chips, salads ...The food's fine, but it's the view that makes this place popular.

Glasshouse $$$
Hilton Dubai Creek, 04 2271111

With a Mediterranean menu overseen by chef Gordon Ramsay and floor-to-ceiling windows overlooking the Creek, this is quite a winner.

Sezzam $$
Mall of the Emirates, 04 3413600

A casual, though slightly busy, family setting with many cuisines including Asian, Chinese, kebabs, burgers, pizzas and more.

Spectrum on One $$$$
Fairmont, 04 3118000

Serving cuisines from all around the world, Spectrum on One has a spacious and attractive setting. The perfect place for large groups.

Spice Island $$$
Renaissance Hotel, Deira, 04 2625555

The food stations here serve a variety of cuisines including Chinese, Japanese, Italian and Mexican. But there might be queues.

Teatro $$$
Towers Rotana, Trade Centre, 04 3438000

The food is great, with a variety of five different cuisines, fantastic service, stylish interiors and a pleasant ambience, though a little busy.

The Market Place $$$
JW Marriott Hotel, Deira, 04 2624444

It's a bustling atmosphere with open kitchens and live-cooking. There's everything from *sushi* and steaks to pastas and curries.

ITALIAN

Al Fresco $$$
Crowne Plaza Dubai, 04 3311111

This value-for-money restaurant with traditional *antipasto, zuppa* and pasta, is a great spot for lunch. Watch the chefs twirling the pizza bases while you wait.

Andiamo! $$$
Grand Hyatt Dubai, 04 3172222

With an open kitchen as the centerpiece of this warm venue, Andiamo offers authentic dishes at reasonable prices.

Bella Donna $$
Mercato Mall, 04 3447701

Taste authentic Italian cuisine including great homemade pastas in a casual environment overlooking Jumeirah Beach. Finish off with a tiramisu.

Bellucci $$
Wafi Mall, 04 3244777

Fresh pesto, freshly made pasta, delicious salads and seafood tagliatelle. It's real Italian and definitely worth a try.

Bussola $$$
Westin Dubai Mina Seyahi, 04 3993333

Sit outside on the wooden deck with a nice sea breeze and enjoy a pizza or order from the special *à la carte* menu downstairs. A romantic setting and makes for great *al fresco* dining.

Bice $$$

Hilton Dubai Jumeirah, 04 3991111

This award-winning, Italian eatery has delightful regional food and classy design. Enjoy freshly made pastas and pizzas and great wine.

Cappana Nuova $$$$

Dubai Marine Beach Resort and Spa, 04 3461111

With indoor and outdoor dining, you have amazing views of the Arabian Sea. A romantic setting with excellent Italian food.

Casa Mia $$$$

Le Meridien, Garhoud, 04 2824040

Right in the lively Meridien Village, the atmosphere is busy. So sit outside and enjoy the superbly traditional Italian food. End with crème brûlée.

Certo $$$

Radisson SAS Hotel, Dubai Media City, 04 3669111

Delicious wood-fired pizzas, freshly made pastas and a signature dish of *linguine*, you'll certainly savour the Italian food here. There's also an amazing selection of 500 wines from around the world!

Cucina $$

JW Marriott, Deira, 04 2624444

Enjoy the rustic old charm about this place as you taste Cucina's homemade pastas, wood-fired pizzas and yummy risottos.

Great areas to eat

Not sure what to eat and looking for a great outdoor atmosphere?

Century Village
Garhoud

A large courtyard with lit-up trees and fountains and restaurants spilling out – you'll feel like you're in Spain. There's great Italian, Portugese, *sushi*, Arabic and more ... and if you fancy heading to an English pub afterwards, Irish Village is right next door.

Le Meridien Village
Garhoud

Tucked away in the back of Le Meridien is a selection of great eateries with a lively atmosphere. There are French, Thai, Japanese and Italian– and the food is some of the best in Dubai. Head to Alpha or Warehouse afterwards, two top spots for lively nightlife.

The Walk at JBR
Jumeirah Beach Residences

This one's fairly new but go there on any night and it'll be busy! It's a very long outdoor stretch of restaurants, cafés and shops. Dinner in the Sky also took place here in May 2009, and should be coming back – so watch out for the table hanging high from a crane. Book with www.bluebanana.com if you want to experience this high-flying dining.

Dubai Marina

Much like The Walk at JBR, this one's on the Marina and most of it is indoor, looking onto the Marina. It's got a good selection of restaurants including Chinese, Indian and Italian.

Madinat *Souk* Jumeirah

This huge souk with winding lanes and shops galore is home to some of the best and most atmospheric restaurants. And the choice is ample! Whether for dinner, coffee, a trip to the theatre or just a roam around, the Madinat is a must for all.

Focaccia $$$
Hyatt Regency, Deira, 04 2091600

Offering beautiful views across the Arabian Gulf, Focaccia serves authentic pizzas, pastas and seafood in a Mediterranean villa setting.

La Moda $$$
Radisson SAS Deira Creek, 04 2057033

This trendy restaurant with chic and stylish décor boasts a menu with all that's good about Italian cuisine. For dessert, try strawberry fondue with amaretto lady fingers.

La Vigna $$
Century Village, 04 2959300

Owned by Umberto, a famous Italian chef, La Vigna offers authentic Italian cuisine with homemade pasta and excellent wines. Sit outside and enjoy the European village-like atmosphere.

Ronda Locatelli $$$$
Atlantis, Palm Jumeirah, 04 4260750

With Michelin-star chef Giorgio Locatelli, you're guaranteed great Italian food from delicious raviolis to thin pizzas.

Segreto $$$$
Souk Madinat Jumeirah, 04 3668888

This is sophisticated Italian fine dining. There's a large outdoor bar area where you can sip cocktails *al fresco*. The dim lighting and beautiful decor make it quite the romantic restaurant.

Verdi $$$

Taj Palace, Deira, 04 2232222

You'll find more than 40 kinds of freshly made pizza along with pasta and risotto dishes from Rome, Milan and Sicily all with a lively Italian ambience.

Sweet treats

Be dazzled by sweets and chocolates, flavoured popcorn and ice cream at **Candylicious** (04 3308700) in Dubai Mall. With 10,000 square feet, it's the largest confectioner in the world.

Dubai's gone crazy for cupcakes. There's **Kitsch Cupcakes** (Jumeirah Beach Rd, 04 3956963), **Sugar Daddy's cupcakes** (Village Mall, Jumeirah Beach Rd, 04 3448204) and New York's very own **Magnolia** bakery (Bloomingdales, Dubai Mall) is the most recent addition.

Dubai has recently caught on to the US-style frozen yoghurt fashion. The latest opening is **Forty Carrots** in Bloomingdale's (Dubai Mall, 04 3505333), straight from New York. Mall of the Emirates houses **Pinkberry** (04 3411378), another famous brand, which boasts pomegranate and green tea flavours. **Red Mango** (04 2328887), currently in Festival Centre, is also opening soon in Dubai Mall. The selection at Dubai Mall seems endless, with yet another – **The Frozen Yoghurt Factory**. And lastly, if you're at Dubai Festival City, try out **Yogurberry** (04 2328289).

JAPANESE

Kiku $$$

Le Meridien, Al Garhoud, 04 2824040

Brimming with Japanese guests, you'll get the real Japanese deal at Kiku. Choose from *sushi, sashimi,* fresh soups, *tempura* and *teppanyaki* and other delightful dishes.

Kitsune $$$$

The Fairmont, 04 3327660

Enjoy contemporary Japanese cuisine prepared by award-winning chef Hiro Nakamura. Along with excellent *sushi* and *sashimi*, you'll also find lobster salad, fried eel and other gastronomic delights.

Manga Sushi $$
Beach Park Plaza, Jumeirah Beach Road, 04 3428300

This has a quirky Japanese-style layout and some of the best *sushi* in Dubai. During the meal, they'll even come and perform a song for you.

Miyako $$$
Hyatt Regency, Deira, 04 3172222

There is of course *sushi* and *sashimi* at this outstanding intimate Japanese eatery, but there are other tasty dishes such as crumbed fried oysters.

Nobu $$$$
Atlantis The Palm, 04 4260760

This famous restaurant needs no introduction. It's one of the best and expensive places to dine with fantastic *sushi* and other Japanese dishes and has dark, beautiful and layered interiors.

Ping Pong $$
Dubai Mall, 04 3399088

This popular restaurant from London, serving steamed parcels of loveliness, has recently opened in Dubai. It's great for delicious little dumplings, sticky rice rolls, tasty mocktails and the flowering teas.

Shogun $$
Al Ghurair Centre, 04 2285568

Right in Deira, this restaurant serves Korean and Japanese cuisine. You'll also notice it's packed with Koreans when you walk in – always a good sign.

Sumo Sushi and Bento $$

Dubai Media City 04 3914141/ Town Centre, Jumeirah, 800SUMO(7866)
Aviation Club, Garhoud 04 2830622/ Dubai Healthcare City, 04 4380661

You'll get fresh *sushi* and *bento* boxes, a great take-away or lunch option. They even make corporate platters for events.

Sushi Sushi $$

Century Village, Al Garhoud, 04 2829908

The Japanese and Oriental food here is great. They serve everything from delicious soups, *sushi* and *teriyaki* to *teppanyaki* stir fries, noodles, and salads.

Tokyo@The Towers $$

Emirates Towers, 04 3198088

At this calm and suave restaurant with wood columns, you can either sit at the *sushi* bar, the live-cooking *teppanyaki* table or just at a normal table. The *sushi* here is fresh and delicious, but so is the *teppanyaki* and every other amazing Japanese dish on the menu. End with a delicious homemade red bean ice cream.

Wagamama $

Al Fattan JBR 04 3995900/ Crowne Plaza, 04 3056060
The Greens, 04 3615757

Fantastic oriental dishes for vegetarians and meat-eaters alike, served at reasonable prices.

Zuma $$$$

DIFC, Sheikh Zayed Road, 04 4255660

This is a hip and minimalist fine dining restaurant serving fantastic Japanese including *sushi* and *tempura*. Portions aren't large and prices are rather high but you'll certainly be satisfied with whatever you order.

MEXICAN

Cactus Cantina $$

Rydges Plaza Hotel, Satwa, 04 3982274

Don't fill yourself up on the free baskets of potato chips and salsa dip. You'll get great Tex-Mex staples such as *nachos, burritos, tacos* and *fajitas.*

Cactus Jacks $$$

Millennium Airport Hotel, Garhoud, 04 2823464

This bright and lively restaurant has fantastic Mexican food and theme nights during the week, with a resident DJ.

El Chico $

Jumeirah Beach Residence, 04 4233828

You have to order fresh *guacamole* as they make it right in front of you. There's everything from *fajitas* and *burritos* to *tacos* and *nachos*. The chocolate cake is pretty deadly and large and, of course, delicious.

Maria Bonita's Taco Shop $$

Umm Suqeim, 04 3954454
Green Community, 04 8853188

Great food at good prices. Speak to the two parrots sitting outside while you enjoy *quesadillas*, soups, *tacos*, salads and beans.

Maya $$$$

Le Royal Meridien Beach Resort and Spa, 04 3165550

This is Dubai's first fine-dining Mexican restaurant with brilliant *al fresco* dining options. You will find more than just the Mexican staples here.

SEAFOOD

Amwaj $$$$

Shangri-La Hotel, 04 3438888

A stylish, blue setting with a menu of fresh international seafood. It's great for a business lunch or even an intimate dinner. With fresh fish flown in from France, gorgeous décor and delicious desserts, Amwaj will not disappoint.

Dinner Cruises

Al Boom Tourist Village

04 3243000, www.alboom.ae

One of the pioneers of *dhow* cruises in Dubai – they're famous for the event halls they have. For the 2-hour cruise, it's Dhs176 per person including dinner with appetizers, meat barbeque and seafoods.

Al Mansour Dhow

04 2057333

For the 2-hour cruise, it's Dhs135 per person including a welcome drink and Arabic buffet. Alcoholic beverages also available separately.

Bateaux Dubai

04 3994994

This plush floating restaurant, encased in glass so you can gaze at the stars, allows you to dine in style whilst enjoying the stunning views. You can choose from a combination of Eastern and Western dishes, and if it's romance you're after, there's a private deck.

Creek Cruises

04 3939860, www.creekcruises.com

This cruise and dinner includes an international buffet dinner with drinks, tea and coffee. For the 2-hour cruise, it costs Dhs150 per person.

Al Mahara $$$$
Burj Al Arab, 04 3017164

This sophisticated signature restaurant is a memorable experience with a submarine ride to the dining area and then a cylindrical floor-to-ceiling aquarium once inside. The dishes are tasty, though expensive.

Aquara $$
Dubai Marine Yacht Club, 04 3627934

Sit on the terrace in this romantic spot overlooking the gorgeous Dubai Marina waterways. Aquara is also great for Friday brunch – there's a live *sushi* and *sashimi* station, a stir-fry station and a seafood bar.

Bu Qtair Caféteria $
Near Burj Al Arab behind Chalet restaurant

This little side stall is a real hidden gem where you'll get the best fried fish in a very natural outdoor Keralite environment. And you'll be eating the catch of the day – no menu. It's a squeeze and it's very cheap.

Fish Market $$$$
Radisson SAS, Deira, 04 2057333

With a lively and bustling atmosphere, this restaurant has an interesting concept. There's no menu. All you do is head over to the fish counter, pick what you want and the chefs do the rest.

Ossiano $$$$
Atlantis Hotel, 04 4260770

This is Michelin star chef, Santi Santamaria's, first restaurant outside of Spain. Sit by the huge aquarium and savour the absolutely amazing food. The prices might pinch, but it's well worth it.

Pierchic $$$$

Al Qasr Hotel, Madinat Jumeirah, 04 3666739

Get a table outside, especially if you're looking for a highly romantic evening. It has brilliant views of the sea, Atlantis and Burj Al Arab ... and of course, fresh and delectable seafood.

Salmontini $$$

Mall of the Emirates, Al Barsha, 04 3410222

A family friendly restaurant with excellent salmon tartare and great homemade smoked salmon. Enjoy the views of the Ski Dubai slopes and the great choice of wines.

STEAKHOUSES

JW's Steakhouse $$$$

JW Marriott Hotel, Deira, 04 6077977

Sophisticated dining with warm interiors offering certified Angus steaks and fresh seafood fished straight from the tank, the best from land and sea.

Meat Co. $$$

Souk Al Bahar, Old Town, 04 4200737

With views of the Burj Al Arab and a simple menu of different steak options, Meat Co. has great food and wine.

Manhattan Grill $$$$

Grand Hyatt, 04 3171234

If you love meat and steaks, you won't be disappointed here. This rather spacious restaurant has booths and large tables, so it's great for a group of people or a business meal.

Rib Room $$$$
Emirates Towers Hotel, 04 3300000

Savour succulent steaks, fresh seafood and great wine in a very stylish setting.

Rare $$$$
Desert Palm, 04 3238888

Whether you sit on the balcony and enjoy the view of the fields or inside the warm interiors, you'll be sure to taste some of the best steaks in Dubai.

Ribs and Rumps $$
Dubai Mall, 04 4340468

Well-aged steaks, mixed grills, fresh seafood and large portions will certainly satisfy.

The Exchange Grill $$$
Fairmont Hotel, Sheikh Zayed Road, 04 3325555

One of the best steakhouses serving flavourful steaks in a relaxed, elegant setting and with a list of 250 wines.

THAI

Benjarong $$
Dusit Hotel, 04 3433333

The only Thai hotel in Dubai, this restaurant serves authentic Thai food. Up on the 24th floor, the views stretch over the desert.

Blue Elephant $$
Al Bustan Rotana, Garhoud, 04 2820000

Regarded as one of Dubai's finest Thai restaurants, Blue Elephant, like its famous London counterpart, offers excellent Thai food amidst waterfalls, flowers and greenery.

Pai Thai $$$$
Al Qasr, Madinat Jumeirah, 04 3666740

This is a peaceful, serene and very romantic restaurant, not least because you'll be brought here on an *abra*. Papaya salad, the usual spicy and tasty curries and *pad thai* are all great here.

Smiling BKK $
Next to Jumeirah Post Office, Jumeirah, 04 3496677

It might be a little difficult to find and it's a pretty dingy place, but the fantastic Thai food is well worth it. Sit in this rather funky, fun and arty setting and eat away.

Soi55 $
International City, France, P13, 04 4221235

Located in International City, this might seem a bit far, but if you're a Thai food lover, you're in for a treat. The décor is stylish and contemporary and the very authentic Thai cuisine is simply delicious.

Sukhothai $$
Le Meridien, Garhoud, 04 2170000

An old time favourite for Thai food lovers in Dubai. With delicious green and red curries, some good meat and seafood dishes, this will be a delectable meal.

Sumibiya $$$
Radisson SAS, Deira Creek, 04 2227171

This is a *yakiniku*-style restaurant with a grill fitted in your table so you can cook your own meat and fish – a fun way to interact with others. The Japanese food is tasty.

Thai Bistro $$
Dubai Marine Beach Resort and Spa, 04 3461111

One of the best Thai restaurants with relaxed ambience, indoor and outdoor seating and with a view of the landscaped gardens, swimming pools and the Arabian Sea.

Thai Chi $$
Wafi, Oud Metha, 04 3244100

As the name suggests, you'll find Chinese and Thai dishes here. You can go for a private meal in one of their rooms or sit outside and enjoy the lively atmosphere.

Thai Terrace $
Trade Centre Road, Bur Dubai, 04 3969356

This is a homely, cosy restaurant with tasty green and red curries, soups and noodles all at reasonable prices.

Thiptara $$$$
The Palace, Old Town, 04 4287961

A wonderful eatery with dim lighting and woods overlooks the hotel's gorgeous pool and offers stunning views of the Burj Khalifa. The Thai seafood, which is picked from a live aquarium, is Thiptara's speciality.

BEST FRIDAY BRUNCHES

Fridays in Dubai are the brunch day as you'll find out as soon as you get here. You may just think of brunch as a random word – a combination of breakfast and lunch at a slightly late hour, but in this city brunch is a social, relaxed, enjoyable Friday.

Sitting in pure decadence, navigating through the endless selection of dishes and enjoying the atmosphere for hours during the afternoon has become quite the pastime. And Dubaians expect a lot from their brunch – good food, lots of it, plenty to drink and a nice atmosphere. With the fantastic displays and gastronomic delights, what better than feast of indulgence after a week of hard work?

Dubai now has so many brunch spots to choose from that it's actually become a competitive sport to have the better buffet, to give more value for money, to have limitless amounts of food to devour.

One of my favourites has got to be the Intercontinental in Festival City. The relaxed mood, bright yet cosy decor, wood-fired fresh pizzas and array of salads make it the perfect place to chill out on a Friday. But wherever you go, just make sure it's on an empty stomach!

Al Dhiyafa, Habtoor Grand Resort and Spa

04 3995000
12:30pm–4pm, Dhs275 with wine, Dhs175 normal buffet, half-price for children 4–12yrs

The Prosecco Friday brunch blends Middle East delicacies with an international menu. It's fresh, healthy and wholesome.

Al Qasr, Madinat Jumeirah

04 3668888
12:30pm–4pm, Dhs495, Dhs395 under 21 yrs, Dhs220 under 12 yrs, free for under 4 yrs

With a hefty price tag, this is one you should save for a treat, and make sure you have an empty stomach. This brunch serves anything and everything you could possibly want. Fresh warm *pretzels*, brownies made in front of you, seafood, *sushi*, curries, fish and chips ... anything else? Well, rest assured you'll get it. There's a vast range of international cuisine. And it's a lively, loud, atmosphere.

Anise, InterContinental Dubai Festival City

04 7011128
12:30pm–3:30pm, Dhs395 with drinks, Dhs295 just buffet, half-price for children 5–12yrs, free for children below 5yrs

With a relaxing and stylish decor, Anise is the perfect way to unwind and enjoy the delectable food. With live cooking stations, delicious, fresh-out-of-the-oven pizzas, *sushi* station and salad counter, this is a sumptuous delight. Enjoy the chocolate fountain flavoured with hazelnut syrup, other tempting treats including cute little boxes of popcorn and a fantastic range of cheeses.

Aquara, Dubai Marina Yacht Club

04 3627900

12:30pm–3:30pm Dhs250 with alcohol, Dhs180 with non-alcoholic drinks, half-price for children

With the Marina backdrop and live DJ music, this makes a delectable Friday brunch. There's a live *sushi* and *sashimi* station, a stir-fry station and a seafood bar.

Beachcombers, Jumeirah Beach Hotel

04 4068999

12:30pm–4:30pm, Dhs225 with Pimms, Dhs185 just buffet, Dhs60 for children

Enjoy beautiful views of Burj Al Arab as you indulge in freshly prepared Asian cuisine with refreshing beverages at the beachside.

Blades and The Tea Lounge, Four Seasons Golf Club

04 6010101

12pm–3pm, Dhs365 with alcohol, Dhs285 without alcohol, Dhs165 for children 6–12yrs

Seafood, Mediterranean dishes and a chocolate fountain. A terrace for *al fresco* dining. For children, there's a special menu, face painting and games.

Ewaan, The Palace, Old Town

04 4287888

12pm–4pm, Dhs390 with alcohol, Dhs245 without alcohol, half-price for children 6–11yrs

Enjoy views of the tallest building while you sit for a long brunch with live cooking stations for waffles, crepes, pancakes and a line-up of other delicious delicacies.

Fazaris, The Address, Downtown Dubai

04 4368923

12:30pm–4pm, Dhs390 with alcohol, Dhs290 without alcohol, Dhs145 for children 6–11yrs

This is one decadent brunch and it's not cheap. With *foie gras*, lobster and langoustine on the menu, it caters to a rich palate. There's Japanese, Thai, Mediterranean, Indian and Arabic cuisine. The chocolate station with a plethora of chocolate desserts is one you can't miss.

JW Marriot, Deira

04 2624444

12pm–4pm, Dhs295 with alcohol, Dhs195 without alcohol, Dhs125 for children 4–14yrs

The best from Asia, Europe and beyond, the JW brunch offers you Asian *tapas* from The Bamboo Lagoon restaurant, Indian and Arabic dishes from Market Square restaurant and sausage salad with gherkins from the German corner, Hofbrauhaus. You'll also find carving stations and seafood salads.

Market Café, Grand Hyatt

04 3171234

12:30pm–3:30pm, Dhs170 with soft drinks, half price for children 6–11yrs

Set in the lush indoor rainforest garden restaurant at the Grand Hyatt, this brunch is exciting with its five open kitchens. Children will also be entertained with the food being tossed and cooked in front of them. Tasty Italian pastas, Arabic dishes, an extensive seafood counter, Indian cuisine and international desserts.

The Cellar, The Aviation Club

04 2829333

12pm–3:15pm, Dhs135 with 1 glass of wine, Dhs50 for children below 12yrs

This is an *à la carte* international brunch in a relaxed and elegant contemporary restaurant with a rustic character, with views of the Irish Village lake. The Cellar offers Dubai's widest selection of wines, and they've recently introduced a Sunday brunch.

The Tee Lounge, Four Seasons Golf Club
04 6010101
12pm–3pm, Dhs365 with alcohol, Dhs285 without alcohol, Dhs165 for children 6–12yrs

Enjoy a wide selection of international dishes and live cooking stations underneath the atrium's swirling glass roof. There's chilled salads, Arabian sensations, a seafood bar, carving and soup stations, and international main courses. Desserts include waffles and blueberry cheesecake. They even have activities to keep the children entertained.

Traiteur, Park Hyatt Dubai
04 6021234
12:30pm–4pm, Dhs550 per person, with champagne

The setting is just beautiful – overlooking yachts moored by the waters. Traiteur serves modern European cuisine, and is classy and stylish and calls for such guests. With theatre-style views of the kitchen, this brunch can be highly interesting. And at the end, you have a delicious array of sweet treats. To complete the day, wander outdoors to the terrace and enjoy the live jazz tunes.

BEST CAFÉS FOR LUNCH

There are plenty of places you can grab a coffee in Dubai, but only a handful which are slightly different, which have a great atmosphere, and where you feel great just hanging out. From the New York style Central Perk to the traditionally Arabic atmosphere of Basta Arts Café, you have quite a quirky selection. Some of the cafés listed below are more food-orientated, hence should be with the restaurants, but they're fantastic luncheon spots, where you can enjoy some wholesome food with friends. The latest to the collection is O Concept which is only partly a café. It also has a gallery, sells clothes and has other random exhibits.

Basta Art Café
Al Fahidi Street, Bur Dubai, 04 3535071
8am–10pm daily

Basta Art Café is set in a leafy courtyard in the historic Bastakiya area and has a uniquely traditional atmosphere. The food's tasty – if you come at lunchtime, try the *halloumi* salad or a jacket potato, but portions are large. And if you're into fresh juices and smoothies, then try Flamingo or Berry Berry, and end with Moroccan tea. There is also a gallery and shop selling local arts and crafts.

Circle

Beach Park Plaza, Jumeirah Beach Road, 04 3428177
Dubai Media City, 04 3915170
8am–midnight daily

HandH bagels are famous in New York and they have now arrived here at Circle. So you will get every kind of bagel and they do taste great. Enjoy smoothies with low fat yoghurt, a hearty salad and cheesecake or any of the other delicious desserts. The interiors are modern, white, funky and spacious.

Emporio Armani Café

Mall of the Emirates, 04 3410591
11am–11:30pm daily

This is as fashionable as you'd expect an Armani café to be with modern, trendy interiors. It's definitely a cool place to hang out. With thin pizzas and pastas, healthy salads and other dishes, the Armani Café is good for lunch or even to try one of the delicious puddings.

Fashion Lounge

Jumeirah Beach Residence, 04 4270268
10am–11:30pm daily

This fusion of gallery, boutique and restaurant is unique, and the stylish, trendy surroundings echo the name. The cuisine is mostly French, but you'll also find an array of meals influenced by other parts of the world. And for dessert, try chocolate fondue and ricotta cheesecake. Check out the one-off jewellery pieces and paintings.

Limetree Café

Jumeirah Beach Road, 04 3498498
7:30am–6pm daily

Here, you'll find everything to be fresh and wholesome, and there's such a large selection of food that you'll want to eat more than just one dish. Various kinds of salads, large sandwiches, delicious banana muffins and don't miss out on the famous carrot cake which is the best in Dubai.

More Café

Al Murooj 04 3433779, Al Garhoud, 04 2830224, Gold and Diamond Park, 3234350
Murooj and Garhoud 8am–10:30pm, Gold and Diamond Park 7am–11pm

Start your day with a More-ish breakfast. There are healthy options, but then there's also the full English fry-up as well as delicious pancakes and a yummy carrot cake. It's a comfortable place with lots of space, where you can work, sit, chill and think. Make sure you try More's own homemade organic bread, and if you're there for lunch, there are various salads, mushroom risotto, paella and then random things like iced Greek coffee. For the slightly more calorie conscious, try the homemade fat and sugar-free ice cream.

O Concept

Beach Residents Building, Shop Number two, Jumeirah, 04 3455557
10am–10pm daily

Part café with stylish chairs, part funky clothes boutique, part home pieces, part art gallery, it's slightly difficult to categorise or define, but that's what makes it so great. It's quite new, bringing a flavour of Paris's Le Marais mixed with Spitalfields Market, London.

Organic Food and Café

Greens, 04 3617974, Dubai Mall, 04 4340577
Greens 8am–9pm, Dubai Mall 9am–10pm weekdays and 9am–12midnight Thurs–Sat

This is one of the only places in Dubai you'll find organic food. It has a relaxed simple atmosphere with lots of plants. The homemade bread is delicious, and the extensive menu includes soups, quiches, pizzas, risotto and stir-fry. There's also organic ice cream and fresh juices, and if you're into milkshakes, try the Peanut Lover and Chocolate. Buffets on Friday are awesome.

Switch

Dubai Mall, 04 3399131

This chic restaurant inside the new Dubai Mall, designed by design master Karim Rashid, serves delicious Mediterranean dishes, but also has an amazing selection of desserts such as the New York blueberry cheesecake and sticky toffee pudding. They also have some great smoothies.

The One Café

Jumeirah Beach Road, 04 3456687
Sat–Thu 9am–9pm, Fri 2pm–9pm

Based inside The One on Beach Road, a famous chain selling gorgeous home interiors, the café has delicious smoothies, sandwiches, tasty ravioli and fresh soups.

XVA Café

Bastakiya, Bur Dubai, 04 3535383
Sat–Thu 9am–9pm, Fri 9am–6pm

With trees and canopies and set in a pretty courtyard, this café has a lovely atmosphere. You'll find great Arabic snacks, salads, soups and sandwiches. There's also an art gallery and they hold film nights.

Chapter 21

Going out

With plenty of cinemas, a number of theatres, hundreds of places you can sit and shisha away, and many bars and nightclubs, there's always lots going on in Dubai and so much you can do at night. Or, if you fancy shopping late in the evening, many malls are open till 11pm.

With a fantastic variety of cosmopolitan bars, Dubai has become quite the clubbing destination. You'll find lively party atmospheres, bars where you can sip on a drink and simply enjoy the breathtaking views and others where you can do some karaoke. And the music is as varied as you'll find anywhere – from garage and pop to Bollywood tunes, Bhangra and Arabic music.

CINEMAS

There are a number of cinemas in Dubai which cater for the international audience by screening Arabic, Hindi and English films. You'll certainly find all the latest releases of American movies either at the same time as they are made available in the US or a just little later. You should also find the latest Bollywood releases in the cinemas. Any films with very explicit sexual images or anything that offends the moral values of the country is censored.

Movie timings are published in local newspapers. Alternatively, call the cinemas to find out.

CineStar
Deira City Centre, 14 screens
04 2949000

CineStar
Mall of Emirates, 12 screens
04 3414222

Grand Cinecity
Al Ghurair City, 10 screens
04 2289898

Grand Cineplex
Grand Hyatt, 17 screens
04 3242000

Grand Festival
Dubai Festival City, 15 screens
04 2328328

Grand Megaplex
Ibn Battuta Mall, 21 screens
04 3669898

Grand Mercato
Mercato Mall, 8 screens
04 3499713

Grand Metroplex
Near Metropolitan Hotel, Sheikh Zayed Road, 8 screens
04 3438383

Lamcy Cinema
Lamcy Plaza, 4 screens
04 3368808

Reel Cinemas
Dubai Mall, 10 screens
04 449 1988

Outdoor movies

Why not watch movies al fresco and in an informal unique atmosphere … at Wafi City Rooftop Gardens (04 3240000)?

SHOWS

Dubai doesn't have the most vibrant theatre scene but, with the growing international community, there are now many more international plays and musicals touring Dubai. The Madinat Theatre and DUCTAC both have good theatre facilities.

Dubai Community Theatre and Arts Centre (DUCTAC)

04 3414777, www.ductac.org

Conveniently located inside the Mall of the Emirates, performances here are centred on dancing and storytelling. It also has a whole host of classes.

Madinat Theatre

04 3666546, www.madinattheatre.com

This modern 442-seat theatre inside the famous Madinat Souk is the first of its kind in the Middle East. It has a busy event calendar throughout the year with past performances including *Nutcracker Ballet, Stomp* and *Umoja*.

Jumana – Secret of the Desert

04 3679500, www.alsahra.com

With stunning audio-visual, pyrotechnics, water and laser effects, this stunning show celebrates Arabia's rich history and culture. The stage is set in a large lake and the show takes place six nights in a week.

The Laughter Factory

04 3551862, www.thelaughterfactory.com

Having pioneered stand-up comedy in the Gulf, The Laughter Factory has become the best international stand-up comedy venue in the region. Every month, three international, stand-up comics are brought here for a string of shows. Buy your tickets early – it's not uncommon to find a 'House Full' sign.

Cirque Du Soleil

This Canadian-based circus has performed in Dubai for a few years and will become permanent at a purpose-built theatre on Palm Jumeirah, sometime soon.

SHISHA

Shisha is a part of the culture and a popular pastime in the Middle East, as it is in Egypt and other places. It's great to enjoy while out with friends in the evening or late night, as *shisha* cafés are usually open late into the night, some till 1am and others till 3am. The most recent and new place is the outside café at The Address in Downtown Dubai, where you can *shisha* away as you watch the breathtaking fountain display dance to music at regular intervals.

This *shisha* pipe, also known as *hookah, nargileh* and hubbly bubbly is filled with flavoured tobacco, such as apple, strawberry, vanilla and many others. The varieties of flavours really are fantastic and endless, so make sure you try out a few. If you want to buy a *shisha* pipe, they come in all colours and sizes and are available in the *souks* and some supermarkets. Just make sure you ask for instructions on how to use one when buying it.

Al Mijana

Le Meridien, 04 7022615
12:30–3pm, 7:30pm–1:30am

Cosmo Café

The Tower, Sheikh Zayed Road, 04 3326569
8:30pm–1am

Elements Art Café

Wafi City, 04 3244252
10am–1am

Ewaan Lounge

Palace Hotel, Downtown Dubai, 04 4287951
6pm–2am

Fudo
Jumeirah Beach Road next to Mercato Mall, 04 3498586
9am–3am

iKandy Bar
Shangri-La Hotel, 04 4052781
6pm–2am

Reem Al Bawadi
Jumeirah Beach Road, near Burj Al Arab, 04 3947444, www.reemalbawadi.com
9am–2am

Samari
Near Capitol Hotel, Al Mina Road, 04 3454511
12midnight–3am

Shisha Courtyard
One and Only Royal Mirage, 04 3999999
7pm–1am

Shu Restaurant
Jumeirah Beach Road next to Emirates Hospital, 04 3491303
10am–2am

Souk Madinat Jumeirah
Central Plaza, Madinat Souk, 04 3668888
10am–11pm

The Courtyard
Al Manzil Hotel, Downtown Dubai, 04 4285930
6pm–2am

QUIZ NIGHTS

El Paso
Dubai Marine Beach Resort, 04 3461111
Wednesdays 9pm–10pm

Fibber Magee's
Behind KFC Building, Sheikh Zayed Road, 04 3322400
Tuesdays 8pm onwards

George and Dragon
Ambassador Hotel, Bur Dubai, 04 3939444
Fridays 3–4pm

Locker Room
Golden Tulip, Al Barsha, 04 5016189
Mondays 8:30–11:30pm

The Boston Bar
Jumeirah Rotana, Al Diyafah Street, 04 3455888
Mondays 8:30–11:30pm

The Dubliner's
Le Meridien, Garhoud, 04 7022508
Tuesdays 8 – 11pm

Most clubs don't really get going till around 11pm and most stay open till 3am. Thursday and Friday weekend nights are the main party nights in Dubai, though there's usually something going on everyday.

BARS

The legal age to enter bars and clubs in Dubai is 21, so it's wise to be carrying some form of ID if you look younger.

Agency

Emirates Towers, Sheikh Zayed Road, 04 3198780
Sun–Thu 12noon–3am, Fri–Sat 3pm–3am

This is an upmarket wine bar attracting after-work professionals. You're definitely not going for the view, but it's got a great atmosphere.

Bahri Bar

Mina A'Salam, 04 3668888
Sat–Thu 1pm–3am, Fri 4pm–3am

Sit outside on the wooden terrace at this stylish bar and absorb the stunning uninterrupted views of the canals, Arabian waters and the imposing Burj Al Arab.

Bar 44

44th floor of Grosvenor House, Dubai Marina, 04 3998888
Fri–Wed 6pm–2am, Thu 6pm–3am

This exclusive and stylish champagne and cocktail bar is located on the 44th floor of Grosvenor Bar and offers excellent views of the Marina and Palm.

Barasti

Le Meridien Mina Seyahi Beach Resort and Marina, 04 3181313
Daily 11am–2am

This beach bar with a wooden deck and great *al fresco* setting is one of the busiest spots in Dubai – popular with expats. It has a real mix of crowds and great bar food – try the Barasti fish and chips and the signature mocktail Mina effect. There's also Indian, Arabian and Italian food and if you fancy *shisha*, just ask. Of course, if you want an amazing pizza, Bussola's right here.

BarZar

Souk Madinat Jumeirah, 04 3666197
Daily 5pm–2am

With two floors and a popular waterside terrace, this place is pretty big and always buzzing. There's a live screen showing sports and a noisy crowd.

Belgian Beer Café

Intercontinental Festival City, 04 7011128
Daily 5:30pm–2am

This has a true European atmosphere and you'll find all the food and beers to be Belgian. There is also a lovely outdoor terrace.

Buddha Bar

Grosvenor House, Dubai Marina, 04 3176833
Daily 8pm–2am

The décor is plush, flamboyant and dimly lit, with red chandeliers, a gigantic statue of Buddha, private coves, floor-to-ceiling windows with great views of the Marina. Enjoy the fancy cocktails at the bar or have some bites in the restaurant area. The Asian cuisine is as tasty as it is pricey.

Cavalli Club

Fairmont Hotel, 04 3329260
Daily 7pm–11:45pm

Italian fashion designer Roberto Cavalli opened the first Cavalli Club in May 2009 with Swarovski-laden walls and his signature animal print throughout. The ground floor will showcase jewellery, watches and accessories. Upstairs is the Italian restaurant and lounge bar.

Double Decker
Al Murooj Rotana, behind Dusit Dubai, 04 3211111
Daily 12noon–3am

This is a real hotspot for the British crowd and has a great mix of music and karaoke all week, and sports on the big screen.

Irish Village
Garhoud, 04 2824750
Sat–Wed 11am–1am, Thu–Fri 11am–2am

This Irish-style pub with an indoor and huge outdoor area serves traditional pub grub and drinks. A good place to go for a British or Irish experience.

JamBase
Souk Madinat Jumeirah, 04 3666914
Daily 4pm–2am

With arty, funky and eclectic décor, South American food and the in-house jazz and blues band, this is a great place for some lively music.

Left Bank
Souk Al Bahar, 04 3684501
Daily 6pm–2am

With minimalist décor, dim lighting and stylish surroundings, this classy new bar has a pretty dressed-up crowd sipping their concoctions of cocktails.

Long's Bar
Towers Rotana Hotel, 04 3122202
Daily 12noon–3am

Quite the remake of an authentic British pub with football on TV, this is a popular venue for expats.

Nasimi

Atlantis, Palm Jumeirah, 04 4262626
Daily 11am–12am

A sophisticated and loungy beach-front setting with a unique location on the tip of the Palm Island. And if you feel like eating, enjoy some delicious noodles at the restaurant. Watch out for some awesome full moon parties here.

Neos

The Address Hotel, Downtown Dubai, 04 4270515
Daily 6pm–2:30am

High up on the 63rd floor, this swanky bar with dark interiors and a futuristic design has simply got the most stunning views – but you won't get a seat by the window if you don't book in advance. Be warned – the prices will really pinch.

Nezesaussi

Al Manzil Hotel, Downtown Dubai, 04 4285888
Sat–Wed 6pm–2am, Thu–Fri 12pm–2am

This is a real sports bar, where you can watch footie, rugby or cricket matches. Enjoy the food from New Zealand, Australia and South Africa.

Oeno

The Westin Dubai Mina Seyahi, 04 3994141
Daily 4pm–1am

This funky bar with stylish and trendy furniture has fine wines and cheese and a good selection of food. There's also a wine wall and a librarian-style bookshelf ladder.

Rooftop Lounge and Terrace

One and Only Royal Mirage, 04 399 9999
Daily 5pm–1am

An unbeatable, beautiful setting, with views of the Palm Jumeirah Arabian sea. Lie back and sip your cocktail on this elegant terrace.

Sho Cho

Dubai Marine Beach Resort and Spa, 04 3461111
Daily 7pm–3am

A hip and trendy place, with a lovely and often jam-packed terrace overlooking the beach. Sit on the stylish white sofas inside and order some fantastic *sushi*.

Sky View Bar

Burj Al Arab, 04 3017442
Sat–Thu 12noon–1:30am, Fri 1pm–4:30pm, 7pm–1:30am

There's a minimum amount you have to spend here of Dhs250 per person and a strict dress code. But for that price, you're in the most exclusive venue with incredible views enjoying live bands.

Warehouse

Le Meridien, opposite the Airport, 04 7022560
Daily 5pm–3am

This is a sleek, stylish bar spread over two floors which opened in early 2009. But it's not just a bar. It's also a pub, wine bar and fusion restaurant.

NIGHT CLUBS

Most clubs don't really get going till around 11pm and most stay open till 3am. Thursday and Friday weekend nights are the main party nights in Dubai, though there's usually something going on everyday.

360°

Jumeirah Beach Hotel, 04 4068744
Daily 4pm–2am

An awesome location with an open air bar, two circular levels and breathtaking views of the ocean and Burj Al Arab. It's a popular hangout for the young and affluent in Dubai but it's closed in the summer.

400 Club

Fairmont, Sheikh Zayed Road, 04 3324900
Tues, Thu, Fri 9:30pm–4am

A very exclusive club for Dubai's elite and in crowd playing a mix of Arabic, house and R&B.

Alpha

Le Meridien, Garhoud, 04 7022640
Tue and Thu 6pm–3am, Fri 4pm–3am

One of the coolest venues around with marble floors, vaulted ceilings and floor-to-ceiling windows. It has everything from funk and soul nights to live Indie bands.

Apartment

Jumeirah Beach Hotel, 04 4068000
Tues–Fri 9pm–3am

This elegant venue has a bar, music room and dining room. It's salsa night on Thursdays and hip hop on Fridays.

Bang

Souk Al Bahar, Downtown Dubai, 04 4397444
Daily 10pm–3am

A chic and luxury club with exclusive cocktails and free flowing champagne magnums.

Boudoir

Dubai Marine Beach Resort, Jumeirah Beach Road, 04 3461111
Daily 7:30pm–3am

This plush club, done up in a French Renaissance style, is a real favourite with all the well-dressed elite of Dubai. You'll find a large Lebanese crowd.

Chi at the Lodge

Al Nasr Leisureland, Oud Metha, 04 3379470
Daily 9pm–3am

A spacious club with four rooms, with a selection of R&B, hip hop, Indie and more, Chi caters for all music tastes. It also has an awesome outdoor Balinese garden and a luxurious VIP room.

Kasbar

One and Only Royal Mirage, 04 3999999
Mon–Sat 9:30pm–3am

This triple-levelled and very upmarket nightclub has intimate alcoves and only allows couples to enter. Admission is also Dhs50 each.

Sanctuary Nightclub

Atlantis Palm Jumeirah, 04 4260561
Daily 9:30pm–3am

This is a state of the art nightclub located in the fantastic Atlantis and has a weekly line up of events.

Zinc

Crowne Plaza, 04 3055533
Daily 10pm–3am

Zinc has a great mix of music including House, R&B and Old School. This is quite a hangout for all the Emirates crew.

Supporting a
Great Cause
Go
For it
Queen International School

Chapter 22

Charities and special needs

Despite appearances, Dubai is not all glitter and superficiality: there are those who care for others and a wide range of charities and support groups for those with special needs.

CHILDREN'S CHARITIES

Below is a list of some charities with most programmes focused on children and how to help them cope with whatever they are experiencing now – whether sickness or poverty. You can volunteer by being a donor or simply by offering your services and time for them.

All as One

04 3116578, www.aaodubai.org

A non-profit organisation that helps the orphaned, abandoned, abused and destitute children of Sierra Leone.

Children's Hope Foundation

04 5111905, www.chfdubai.org

Raises money for various children's charities providing medical, educational and leisure facilities for children suffering from illness, disability or poverty all around the world.

Dubai Cares

800 DXBCARES(39222737), www.dubaicares.ae

A charitable establishment launched in 2007 by Sheikh Mohammed bin Rashid Al Maktoum with the aim to improve children's access to primary education in developing countries including Bangladesh, Maldives, Sudan and Yemen.

Helping Hands

Elle and Roger on 050 5671434, info@helpinghandsuae.com, www.helpinghandsuae.com

This charitable project began in 2006 by Roger and Elle Trow, with the aim of making a difference to the lives of the neediest people from the lowest paid migrant workers to the most disrespected.

Make-a-Wish Foundation

04 3680217, www.makeawish.ae

An organisation which assists children with life-threatening illnesses by granting their most cherished wish.

Riding for the Disabled

lessons@rdad.ae, www.rdad.ae

A non-profit organisation that relies totally on donations of time and money.

SPECIAL NEEDS SERVICES

Below is a list of some of the programmes provided for people with special needs. Most cater for all special needs using a variety of education programmes within their programme. All of these are relatively new with the oldest founded in 1979. Dubai is only now catering more for those with special needs, though programmes and organisations are still growing.

Dubai

Al Noor Centre for Children with Special Needs
Behind the Mall of the Emirates, Al Barsha, 04 3404844,
alnoorspneeds@alnooruae.org, www.alnooruae.org

Al Noor is run under the auspices of the Ministry of Social Affairs and is passionately committed to helping special needs children from their infancy to adulthood, its goal being to integrate its students into society.

Child Early Intervention Medical Center
Al Razi Building, Dubai Health Care City, 04 4233667, www.childeimc.com

CEIMC is a clinic that provides a variety of services to all children and families with children who are disabled, at-risk or who have special needs from birth to the age of 12. They offer a wide range of therapeutic, educational, and family support services.

Dubai Autism Center
Villa 20, Al Diyafah Road, 04 3986862, info@dubaiautismcenter.ae,
www.dubaiautismcenter.ae

This is the largest non-profit organisation in the UAE serving children with autistic-spectrum disorders. They provide training for parents of children with autism and have classes and therapy for children.

Dubai Center for Special Needs
Sheikh Zayed Road, before Safa Park, behind Gulf News, 04 3440966,
dcsneeds@emirates.net.ae, www.dcsneeds.ae

This non-profit institution provides specialised education and therapy for children with various disabilities. The biggest special needs groups are Down Syndrome and Cerebral Palsy, but they cater for many special needs groups.

Dubai Club for Special Sports

Al Nahda Road, beside Lulu Hypermarket, Al Qusais, 04 2988205, www.specialsports-dubai.com

This sports club is for people of all ages with various special needs. They compete with other teams from the UAE and from around the world. Sports include wheelchair racing, basketball, powerlifting, volleyball, table tennis, and football. They also have a women's club section, where many of the women have graduated as fashion designers.

Foresight

www.foresightrp.com, info@foresightrp.com

Foresight is helping to accelerate a cure for blindness caused by hereditary eye disease which affects millions of people worldwide, particularly retinitis pigmentosa. Blindness is the most common disability in the UAE.

Start

04 3681128

This art education charity focuses on bringing art to special needs children in Dubai. They often meet at the Jam Jar and children with special needs can indulge in painting activities.

The Rashid Pediatric Center

next to Mall of the Emirates, 04 3400005, rashidce@emirates.net.ae www.rashidc.ae

Provides quality education and therapy services to children with special needs aged 3 to 15 years. They teach children with learning difficulties, physical disabilities and those who are severely hearing impaired, with the language of instruction as English and an auditory-verbal approach.

Sharjah

Al Amal School of Humanitarian Services

06 5671117, www.schs.ae/index.html

SCHS is a large school that provides education, care, training and rehabilitation to children and adults with special needs, regardless of the level of disability. They provide services for more than 2000 persons with disabilities and have a separate school for the deaf, on campus.

Awladouna Center

06 5387538, awc72002@emirates.net.ae

This centre for learning and rehabilitation offers consulting services, occupational therapy, educational teaching services aimed at integrating special needs children into mainstream schools, and speech and language therapy. They teach children aged 3–16 and teach in Arabic and English.

Sharjah Autism Center

06 5243131, autism@emirates.net.ae

This centre provides services for various degrees of autism in the Sharjah area.

The Modern International Center for Speech

06 5536344

MICS offers speech therapy on a one to one basis for those suffering from genetic deficiencies, hearing impairments, learning disabilities, stuttering and other speech impediments. Languages include Arabic, English and Hindi.

OTHER CHARITIES

Emirates Environmental Group

www.eeg-uae.org, 04 3448622

This is an organisation devoted to protecting the environment through the means of education and community involvement. They sort through all the waste in the recycling centres, increase the level of awareness and educate the public on environmental issues.

Feline Friends

www.felinefriendsdubai.com, felinefriendsdubai@yahoo.co.uk

Their goal is to bring relief and care to the stray, domestic and abandoned feline population in the UAE by rescuing cats from the streets, providing guidance and support for cat owners and educating the public to care for and respect the cat population.

Go Green

www.gogreen.ae, info@gogreen.ae

An organisation for sustainability and renewable energy with an aim of collecting empty, unused, defective and discarded printer cartridges of all makes and models in order to recycle them.

Take My Junk

www.takemyjunkuae.com, 050 1794045
junk-uae@gmail.com

If you're throwing out any items that you don't need anymore, contact Faisal Khan. Someone will come to pick up your items and they will be reused for low income labourers.

Volunteer in Dubai

www.volunteerindubai.com, 04 4321876
info@volunteerindubai.com

This group is aimed at bringing together any organisation, good cause or individual effort in the UAE, with people willing to help out. Get in touch with them if you want to volunteer for an hour or a day or just do a one-off voluntary act.

Conclusion

Dubai is a city that never fails to surprise, that is constantly moving and forever changing. The sheer scale of development it has undergone over the past decade and the 40-year transformation from a fishing port to the sumptuous city that it is today is astounding and remarkable.

It is exciting to be a part of this new city, which is still taking shape and is home to some of the most stupendous projects in the world including the Palm, Burj Khalifa tower, an underwater hotel and so much more. The most recent addition to Dubai's wondrous projects is the futuristic-looking Metro, which has made travelling around Dubai easier.

While Dubai slowed down in 2009, it seems the worst is over, there are more jobs available and the situation is getting better. In fact, Dubai has become more realistic as a result of the recession – in terms of prices, achievables and the scale of projects.

Essentially, Dubai is a safe, liberating and young city, a city which never sleeps. With people of all nationalities continuously moving in and out, everyone's out to enjoy themselves, to make new friends and earn high, tax-free salaries. Dubai really is a bastion of pleasure.

There is also a snaring energy about Dubai that captivates, mesmerises and makes you just want to stay. And while it has often been criticised for being devoid of art and culture, there is now a rapidly evolving arts scene, an emergence of art galleries, events such as the Literary Festival of Dubai, Dubai International Jazz Festival and Art Dubai, as well as the timeless old *souks* and various museums.

When you have had your fill of sea, sun, desert, shopping and brunches, the other emirates are within driving distance and there are so many countries close enough to fly to for weekends away. It is the sheer number of destinations Emirates flies to that has made Dubai into such a hub. Not only has this aided tourism, but it is also a real advantage for Dubai residents, whether they need to travel for business or holiday.

If you're moving here, this book will help you ease into Dubai, explain what you need to do initially, the activities you can get involved in, where to eat, where to shop and everything that you need to know.

Immerse yourself in this pleasureful city ... Enjoy Dubai!

Index

How To Books are available through all good bookshops, or you can order direct from us through Grantham Book Services.

Tel: +44 (0)1476 541080
Fax: +44 (0)1476 541061
Email: orders@gbs.tbs-ltd.co.uk

Or via our website

www.howtobooks.co.uk

To order via any of these methods please quote the title(s) of the book(s) and your credit card number together with its expiry date.

For further information about our books and catalogue, please contact:

How To Books
Spring Hill House
Spring Hill Road
Begbroke
Oxford
OX5 1RX

Visit our web site at

www.howtobooks.co.uk

Or you can contact us by email at info@howtobooks.co.uk